LAST ...

Born illegitimate... Jameson was ed... ...mentary schools in East London and started work as a Fleet Street messenger at the age of fourteen. He rose to become managing editor of the *Daily Mirror* and editor of the *Daily Express*, the *Daily Star* and the *News of the World*. Since 1984 he has achieved nationwide fame as a TV and Radio 2 presenter. Penguin also publish the first volume of his autobiography, *Touched by Angels*.

Derek Jameson has been married three times and has a daughter and three sons. He lives in London.

What they say about Derek Jameson:

'Fleet Street's loss was television's gain. The great personality of today' – David Frost

'Should do well in a shop' – Bertram Cartwright, Headmaster

'He is one of the best public speakers the profession of journalism ever produced' – Sir Edward Pickering, *The Times*

'A great natural broadcaster' – Terry Wogan

DEREK JAMESON

LAST OF
THE HOT METAL MEN

FROM FLEET STREET TO SHOWBIZ

PENGUIN BOOKS

PENGUIN BOOKS

Published by the Penguin Group
Penguin Books Ltd, 27 Wrights Lane, London W8 5TZ, England
Penguin Books USA Inc., 375 Hudson Street, New York, New York 10014, USA
Penguin Books Australia Ltd, Ringwood, Victoria, Australia
Penguin Books Canada Ltd, 10 Alcorn Avenue, Toronto, Ontario, Canada M4V 3B2
Penguin Books (NZ) Ltd, 182–190 Wairau Road, Auckland 10, New Zealand

Penguin Books Ltd, Registered Offices: Harmondsworth, Middlesex, England

First published by Ebury Press, an imprint of the Random Century Group, 1990
Published in Penguin Books 1991
1 3 5 7 9 10 8 6 4 2

Printed in England by Clays Ltd, St Ives plc

Contents

FOR ELLEN
who took my hand and walked
into the light

Preface

THIS volume concludes the story of my life. It has never been less than turbulent; some would say completely barmy. *Touched by Angels*, the first part of my autobiography, traced my progress to the top of the Fleet Street ladder in the most unlikely circumstances. I was a product of London's East End, a slum kid of dubious parentage who had grown up in a home for waifs and strays. That story ended in the editor's chair at the *Daily Express*. 'Oh well', I concluded, 'the angels have brought me this far. Now I guess it is really going to get tough.' That it did. More than once I was to find myself out on the cobbles, broke and unemployed. The old Fleet Street was fading fast and me with it. The last of the hot metal men, I called myself. Nobody could argue with that. I had given forty years of my life to the place and now my day was done. Not to worry. The bright lights were beckoning. At the age of fifty-five, I picked myself up once again and set out to conquer the airwaves. The angels were always there, shining down on me. I was to become the breakfast toast of ten million Radio Two listeners and Rupert Murdoch's chief test pilot on SKY Television. The highest paid man in show business, according to those rascals back in Fleet Street. Not that my troubles were over. Along the way, though my public never knew it, I was locked in the biggest battle of them all. The love of my life was drinking herself to death. As I said, a turbulent life. This is the story of those years . . .

MY apologies to those who passed my way, but somehow got missed out of the book. I must have worked alongside some 7,000 people in Fleet Street alone. It is not possible to give due recognition to everyone who became part of my story. What I can do is send love and thanks for their splendid company. In the same spirit, these memoirs are a personal reflection and not intended to cause distress to anyone. If unwittingly that has happened, I am truly sorry.

– 1 –

The Most Exciting Place on Earth

LOOK at the carved wooden plaque, children. There on the wall of The Cock tavern. It's about the old days. *The Cartoonists' Club of Great Britain – Golden Joker Award. Presented to Derek Jameson 6.12.89 to commemorate the passing of a Golden Age called Fleet Street.*

That's my home they're talking about. I was the biggest joker of them all. Forty years, man and boy, up and down that narrow, crowded half-mile of malevolence and magic. Now the spell is broken and the old place has gone, lost for ever. There wasn't even a memorial service. They say there was nothing left to mourn. Mind you, something remains – it is still the generic term for a bunch of newspapers. A piece of grammatical shorthand on a stranger's lips.

Fleet Street. The name lives on. There are those who will want to know what it was all about. Perhaps they will have heard of our love and devotion. The way it was in my day when the Street was puffed up with pride, a place of writers and craftsmen where on a balmy night your nostrils picked up the stink of printer's ink and oil from the rolling presses.

Just being there made people special. An argumentative, inquisitive, anarchistic and outrageous camaraderie of know-it-alls who claimed the right to be party to everything happening in the world that mattered a damn. What's more, they would decide whether they *wished* to know. To publish – or forget it. Much of their waking life would be consumed by a fierce debate on their latest story, picture, page or paper. This rag, tag and bobtail of life, drawn from Eton or Wagga Wagga, never stopped talking, drinking, smoking, swearing

11

and – most of all – laughing. In between times they would get on with the business of producing words and pictures for the edification of the millions who daily paid for their services.

Yet it was never much, this most exciting street on earth. One short artery interspersed by dark, cobbled alleyways turning into squares and narrow streets. They reach north towards Holborn or conversely run south down a hill to the banks of the Thames. To the east lies St Paul's Cathedral, while the west leads to the Royal Courts of Justice and the Strand. High on the walls, should any stranger doubt he treads the pavements of history, an occasional crusader's shield proclaims this territory as being under the auspices of the City of London.

Lording over it all were the great stone monuments created by the Press barons to house their chattering armies doing battle day by day with a torrent of words and pictures aimed at the heart of the man on the omnibus in Wigan and his like. The prize – the small change he was prepared to pay for a newspaper.

On the south side of the street, a cluster of sooty buildings formed the empire of Lord Northcliffe, the flawed genius – he once made his liftman an editor – who was perhaps the first to fathom that universal education equals mass circulation. His flagship, the true-blue *Daily Mail*, now resides amid the glitzy department stores of Kensington. Only the ghosts remain behind the grey portals of the *News Chronicle*, strange fruit of the Cadbury family, assassinated and handed on a plate to the rival *Mail* in 1960. Along the same Tudor Street were the offices of *The Observer*, a cuckoo in other nests in the sense that it never possessed its own printing presses, but was always run off by rival outfits like *The Times*. The Old Thunderer kept very much to herself in Printing House Square, on the other side of Blackfriars Bridge, until she acquired a sister late in life, the *Sunday Times*, and moved into the family home in Gray's Inn Road to the north of Fleet Street. Nowadays *The Observer* comes out of a glass bubble in Battersea and the *Times* sisters share the bed of *The Sun* and *News of the World* in a computerised mausoleum at Wapping, in London's Dockland.

These two popular entertainers were previously to be found up the cobbled hill in Bouverie Street, where the two faces of a giant clock served as warning to every scoutmaster on a grave charge that the *NoW* never sleeps. The old Queen of Fleet Street was the first British conquest of Rupert Murdoch after his arrival from Australia in 1969. She grudgingly made room months later for his new baby, *The Sun,* acquired from the Mirror Group for a mere £750,000.

Step a few paces northward and there is Fleet Street proper, which oddly enough was home to only two of the newspaper giants. On the north side were the majestic *Daily Telegraph,* marble without and slum within, and a few paces along the kinky black glass of the Express Group. Today the *Telegraph* papers also come from Dockland. The *Express* has stayed closest to home, occupying a custom-built headquarters on the wrong side of the Thames south of Blackfriars Bridge. The *Daily Mirror, Sunday Mirror* and *Sunday People* remain in their blue and orange mini-skyscraper at Holborn Circus, a half-mile north of Fleet Street, though the papers are printed elsewhere and the editorial departments are also moving to more economic premises.

These were the big boys who ruled Fleet Street for the greater part of my days. Alongside them, of course, the ancillary services: the giant news agencies like Reuters, where I learned my craft, and its cousin, the Press Association; typesetters, blockmakers, photo agencies, freelance hacks and public relations types.

I knew it all. This was my life. Every last pub, club, editorial, press hall, every twist and turn. The very paving stones themselves were home to me, a poor kid from the back streets of the East End. If the Street belonged to anyone, I have to be prize claimant to the throne. I did more jobs, worked there longer, in more places, and knew more people than anyone else.

At fourteen I was running those blitzed streets with my satchel of messages, dodging doodlebugs, though still considered too young to enter Reuters' head office. Outdoor messengers like me, the lowest form of life in the Street, were confined to an outside annexe. I grew up to be man enough to buy my first round in the scruffy old King and Keys, rubbing shoulders with the editor of the *Daily Telegraph* – and him a Harrow man. Before calling it quits in 1984 I had been through the ranks as a reporter, feature writer, sub-editor and on to the higher echelons until eventually I was managing editor of the *Daily Mirror,* and editor of the *Daily Express, Daily Star* and *News of the World.* Along the way I laughed a great deal, cried a little, and tasted all that life could offer in that street where certainly I never saw any shame. I've been talked out of going for a manager's throat because he refused to change a page, spewed out my guts clutching the white tiles in the cellar bog of the Poppinjay in a strike that wouldn't go away, screwed myself silly under more than one executive desk because it felt so good to be there sharing sensations with a beautiful lady in newspapers.

Dear heart, who knows me so well, scatter my ashes in some dark alley beside what is now a Japanese investment bank. Who knows, the breeze might carry my mortal remains to an unseen crevice, some forgotten ledge, where my spirit will again hear those laughing voices in the night.

Compositors coming back from the pub in time to sort the type, all fingers and thumbs, for the late London edition. They are nut-brown men fond of gardening and fishing. There is daylight saving aplenty in their trade. Behind them, perhaps, a pair of big, beefy stereotypers – the tattooed foundrymen who cast from molten lead the plates that whizz round in the night printing the news. Or warehousemen from the publishing hall, hurrying to be on time for the whistle that tells them the presses are rolling. Papers spilling out of the overhead gantries, a great cascade of pulp turned into print. Wrap them quick, twenty-four to the quire and one for luck, and send bundles racing to catch the night express to the corners of the land. Sub-editors, busy as bees, heads still buzzing with some typographical marvel created in seconds and blown out of all proportion by three pints at the pub. Four decks of upper and lower case, 24-point Century Bold across single-column. Otherwise known as 4/24CB CLC X1. *Lousy count on Century*, they tell each other, *you get nothing to the single column. How the fuck do they expect us to write decent headlines with that stuff?* Reporters scurrying back for an early copy, eager to see what they've made of the story they were working on at six o'clock this morning. *Have I got it to myself, or is it on PA?* Reporters live in perpetual fear that the Press Association somehow has got hold of a story that should by rights be his or hers alone and not given to some news agency to be shared by the world through the marvel of the teleprinter. Photographers off on a late story, out of the pub and into the car that's never parked far away. *Who knows? This could be the big one. A fire in Wandsworth. Can*

*get some great shots in a fire. Birds jumping out of windows with no
clothes, that sort of thing. Hope Monty's not on it . . . the bastard's
got that 400 mil.* Firemen, messengers, managers, machine minders,
lawyers, proof readers, engineers, electricians, bookies' runners and
union bosses, wine waiters, advertising clerks, cashiers and canteen
ladies. All these and more are Fleet Street. Spreading the word,
bringing the news. ''*Ere are, Guv! All the latess . . . Ex-TRA!
Stannard.*'

Oh, God above, the characters! The simply amazing, extraordinary, eccentric and beloved people who were part of the Street,
one of the gang. The first among them for me was Hannen Swaffer,
the greatest pundit of his day. Spiritualist, socialist, crusader for
anyone's rights. Just look at the man in his black smoking jacket,
fag ash on each lapel. Penetrating eyes taking in the world behind
the magnified lens of thick glasses, big red hooter like an island in
the battered sea of his leonine head, grey hair thrown back like some
Greek philosopher.

As a boy I would collect his copy from his eyrie on the top floor
overlooking the statue of nurse Edith Cavell at the bottom of St
Martin's Lane. One glance from him and I froze. For weeks he left
me standing there at the door of his flat while he finished his column.
It could take a minute or an hour. After a time he relented and left
the door open with a grunted 'Come in'. I would stand in the hall
filled with wonder. Through every door, on every shelf, on the floors
piled up against the walls, there were books and still more books.
It seemed that every inch of flat space was a potential shelf.

'It's like a bloody library in here' were my first words to him
beyond 'Good morning, Mr Swaffer'.

'Can't get rid of 'em,' he said. 'People keep sending them for me
to read. They want a mention . . .'

'Chuck out the ones you don't want,' I told him. 'I know a place
in Fleet Street. Tanner a copy, so long as they're new.'

We put together a suitcase full. It weighed a ton. I got a quid for
the lot. When I handed him the money the following week, Swaff
stared at it in his hand and asked, 'What's this for?'

'The books,' I said. 'I sold the books.' For a second I thought he
had no intention of taking the money, that it would be all mine. Not
likely. Understanding dawned on him. He burrowed into his trouser

pocket for loose change. I got sixpence. Hard labour, I called that.

One day he asked me what I wanted to do when I grew up. 'I want to be a journalist, Mr Swaffer.' I added hastily, 'Like you.' Who knows, the old bugger might give me a helping hand.

'Don't be stupid, sonny,' he said. 'Get yourself a decent job in a garage or something.'

You have to be slightly bonkers to work in Fleet Street. Timid souls need not apply. It has little to offer solid, straight, respectable folk whose day revolves around the 8.10 from Chislehurst every morning, though to be sure we would spend much of our time envying them their ordered lives.

One of the joys of the place is that nobody actually cares who you are or where you come from just so long as you are a fellow addict, hooked on what the Irish call the crack – the mad, impetuous, cynical, curious, questioning and self-deprecating world of journalism. It helps to have more than a passing fancy for the language, printed and spoken. Self-doubts are not permitted. For those who ask *What am I doing in this lunatic asylum?* it is time to move on to public relations or father-in-law's toy business. There they will spend the rest of their days telling the way it was when Fleet Street really meant something.

I remember Lionel Crane, one of the best feature writers in the business. A *Mirror* man who had spent a great chunk of his life reporting Hollywood follies for a public that still went to the pictures. Brought back home in the age of television, he would hold us spellbound in the pub with his stories of the great stars that had been too hot for the presses.

He was a short, intense man, a born storyteller, like all great journalists. 'She couldn't act to save her life, old boy, and her English was dreadful. They had to hold up a bloody great card in front of the camera with every word spelled out phonetically. So when this lad from the *Express* starts taking her out, we sent over a huge parcel to the restaurant where they went for a spot of footsies under the table at every opportunity. He unwraps it there and then, in front of all the other diners, waiters and the rest . . . and there on this sheet of cardboard was written in big capitals: DO U WANT TO FUK???'

Lionel's great dream was to retire to a little property by the rolling

Sussex Downs with a winding lane running down to the village pub. He almost made it. Lionel got as far as Brighton. He even wrote a column in the local *Evening Argus* for pocket money. Lionel always used to shake his head in wonder at the profligacy of national newspapers. 'What they don't realise, old boy,' he would say with his gleeful laugh, 'is that we would do the job for half the money!'

The thing that puzzled me about Lionel's retirement was that he kept turning up in the *Mirror* pub at the top of Fetter Lane, the White Hart, known to all as *The Stab*, being the place executives went for a drink with those they planned to stab in the back. One day I bearded him about it. 'What happened to the country pub at the end of the winding lane?' I asked him.

'Well, the truth is, old boy,' Lionel told me sadly, 'I get more good conversation, more stimulation, in five minutes in this place than I would get in a fortnight in my local!' Then that great guffaw so frequent in the newspaper business. *Sod 'em all*, it says. *This is me. This is where I belong.* On the *Sunday Mirror* we bylined Lionel as 'The man with a passport to the world'. That gave me a laugh when I took him to the Savoy for lunch and he started eating his artichoke – with a knife and a fork!

Fleet Street pubs were filled with magic. The best ideas bounced off the walls in those hot, overcrowded, noisy and smoke-filled parlours. It was the place to be for good chat, spiced with gossip, to hear the latest jokes and scurrilous stories. Most of all they were rumour factories with the editor's prospects of survival the main topic. Every newspaper had its own pub or pubs, usually within spitting distance of its walls. We used to say that some enterprising soul should park a pantechnicon loaded with booze outside the back door. Rabbiting away, the workers would stream into the van and order their pints and vodka tonics, totally unaware of their surroundings.

Our strange hours were a gift for the licensed trade. At lunchtime the pubs would be heaving with reporters and photographers waiting to go out on a story, daytime workers from the news, pictures and features departments, accounts or advertising clerks, secretaries galore giggling away. Come evening the drink would still be flowing, but the cast somewhat changed. Sub-editors on their break would now form the biggest group and there would also be a few comps and other inkies – printworkers – here and there, though they tended to find pubs of their own. Still plenty of reporters and photographers about and, of course, the drinking classes. The lost and lonely with no homes they cared to go to. Most of the executives would pass through at some time or other. They seemed never to go home. What makes standing at bars such an important part of newspaper life is the long gap between last copy and pictures going to the printer, usually about 7 pm, and the first edition coming off the presses some three hours later.

Even Fleet Street pubs closed their doors eventually. That was when the clubs came into their own. Drinking dens turned up all over the place, some lasting only months and others making a big success and packing them in year after year. They tended to be run by people working in newspapers, well versed in the strange ways and hours of the industry. Top of the tree was the old-established Press Club, though that foundered through lack of interest. The younger journalists regarded it as the redoubt of old fogeys endlessly wittering on about the great stories they had covered yonks earlier.

There was a time when the backbenches of rival newspapers – the executives who mastermind production of the paper editorially – met around midnight at the Press Club bar to exchange banter and gossip, decrying each other's best efforts.

Some deputy night editor of the *Mirror* would hold up the *Sun's* front page and claim shrilly: 'Look at that! What a load of bollocks. And the picture's old . . .we ran it weeks ago.'

To which the chief sub of the *Sun* would sneer: 'Hah! Bet a fiver you lift that splash for the late London edition. Every decent story you've had for the past month has been pinched from us.'

After an hour or two of this elevated chat, the drink flowing smoothly down throats parched by hours of frantic activity, they would retire happily to the games room and attempt to thrash each other at snooker. Each ball potted would be seen as a triumph for one paper over the other. There's many a mediocre sub-editor been promoted to the backbench because he was wizard at potting reds.

The last stragglers would be there until 4 am or so, making their way home only after Sean, the night steward, had said in his soft

Irish for the umpteenth time: 'For God's sake, gentlemen, have you no beds to go to?'

As if anyone in his right mind would want to go to bed when there are newspapers to talk about.

2

So You Want to Be an Editor

THE demon ambition makes fools of us all. Why else would anyone volunteer for the lunatic asylum by becoming an editor? The wages never match the demands of the job, though bosses are more generous these days. They no longer have print unions gobbling up most of the profits.

Before the Wapping revolution of 1986 there were constant screams of pain from management about editorial costs, and our salaries were kept relatively low. It was a kind of penance. If the National Union of Journalists was making outrageous demands, such as seeking parity with printworkers, then it must be the editor's fault for employing such appalling people.

Although it was our responsibility to generate sales and advertising revenue by the million, in my day editors were kept at about the level of a linotype operator on the *Financial Times*. Plus expenses and a chauffeur-driven car, of course. One has to keep up appearances. So you don't take on one of the toughest jobs in the world for the money. It is ego more than anything else. The desire to succeed, to be best. I suppose we all like to be noticed and regarded as special, though others are not daft enough to volunteer to be a human coconut shy. Not that any such thoughts cross your mind when the call comes.

This is it. The big one. The power and the patronage make it about as close as you will get on earth to playing God, though there is no script for the part. You simply fly by the seat of your pants and hope to get it right. Otherwise the guv'nor might have to shell out a million quid in libel damages. They do not take kindly to that.

It is not wise for an editor to let his omnipotence show. The proprietor is likely to get jealous, the staff contemptuous. Not forgetting the readers. They like to imagine the person behind their favourite newspaper is not much different from themselves. We like to think so too.

Why me? you ask yourself a thousand times, though obviously it is not a thought you pass on to the rest. For years you have been part of the highly concentrated effort and collective lunacy that goes into the pages of a newspaper. Now *you* are the paper. It is there to reflect your experience, standards and instincts. You have spent half your days and nights with these kindred souls who have chosen to live by the pen. Now you have been planted in the editor's chair. It's you they're looking at, mate. What are you going to do?

The answer could determine the course of their lives. Since I was very much a *Mirror* man, there must have been a great deal of head-scratching when, eager for battle, I arrived on a hot August day in 1977 at the black glass palace that was then the Fleet Street headquarters of Express Newspapers.

At last I had made it. Editor of the *Daily Express*. For me, the greatest achievement of all – though I had known from the age of twelve that it was something I would do.

As I wrote in the first volume of my memoirs, *Touched by Angels*, I was an evacuee in Hertfordshire at the time, a poor boy from the East End abandoned by what family I had and yet determined to become a journalist. Nobody gave me the slightest chance. I alone believed, no doubt because of the psychic awareness that has always been with me. Put it down to the angels looking after me. They convinced me that I should be not only a journalist, but also editor of the biggest and most successful newspaper of those wartime days, the *Daily Express*. The twist in the tale is that I never wanted the *Express*, much preferring the more popular tabloid *Daily Mirror*. I had actually learned to read through the comic strips in the *Mirror* – it was very much a working-class paper and its Labour politics appealed to my left-wing idealism.

I spent sixteen happy years with the Mirror Group, going through the ranks to become managing editor of the *Daily Mirror*. Nevertheless, it seemed the final prize would elude me, not least because I was second-in-command to the highly regarded Michael

Molloy, who was ten years my junior. In the event, he remained editor of the *Mirror* for another decade after my departure.

One of the joys of making it to the No. 2 spot is that you can be sure rival newspapers will put your name high on their list when they are looking for a new editor. As Northern editor of the *Mirror* in Manchester, I had gained a big reputation as a circulation builder and beaten off the early forays of the soaraway *Sun* in my territory. Those successes had landed me a plum job in London. Now it was only a matter of time before I got an editor's chair. Rupert Murdoch took me to lunch at the Savoy and we agreed I would join him if he came up with the right job. There was also talk of my taking over the *Sunday People*.

So it was no surprise when the phone rang in my *Mirror* office and Charles Wintour, guru of Express Newspapers and a famous former editor of the London *Evening Standard*, invited me to lunch. I knew before putting the phone down that the *Daily Express* was coming my way. The paper was on the skids and the Express Group had been bought five weeks earlier at the knockdown price of £13.6 million by Trafalgar House, the consortium of construction, hotel and shipping interests.

Within hours Charles Wintour was ushering me into the presence of Victor Matthews, the poor boy from Islington in North London who had become one of Britain's leading entrepreneurs with his partner at Trafalgar, Nigel Broackes. Matthews had taken over as chairman of Beaverbrook Newspapers and here he was in a private suite at the Hotel Bristol, off Piccadilly, looking for someone to save his flagship.

Charles records what happened next in his book, *The Rise and Fall of Fleet Street* (Hutchinson, 1989): 'Jameson's anecdotal style, cockney beginnings and total self-confidence in his own talents seemed to cast a spell on Matthews. I soon felt as surplus to the lunch as a mother-in-law on honeymoon and left them talking long after the meal was over.'

It was supposed to be a reconnaissance, but Victor went ahead immediately and made me editor without consulting his top managers, notably the aristocratic and tempestuous Jocelyn Stevens, the group managing director. Jocelyn had encouraged Trafalgar to buy the Express papers to keep out Rupert Murdoch, who had offered £10 million for a minority stake in the papers and management control. Jocelyn had been pulling all the strings for years until Matthews' arrival and now he was having to take orders. I don't think he ever forgave me for getting the job without first seeking his permission.

His contempt for journalists was total – and that included editors. Mind you, he had plenty of justification. A succession of poor editors had dragged the once mighty *Express* deeper and deeper into the mire. At its postwar height, it sold well over four million copies a day. Now it was struggling to hold two million and was looking drearier than ever in a new format. The *Daily Express* had turned tabloid just before the Trafalgar takeover, but lacked the expertise that would enable the paper to compete with its more popular rivals.

That's why Jameson, a *Mirror* man of all things, had been brought in. Would he prove as useless as the rest at turning round the circulation? No wonder Stevens sniffed. Ten editors in twenty years and the sales lower than ever.

Our first encounter was so ugly it cast a cloud over all future relations between us. Having been summoned imperiously on the internal hotline, I entered Jocelyn's chrome-and-leather sanctum to find him haranguing two or three of his executives while lying on his back on the floor, his head propped up in the seat of a low chair. His piercing blue eyes appraised me coldly.

'Ah, I thought it might be useful to make one or two things clear to you, Frank,' he bellowed.

'Derek,' I volunteered.

'You see, Frank . . .'

'Derek,' I said, getting louder now.

'What's that? De-wekk! De-wekk! No, I shall call you Frank . . .'

'Derek. My fucking name is Derek! All right, Josh?'

'Ah, well, you see, old boy, nothing personal. Just that editors come and go so quickly around here that we call them all "Frank". Makes life so much simpler, don't you see?'

It never was going to be my favourite joke, but I laughed dutifully with the rest of his minions. He called me *De-wekk* after that on those occasions when we were still speaking. Sir John Junor, my venerable counterpart on the *Sunday Express*, was said never to speak to Stevens and to have banned him from his editorial floor.

Jocelyn's demonstration of managerial skills, Fleet Street style, did not end there. Before departing, he wished me to know: 'I loathe and detest ALL journalists.' He spat out the words, his lips pursed.

'I'm glad you told me that, Josh,' I retorted. 'It explains something that's been puzzling me. I've only been here a few hours, but already I've learned that all journalists loathe and detest you.' He loved the thought of that. As I bolted, his roar of delight followed me down the corridor.

It was a dreadful beginning. No wonder this outfit has such a lousy reputation, I thought to myself. By contrast, the cosy old Mirror Group was like a benevolent society. Ah well, I thought to myself, balls to them. *Let's get on with it . . .*

The first thing an editor must do on taking over is identify his target, to define just how and where he is going to find new readers. One of the problems of the *Express* under the succession of editors preceding me was that it had totally lost its sense of direction. In my view it was very much the paper of the working/lower-middle-class Tory voter. Sounds like a contradiction in terms until you realise that Tory votes of 40 per cent-plus are common in the poorest constituencies. These people presumably read a newspaper. Surely it should be the *Express*, the paper of the masses created by its most famous editor of all, Arthur Christiansen.

Newspaper bosses tend to share certain characteristics. None of them are of much use when it comes to selling newspapers. They crave respectability, yearn for honours and patronage and are extremely cautious. Despite the fact that the *Mirror* and *Express* were traditional rivals, for years the top brass at the *Express* had bled the company white in a costly and futile chase after the readers of the *Daily Telegraph* and *Daily Mail*, both of them firmly entrenched in millions of middle-class homes. Like his predecessors, Victor Matthews inclined in this direction. He used to drive me potty by shaking his head gravely and declaring in tones that suggested he knew what he was talking about, that the *Express* should never have gone 'tab-o-loid', something that had happened a few months before our arrival. It was too late to turn back the clock now. He also coveted the *Telegraph*'s lucrative classified advertisement revenue.

I put all my powers of persuasion to work to talk him round to my point of view.

'It doesn't make any sense,' I told him in our early chats. 'Why should we go after fish smaller than ourselves?

'We've got to chase the Mirror! It's so busy fighting off *The Sun* that it has completely neglected the top end of its readership. On top of that, more and more of its readers are turning away from Labour and the unions. This is the perfect time to create a strong, lively and vigorous paper without the tits and trivia. Working-class Tories aspiring to become middle class.'

Matthews backed me. He was so hungry for new readers, for an *Express* success story after years of failure, that he was willing to try anything. I also cheered him with the thought that we would pick up some readers from the *Daily Mail*.

'It's a soft paper, directed at middle-class women,' I told him. 'David English [the *Mail*'s brilliant editor, Sir David English] has won ninety-four awards and his paper has absorbed the *Daily Sketch* and *News Chronicle*, but the circulation has hardly moved at all. It's so neat and tidy and feminine,' I said derisively. 'About as much use as a ballet dancer playing for Arsenal.' Matthews understood language like that – and Arsenal was his home team.

I sent a rocket round the editorial on the first day. 'Make all the pictures at least one column bigger,' I ordered. 'Put the headlines up two sizes. At least let's look as if we mean business.'

It transformed the paper overnight, much to the delight of the staff. They were a talented bunch, eager to prove they could compete on equal terms with the best in the Street. All those editors coming and going had left them on the ropes, their morale shattered. Now this bloke had arrived from the *Mirror* talking their language and urging them once again to get up and carry on the fight. They couldn't wait.

Express columnist Jean Rook, the first lady – or bitch in some eyes – of Fleet Street, tells the impression I made on the staff in her memoirs, *The Cowardly Lioness* (Sidgwick & Jackson):

> Because he sounds like an overturned barrow in an East End gutter full of damp cabbage leaves, people initially judge Derek Jameson to be as thick as a shorn-off plank. In fact, Jameson was a brilliant, intuitive editor. As well as a one-man Palladium show. At Jameson's editorial

conferences, you couldn't get a word in edgewise among his endless streams of jokey chat. Every morning we just sat there for an hour, with our mouths open to no avail, listening to what was to become Radio Two . . . As an editor, Jameson was inspirational, and ran the paper like a knees-up at which everyone, from the highest to the lowest office boy he himself once was, was invited to join in the fun.

One of the problems had been that the paper had 'gone tabloid' without paying any heed to the rules. The executives had simply miniaturised the big broadsheet pages, failing to comprehend the simple tabloid truth that the smaller the page, the bigger the pictures and headlines. That is the tabloid philosophy. To be big and bold does not mean to be cheap and sensational – as the knockers would have it – but rather to give the paper more powerful impact.

My first appointment was going to be the most important of all. I needed Vic Giles, a key figure at the *Sun*. He was the paper's art director, highly regarded by Rupert Murdoch and architect of those brilliantly designed pages that gave the *Sun* its soaraway pace and punch. Of course, I did not want the *Express* to model itself on the *Sun* – they were aimed at totally different markets – but I wanted my paper to have a strong, distinctive look of its own. In the highly mobile world of newspapers we're well attuned to frequency changes and soon learn to cut our coats according to the cloth. Vic would know exactly what I had in mind.

The problem was how to woo him from the rich pastures of Bouverie Street, where the *Sun* and *News of the World* operated in cramped quarters in an atmosphere of open warfare between management and unions. In true Fleet Street style, I took him to lunch, told him he was a genius and obviously poorly treated on his own paper. I tempted him with a big salary, way beyond what he was getting on the *Sun*, and for good measure promised to make him an assistant editor. As further flattering evidence of my faith in his talents, I asked him to design a new masthead for the paper, making *Daily* small and *EXPRESS* big so that the paper stood out on the newsstands. Vic was delighted. The masthead is sacred territory in the newspaper world, the logo at the top of the front page that shouts the paper's name day in, day out. He joined us in a matter of weeks.

It wasn't too difficult. Vic is among my closest and dearest friends.

He had taught me all I know about typography on the weekly *London American* years before and subsequently I worked for him as a picture editor in the mid-60s when we were both at the *Sunday Mirror*. It's a small world, newspapers. These days he runs his own consultancy business.

Having sorted out the *look* of the paper, now to breathe some new life into the contents. At my first conference of the paper's executives I had asked 'What have we got in the pot?' In newspaper terms that means what has the paper got lined up for the future. It could be a feature series, a book serialisation or some major promotion.

'Not a lot,' said the features editor, Bill Spicer. 'We've got an option on Peter Townsend's book and that's about it.'

'What, THE Peter Townsend?' I asked incredulously. 'Princess Margaret and all that?'

'That's the one,' he said. 'It's only an option. It will cost us £70,000 if we take it up.'

'Buy it,' I told him urgently.

'He hasn't finished it yet . . . it might be a load of rubbish.'

'I don't care if it's gold-plated horse manure,' I told him. 'We must have it! I can do things with the name "Group Captain Peter Townsend".'

This was perfect tabloid fodder. Already I was writing the headlines in my skull: THE ROYAL ROMANCE OF THE CENTURY. My brain automatically blanked out all memory of the Duke of Windsor and Mrs Simpson. Princess Margaret, fun-loving younger sister of the future Queen, desperately in love with the dashing royal equerry, wartime RAF ace Peter Townsend.

Peter's book was anything but rubbish. It turned out to be a beautiful love story, related with discretion and dignity. He told of his first meeting with Margaret in 1944 in a corridor at Buckingham Palace after his audience with her father, King George VI, for his appointment as equerry. The Princess was fourteen years old at the time and it was obvious that the air ace, a mature married man, was smitten from the start.

She was a girl of unusual, intense beauty, confined as it was in her short slender figure and centred about large eyes, generous, sensitive lips and a complexion as smooth as a peach . . . She was coquettish, sophisticated.

But what ultimately made Princess Margaret so attractive and lovable was that behind the dazzling facade, the apparent self-assurance, you could find, if you looked for it, a rare softness and sincerity.

Sensational stuff. UNDER THE SPELL OF PRINCESS MARGARET was the obvious headline for such poignant memories. The story got better as it progressed. They fell heavily in love. There was no way in those days that the Establishment would allow a royal romance with a commoner – and married at that!

In 1953, by now divorced, Townsend was forced into exile as air attaché in Brussels for a cooling-off period. Two lonely years destroyed their love. Princess Margaret ended the affair in 1955 couched in the language of the Establishment:

> I have been aware that subject to renouncing my right of succession, it may have been possible for me to contract a civil marriage but, mindful of the Church's teaching that Christian marriage is indissoluble and, conscious of my duty to the Commonwealth, I have resolved to put these considerations before any others.
>
> I have reached this decision entirely alone and in doing so I have been strengthened by unfailing support and devotion from Group Captain Townsend.

How times change! The Commonwealth now exists virtually only on paper and Princess Margaret was herself later to divorce Lord Snowdon, unmindful of the Church's teaching. The fact that she and Townsend could have defied the powers-that-be with the full support of the public made this a tragedy of Romeo and Juliet poignancy.

Townsend today is a cool, charming farmer and author – he wrote the blockbuster *The Last Emperor*. He is married to a Belgian heiress, Marie Luce, and lives in France with his wife and three children.

Though he was telling his story of the royal romance more than twenty years after the event, he steadfastly refused to write a word that might offend the Princess. Naturally it was the bits he left out that interested me most. Like just how far had they taken their love – and where and when?

'I wouldn't tell you that for £1 million,' Peter told me with a grin.

In my view the magic moment probably came on her first official trip. She went to Belfast accompanied by royal equerry Peter

28

Townsend. Margaret was seventeen at the time, Townsend twice her age. I didn't publish my conclusion. I couldn't bring myself to upset such an upright gentleman.

Anyway, the story was splendid as it was. I had told Messrs Matthews and Stevens that I would not call on them for the vast sums of money it costs to promote a newspaper's wares by way of television commercials until I had something worth advertising. They could not refuse me now. A royal romance, especially with a hint of scandal, is No. 1 on the list of the public's favourite reading, especially among women.

The management swiftly approved a promotion budget for the Townsend series – it was something like £420,000, six times the cost of the book – and we were in business. We hired a top director to make the commercial, Alan Parker of *Midnight Express* fame, and he did a brilliant job.

We printed three million copies of the paper on the first day of the series. Circulation reps reported a big response, with the paper selling out in many areas. Not a bad start. On my arrival six months earlier the *Express* was having trouble selling two million copies a day. Once the dust had settled I reckoned we held on to 165,000 of the new readers attracted to the paper by the Townsend story. Clear evidence, if any were needed, that my policy of going after the popular market was correct. Most gratifying of all was that the *Sun* ran what newspapers call a 'spoiler', their own version of the royal romance. They normally saved such tactics for the *Mirror*. It was the first time Sir Larry Lamb, the *Sun*'s highly successful editor, had taken a swipe at the *Express* and it cheered up the troops immensely. For the first time in years we were being taken seriously by the opposition. Once again we had become a *real* newspaper.

'We like to think the *Express* is competition for once,' Sir Larry told the trade journal *Campaign*. 'Derek is a very able tabloid journalist. He thinks journalism should be fun. And so do I. So long as they stay a million or so behind us, we're only too happy to see them doing well.'

The battle was joined. We were now a force in the marketplace, fighting all the way, aggravating our rivals and making an impression on the public. For the first time in decades the circulation was going UP instead of down.

Even Mrs Thatcher caught on to the mood, visiting the *Express* office for ninety minutes in April 1978 after asking 'to meet the backroom boys who produce the paper'. I told her: 'That makes good sense – I was getting worried about my sub-editors calling you "Maggie" without having met you.'

We set the Street alight again weeks later by tracking down the runaway Joyce McKinney, who had dodged bail on an abduction charge, at a hideaway in Atlanta, Georgia. For weeks the whole pack had been looking for her. Finding Joyce meant that we were on equal terms with the big boys.

THE CASE OF THE MANACLED MORMON attracted immense interest in the summer of 1978. The sensational McKinney, a blue-eyed blonde with a Southern-belle voice, had fallen for a Mormon missionary named Kirk Anderson. He was not interested. So she kidnapped her man, chained him to a bed in a rented cottage in Devon and had her way with him. It was all part of a love ritual, Joyce told magistrates at the preliminary hearing. 'I loved Kirk so much I would have skied down Mount Everest in the nude with a carnation up my nose.'

What a picture! Released on bail, Joyce did a runner while the trial was pending. She disappeared after covering her tracks by making a highly publicised visit to a film première on the arm of Peter Tory, then editor of the *Express*'s now defunct William Hickey column. It was the enterprising Tory who found her in Atlanta weeks later. A little wounded pride can go a long way. We were able to run huge headlines of the WE FIND JOYCE variety accompanied by stunning pictures of the lovestruck girl in her many guises. A notable scoop, though the *Mirror* was later to take the gilt off the gingerbread by a series of its own suggesting she had sold kinky sex in earlier years.

Even before the furore over McKinney faded another exciting promotional exercise turned up trumps. A petite blonde in her late twenties stepped into my office soon after my arrival at the *Express* and asked me to sponsor her on a lone yachting trip around the world.

Newspapers are approached almost daily to support this or that epic journey or adventure to the far-flung corners of the world. Most are denied on the grounds that they have scant prospect of success or cost too much. This particular venture did not seem a likely proposition. The girl so eager to traverse the globe single-handed was Naomi James, married to a famous yachtsman, Rob James, who was to die tragically young in a freak accident in harbour a few years later.

Naomi was not a particularly experienced sailor. I made enquiries and was told she wasn't likely to get past the Needles. But I liked her slow grin and the determined look in her eye. She also was from New Zealand. They seem to be special people. A New Zealander had won the Victoria Cross twice in World War II; and look at Sir Edmund Hillary. I decided to back Naomi, though I could offer her only £14,000 and some practical help from our staff and contacts around the globe.

She sailed triumphantly into Dartmouth on 8 June 1978, aboard the *Express Crusader*, my name for her 53-foot yacht. The Devon port went wild. She had travelled the globe for 30,000 miles on her own, an epic journey of 271 days 19 hours 20 minutes. A world record-breaker and a woman. She had clipped more than two days off the previous record held by Sir Francis Chichester. She, too, was given a handle and became Dame Naomi. The story at the start of summer captured the public's imagination. There was massive coverage by the media, including television news reports. Everywhere the *Express Crusader* was mentioned and *Daily Express* banners were flying. It cost the paper less than £20,000. The publicity was worth half a million.

At last the *Express* was making headway. Month after month healthy circulation gains were generated by the excitement stirred up on the paper. The audited average sale in the second half of 1978 was 2,516,677, a 25 per cent increase in my first year, a notable achievement in such a tough market. We were going like the clappers and on course for three million.

3

Masters and Servants

IT was obvious from the minute we met that I was going to have trouble with Jocelyn Stevens. Chewing up editors had become an everyday part of his job over the years as he fought valiantly to keep the *Express* papers afloat. Journalists are a high cost factor on newspapers, though not as expensive as the paper and ink. Editors in those pre-Wapping days were under severe restraint to keep within tight budgets.

Constant sniping about costs created an insuperable gulf between management and editorial in newspaper offices. Editors are munificent by nature and usually act dumb on matters of finance. They take the view that the more money you spend, the better the paper. And that in turn means more people are going to read it. Well, that's the theory.

Stevens, arriving in his eyrie in the morning, would go apoplectic as he went through the overnight production report. When you are counting every penny it doesn't help to learn that the publisher has spent £5,300 on supplementary road transport because the editorial missed the pooled rail service.

'Why, why, WHY?' he would scream over the intercom. He usually managed to come through bang in the middle of my editorial conference. My executives could hear every word and these morning slanging matches created some meaty gossip for the rest of the day . . . and the rest of the Street.

'Because I wasn't going to the Midlands without the Birmingham City and Aston Villa football results,' I would scream back. 'What d'you want to do, make us a laughing stock? It's YOUR bloody composing room that's to blame. Takes them two and a half hours to change a page they should be able to do in forty minutes!'

On one occasion I hung up on him mid-sentence. Jocelyn was back in a second and spat out with slow menace: 'Don't you dare, so long as you live, ever bang the phone down on me again . . .' What could I do? My executives were sitting on the edge of their seats waiting to see how the editor was going to handle this one. 'Wanna bet?' I snarled, slamming the phone down.

Jocelyn also kept up a bombardment of rude, cryptic memos implying that the recipient was a complete and utter disaster, incapable of doing the job for which he was employed. Here are some samples of the crossfire between managing director Stevens and editor Jameson:

From Managing Director to D. Jameson, 6 Feb. 1978: I continue to be depressed by the inability of the *Daily Express* to go to press on time. *(Sgd.) J.E.G. Stevens*

From the Managing Director to D. Jameson, 8 Feb. 1978: The Chairman would like a full explanation in writing for the lateness of the second and third editions last night. *(Sgd.) Jocelyn Stevens*

From Editor to Chairman, 8 Feb. 1978: The problem is that I am asking the staff to cope with too much work. What is far more damaging to the success of this newspaper is the bullying, arrogant and insulting way in which Mr. Stevens treats my executives and particularly myself. His latest outburst is to pledge himself to get rid of me as 'an absentee editor, always out wining and dining.' Most weeks I am in the office six nights and most days I am in at 10 am and home at midnight. That is the 'absentee editor.' *(Sgd.) Derek Jameson*

From F.L. Tyler, Company Secretary – Addendum to contract dated 19 Dec. 1978: You are not permitted to take part in any radio or television programme without the prior consent of the Chairman, or in his absence the Deputy Chairman.

From Derek Jameson to Deputy Chairman and Managing Director, 12 Jan. 1979: The restriction on my right to speak before a microphone without permission is most serious. Free speech is the fundamental right of everyone, not least the editor of a newspaper.

For all his bombast, I came to love Stevens. In the end everyone fell under his spell. Some of the toughest union leaders in the business, men who would lead a walkout if the canteen tea wasn't hot enough, wept openly when Stevens fell out with Matthews and quit newspapers. I wonder whether they love him as much now he is rector of the Royal College of Art? He was the ultimate gaffer. Tall, blond, powerfully built with blue eyes that labelled him instantly as someone from the top drawer. He was of the fading patrician breed that once ruled Fleet Street. His mother died in childbirth and he was brought up as the ward of his uncle, publisher Sir Edward Hulton, who owned a string of provincial papers and the famous *Picture Post*. Jocelyn grew up with the smell of printing ink in his nostrils and cared passionately about the Beaverbrook dynasty and its declining fortunes. They were like family to him.

By persuading them to sell off to Trafalgar, Jocelyn surrendered much of his own power to someone a million miles removed from his own background. Victor Matthews, like myself, was a poor London boy who made it to the top by hard graft and street cunning. Both of us grew up without knowing our fathers, left elementary schools at fourteen years and finished our education at night classes. Since we came out of the same mould he took to me instantly, and must have given me a great deal of protection in those early months when I was turning the *Daily Express* inside out to make it a competitive tabloid.

Just how much he helped is something of a mystery. Matthews was not a person to weaken his hand with any display of emotion. Once I got angry because the *Express* had managed to scoop its rivals on a big story and the proprietor seemed to think it was of little consequence. 'You never say "Thank you," do you?' I said to him. 'We worked night and day to land that story.' He stared at me with his bootblack eyes for a second or two, then said as if explaining to a child: 'The fact you are here, working for me, is "Thank you".'

He was only a little bloke, but had such a commanding presence that nobody summoned to his office would dare sit down unless invited to do so. You could tell in a second if he were annoyed by the number of people standing in front of his desk, feet twitching, waiting for the invitation that clearly was not going to come.

Even Jocelyn Stevens would defer to this builder from Islington sitting there quietly puffing away on a low tar Silk Cut, careful that no ash sullied his snow-white shirt with cutaway collar, elegant double-breasted suit and patterned silk tie to match. From the tip of his jet-black oiled hair to the toes of his black brogues, he exuded calm sanity in a world gone mad. I never once heard him raise his voice, nor was there anything about his office to suggest we were at the heart of a newspaper empire. Most of the time he would have just a single piece of paper on his desk, presumably telling him where he was due next.

He didn't even lose his composure when Jocelyn and myself almost came to blows in his office over a picture spread I had run in the *Express* of Princess Margaret in a sunsuit on holiday at the Florence villa of an Italian nobleman. What made the story particularly appealing was that she had recently broken with gardening expert Roddy Llewellyn and was supposedly in Italy getting over the affair – pure speculation on our part.

Stevens went potty when he saw the pictures. He thought they were intrusive and in bad taste. On top of that, there was no truth in the story that she was 'getting over' Roddy Llewellyn and we were wrongly implying a romance with the Italian. 'It's all complete and utter balls' was how he put it. I had no doubt he was right. Jocelyn was a personal friend of Princesss Margaret and his former wife was her lady-in-waiting. He must have received a telephone call before storming in to Matthews.

'Rubbish,' I said. 'Everyone knows she's upset about Roddy, even if she isn't saying so, and we thought they were a bloody marvellous set of pictures. Every newspaper in Fleet Street would have run them without a second's hesitation.'

'Oh God, oh God!' screamed Jocelyn as if he had been shot. 'I can't talk to this man. He's the most arrogant person I ever met.' At this unlikely proposition, he banged his head forcibly two or three times on the cabinet of the proprietor's twenty-six-inch television set.

'Calm down, calm down, the pair of you,' said Matthews. 'Derek, in future when you get anything like this, don't do things on your own. Have a word with Jocelyn. He knows people, understands what's going on. He's here to help . . . And you, Jocelyn, don't get into such a state. Derek wasn't having a go at you . . .'

I headed for the door. 'Now for the bad news,' I told them on my way out. 'The pictures are a scam. We were conned by an Italian picture agency. They are at least two years old. I should have thought Jocelyn, with his vast knowledge of such matters, would have noticed . . .' I didn't wait to see whether they laughed.

It was the kind of newspaper madness that baffled Matthews. He was strictly a manager, proud of his past as a top builder, and had no intention in his sixties of starting to learn the newspaper business. He regarded us as a bunch of wild men, anyway.

I remember pulling his leg about Princess Margaret on another occasion. The Princess and I held up the entire yachting world, half the dignitaries in London and Matthews and his chums for thirty minutes. It happened at the Boat Show at Earls Court and it was all on account of the cigarettes she was smoking as we sipped champagne before the opening ceremony. John Players. Plain.

'That's a rough old fag you've got there, Ma'am,' I said to her.

'What d'you mean?' she demanded.

'Well,' I said, 'they're plain and very strong. You'll do yourself a mischief smoking those. Top of the coffin nail league.'

'No, they're not,' she shot back. 'Capstan Full Strength are much worse.'

She was quite right, too. We got talking about our vain efforts to give up the noxious weed, how to learn to love tipped cigarettes, whether cigarette holders are any good, and so on. The Boat Show, sponsored by the *Express,* was a little late getting down the slipway that year. The brass band was beginning to fidget.

'What was all that about?' Matthews growled at me afterwards. 'Holding everybody up.'

'Not my fault, Guv'nor,' I told him. 'It was that Princess Margaret. Chatting me up.'

'Why should she chat you up?' he wanted to know.

'Well, stands to reason, doesn't it? Group Captain Townsend, Antony Armstrong Jones, Roddy Llewellyn, Derek Jameson.'

The building tycoon looked bewildered. 'What have you got to do with that lot?' His eyes bored through me.

'Obvious, innit?' I told him. 'I'm just like them, only rough with it.'

It was Matthews' total innocence that endeared us to him so much. In the three years I worked for the man he never once to my knowledge visited the editorial floor where the paper is produced. He would buzz me on the internal hotline and say 'Come down' when he wanted to see me. The fact that I was on the second floor and he was above me on the third was lost on him.

So was the strict timetable every newspaper must adhere to if it is to come out on time. He usually summoned me for a chat at around 5 pm, just as I was about to gather with the news production executives to decide the all-important question of what stories and pictures should run on the front page, showcase of the newspaper. To be honest, despite problems with the clock I enjoyed our lengthy confabs together. He was completely at ease with me, no doubt because of his conviction that someone from Hackney must be inferior to himself, a lad from Highbury Corner in Islington, two miles up the road. 'You wouldn't understand, coming from Hackney', he was to say to me on more than one occasion. Similarly, he objected if anyone said he was a cockney or came from the East End. 'I'm from North London', he would tell them importantly.

Matthews told me some extraordinary stories. Of his climb to the top from costing clerk at the old-established City builders Trollope and Colls to deputy chairman and managing director of Trafalgar House and now chairman of Express Newspapers. He might well have stayed a clerk forever, but for a mean employer. Matthews had worked hard, gone to night school to become a surveyor, and was delighted one day to be entrusted with the takeover of two relatively small building concerns. I think he paid something like £1 million for them. In their first year, they produced a return of £300,000 profit. So it was clearly a good deal for Trollope and Colls.

'How much d'you think they gave me for my part in it?' Victor asked me.

'What, you mean like a bonus?' I said. 'I wouldn't know. The building trade's foreign to me. About twenty grand, I guess. Perhaps £25,000.'

'Not a light,' said Victor. 'Not two ha'pennies to rub together.' He rubbed his forefinger with his thumb, Fagin-style. 'So I thought "Sod 'em, I'll set up on my own". And I did.' Although well into his thirties, he borrowed that little 'something for a rainy day' that working-class mums of our generation usually kept under the mattress and took it to a friendly local bank manager, who agreed to a loan. Eventually Victor put together enough capital to purchase a small builder's yard in Brixton, South London.

The great postwar building boom was in full spate and Victor quickly built up a reputation as a first-class builder who delivered on time and guaranteed high quality work. His speciality was gutting and rebuilding old properties, a rich field of endeavour that finally brought him alongside City whizzkid Nigel Broackes.

They were chalk and cheese, but became close partners. Victor the builder and manager, Nigel the negotiator with a keen eye for a good deal. Ultimately they were to own Cementation and other construction companies, the Cunard shipping line and its prestigious *QEII*, and a hotel chain with the Ritz as jewel in the crown. Among the companies they took over along the way was Trollope and Colls.

As owner of the *QEII* and chairman of Cunard, people naturally assumed that Victor was enamoured of the sea. He had spent the war years in the Royal Navy. In fact, he confided in me, he was a lousy sailor and frequently seasick. Which perhaps explains why one of the nation's captains of industry managed to serve through World War II with but one promotion – from ordinary to able-bodied seaman.

Nigel Broackes could not have been more different. Upper class, in the Jocelyn Stevens mould. Stowe public school and the 3rd Hussars. Victor talked of him often. 'My chum', he called him. His deputy chairman was deeply wounded, though too proud to show it, when Nigel produced a remarkably candid autobiography, *A Growing Concern* (Weidenfeld, 1979), in which he cast Victor as a dour and humourless manager with whom he did not mix socially. It turned out they had never visited each other's house. Those of us working for the Trafalgar empire at the time were astonished by Nigel's admission that he had dodged paying fares on the Underground in his earlier years.

'I can't understand why he's saying such things,' Victor told me, shaking his head ruefully. 'It's not as if he has to write a book – he doesn't need the money.'

Sniffing a good story, Charles Wintour persuaded Matthews to review *A Growing Concern* in the columns of the *Evening Standard*. It was an extraordinary piece, a cry of pain over errors and omissions in the book. Relations between our two bosses, partners for more than fifteen years at the top of one of the nation's biggest conglomerates, seemed to be down to the level of icy politeness.

Astonishingly, they had gone public on their differences. Throughout the Trafalgar empire executives almost fell over each other as they rushed in and out of offices clutching the paper and crying 'Christ! Have you seen this?'

In his piece, Matthews wrote that initially he had declined an invitation to review the book. He changed his mind when Nigel presented him with a copy and he turned to the flyleaf, anticipating some well-phrased inscription, but found it blank. 'Then, I must confess, I opened the index and found there were numerous references to myself – some flattering, some less so. I thought it was an autobiography, but as I read through the book I wondered whether it wasn't partially my biography and not in the way I would have put it.'

After complaining that Mr Broackes, as he called him, had failed to check his facts with the parties concerned (presumably himself), Matthews said it was his contacts as a builder with the Beaverbrook family that laid the seeds for Trafalgar's takeover of the *Express* papers.

'He describes why he was anxious to acquire Beaverbrook, referring to my alleged moroseness and morbidity at that time. (Boredom would be a better word; I was chairing twenty-four subsidiary board meetings in twenty working days and found it almost impossible to take a day off for any purpose whatsoever.) I was not opposed to acquiring Beaverbrook, but I had considerable doubt as to whether I wished to assume responsibility for it personally.'

Poor old Victor. He was most upset by Nigels's suggestion that he was a misery guts. It is true that he smiled rarely and never got excited about anything, but this he put down to his cautious nature. Certainly he liked to get away from the boredom and bureaucracy at the top of so many big corporations. Reams and reams of paper, endless meetings and appointments with people who were after something.

He was the only man at the top I ever met who hated being bothered at home, which endeared him to me all the more. As his editor, I was allowed the phone number of his farm at Enfield, outside London, with strict instructions not to call him after 7 pm unless it was essential. 'He doesn't like to be interrupted doing the washing up' I would tell people.

Once I called him to report that the electricians' chapel was playing up and we were not likely to get the *Daily Express* on the streets next morning. 'The labour relations people are talking to them, but it doesn't look very hopeful,' I told him. 'I'll try to get a late London edition, but don't put any bets on it.'

'Bloody idiots,' Victor said. 'I've already given them my last word. They never learn, do they? What did you call me for?'

He reckoned he put in a day's work at the farm before coming into Fleet Street. Some said unkindly that he got many of his ideas about popular newspapers from his cowman. More likely the *Daily Mirror*, I thought. He was always quoting the paper to me, unfailingly prefacing his remarks with: 'The wife read in the *Mirror* today . . .' I reckon it was his favourite paper, too, followed by the *Financial Times*. According to *Private Eye* it was the shadowy cowman who complained to Victor about my frequent appearances on television. 'That Jameson's not doing you any good shooting his mouth off on the box,' he is supposed to have said.

Outside the farm, Matthews liked to slip away at least once a week to play golf. When I dared suggest it was all right for some, playing golf while others worked night and day seventy hours a week, he exploded all over the office.

'Play? Play! I don't go there to play,' he said. 'Everyone knows that much of the business of this country is done on the golf course.'

Matthews had a great passion for sport. His wife Joyce and son Ian were heavily into training racehorses. Ian was their only child, a chubby young lad who worked in various departments at the *Express* without making much impression. My only contact with him came when he parked one of father's cars, a Jaguar, in the space specially reserved for the editor of the *Daily Express*. I screamed blue murder and had it removed. 'You know what youngsters are,' his father said to me. 'I don't know what he gets up to half the time, and I'm doing all this' – he swept his hand round the huge office – 'for him.'

There were to be suggestions that Trafalgar had bought Express Newspapers as a toy for Victor to while away his twilight years in business while others got on with running the conglomerate in his place. Whatever the motives, it was to become the biggest triumph of all for the little builder turned newspaper tycoon. It won him a peerage in 1980, years before Broackes got a knighthood for his work developing London's Docklands. More importantly, Matthews floated the group away from Trafalgar and strengthened it to the point where it was bought in 1985 by United Newspapers, a provincial chain that included *Punch* among its assets. They paid £317 million – a startling advance on the £13.6 million Trafalgar had paid for it eight years earlier. Matthews' personal holding was worth £8 million and he also collected another £10 million or so in Trafalgar stock before retiring to the Channel Islands.

I was delighted for him. Victor had always moaned to me, knowing my socialist leanings, that the Labour government of Harold Wilson had cost him personally £7 million in taxes. Politics were always a barrier between us, and I might well have survived better at the *Express* had I been prepared to jump on the Thatcher bandwagon personally as well as in the paper.

Mind you, I never once let him down on politics. At our very first meeting, in the Hotel Bristol, I told him how flattered and delighted I was to be offered the job, but that there could be a problem in view of the fact that, like most *Mirror* executives, I was a Labour supporter. He pointed out that Lord Beaverbrook made a tradition of employing socialist editors, notably Michael Foot and Robert Edwards, and he could see no reason why he should not do the same. 'You wouldn't be daft enough to try to turn it into a Labour rag,' he said. I readily concurred.

Politics was the last thing on my mind as I set about turning round the *Daily Express*, though I had to go through the ritual of approving Tory editorials with the leader writers every day. It wasn't too difficult. Half the time I couldn't see the point they were trying to make, and I also knew that the vast majority of people reading newspapers ignore leader columns. Quite right too.

The first priority in my mind was to get punch and pace into the paper. Everyone gave me the benefit of any doubts – the editor's prerogative – and the word quickly spread: 'This bloke from the *Mirror* knows what he's doing'. Which is more than could be said for many of my predecessors. Everyone knew that the circulation was going down the drain. Officially, we were just above two million copies daily. The paper was haemorrhaging so badly that the advertising department had to offer clients a rebate if it dropped below that figure.

The *Express* staff also took comfort from the fact I had been a sub-editor on the *Daily Express* for a couple of years in the early sixties, having been discovered by the man they admired most, the legendary Arthur Christiansen. He got me the job there when the weekly *London American* I was editing under his tutelage folded through lack of capital.

'The *Express*'s new Crusader', said a profile in *The Guardian* on my appointment. 'He is, in short, a popular newspaperman down to the last four-letter word (strictly not for publication). The *Express* has come full circle from the highbrow Alastair Burnet, who finished his uneasy stint, shell-shocked and bearing the scar of shingles, to a protégé of Christiansen . . .'

Arthur Christiansen has always been my guiding light in news-papers. One lesson I failed to learn from him was to steer clear of the murky waters of politics and the class system. With his powerful domed head, bulldog jaw and barking laugh, he was to inspire many newspapermen and women of my generation. The great thing about Chris, as we called him, was that he knew exactly what he was doing and what was best for his newspaper. Doubt, indecision and second guessing never entered his mind.

Like most editors, he took a lot of stick over the years from his proprietor, Lord Beaverbrook, the Canadian entrepreneur who gained control of the *Express* in 1916 by buying out the chief shareholder for £17,500. But Chris never wavered in his loyalty nor blotted his copybook by poking his nose too deeply into the muddled politics of the crafty old imperialist. He couldn't be bothered with all that nonsense.

The love affair between the empire builder and the apolitical newspaperman began in true romantic style in 1930 when Christiansen was deputy editor of the *Sunday Express*. He had already finished work and gone home to his flat in Chelsea when the late-duty reporter called in the early hours to say there were unconfirmed reports that the famous R101 airship had crashed. Chris was back in the office by the time the report was confirmed. He stopped the presses and produced a late-extra edition carrying the full story with pictures. It was on the streets at 8 am, something the unions never would have permitted in later years.

Beaverbrook rang at 9 am. 'You have secured a wonderful feat of journalism,' he said. 'I am proud to be associated with the newspaper on which you work. Goodbye to you.' Three years later Chris was editor of the *Daily Express*.

Chris died in 1963 at a relatively early age, victim of the weak heart that had led Lord Beaverbrook to drop him as editor six years earlier. He had his first heart attack while staying with the Beaver, who removed him from office during his convalescence. The problem was that he lacked the courage to tell Christiansen, the editor who had made his newspaper so successful and to whom he owed so much, that he was finished. Chris turned up at the office to resume normal business unaware that he was out of a job. When he finally caught up with the proprietor, Beaverbrook told him he had no alternative in view of Christiansen's heart condition. 'I don't wish to be shunned at your funeral,' he said.

Chris was offered a sinecure and a fancy office in the usual fashion. He brushed them aside and set up shop as an editorial consultant. He even tried his hand at show business, playing himself as editor in *The Day the Earth Caught Fire*, a film I have seen many times. It wasn't the Chris we all knew and loved. He was far too stilted and self-conscious. Nevertheless, that sci-fi film planted the seed in my mind: if all else fails, try show business.

In his role as consultant, in 1960 Chris took on the commitment of guiding and encouraging a bunch of young journalists involved in a short-lived weekly called the *London American*, a newspaper aimed at Americans in Britain. I was editor and was only too happy to appoint myself to the task of calling on Chris to go through the proofs together. For two or three hours each week I would sit at the master's feet, hanging on to every word. In this way I was able to pick the brains of the greatest journalistic craftsman of the age, discovering his thoughts and feelings about newspapers and the business of editing. It was an education that was going to be invaluable in future years. I put this remarkable opportunity down to *upstairs*, the angels who have always looked after me and determined my fate. They always make sure I am in the right place at the right time.

The undercapitalised *London American* folded after fourteen months. Chris, much concerned about the staff, immediately called Bob Edwards, one of his successors as editor of the *Daily Express*, and suggested that he would do well to hire a likely lad named Jameson. Within minutes I was ushered into Bob's office in the Black Lubyianka, as we all called *Express* headquarters, and appointed a sub-editor in the features department at a salary of £35 a week – a tenner less than I had been getting at the *London American*. It did not matter. I was now on the staff of 'the world's greatest newspaper', as it proudly proclaimed itself.

It was true enough in Christiansen's time. His influence was still everywhere when I first arrived, though the decline that would take it from his peak of 4.3 million daily to less than two million today was already evident. The top brass was already engaged in the lunatic process of hiring and firing editors willy-nilly, the sure sign that a newspaper – or its management – has lost all sense of direction. Chris had been editor almost twenty-five years, from 1933 to 1957. There have been more than a dozen in the three decades since.

Hard news and strong features, brilliantly projected, was the Christiansen recipe for success. He also believed in the power of pictures. The first thing to catch the eye on entering the *Daily Express* editorial was a banner proclaiming: *One good picture is worth 10,000 words*. He also issued bulletins several times a week giving his views on the paper and dishing out kicks and kudos in equal measure. His words illustrate the short, staccato sentence style of writing that the *Express* papers much favoured in those days. Whether they originated from Christiansen or Beaverbrook himself is not clear, but they were employed to devastating effect. Here are some of the thoughts of Arthur Christiansen:

Good stories flow like honey. Bad stories stick in the craw. What is a bad story? It is a story that cannot be absorbed on the first time of reading. It is a story that leaves questions unanswered. It is a story that has to be read two or three times before it can be comprehended. And a good story can be turned into a bad story by just one obscure sentence.

Let's make war on adjectives. The first edition Diary today says that Miss Bride is 'a well-known flower painter.' There is no need for the adjective. If she is not a well-known flower painter, then the adjective is a lie.

I have the idea that we are striving a bit too hard on make-up in some parts of the paper these days. We should keep layout tricks under control. There is much virtue in simplicity. Always the reader OUTSIDE Fleet Street should be considered.

Yesterday in a story about a broken romance we referred to the girl's occupation as that of bottler in a lemonade factory. We used to have a rule that we did not refer to the occupations of people in lowly stations when romance or broken romance was involved. It is a good rule and should be revived.

It would do everyone connected with Fleet Street (especially editors) a power of good if they spent an occasional day off in unfamiliar territory seeing the newspaper reader as he is at work and play. In familiar territory in the neighbourhood of your own home you don't get the same perspective.

I journeyed from Rhyl to Prestatyn on Sunday past lines of boarding houses, caravans, wooden huts, shacks, tents, and heaven knows what else. In every one of them there were newspaper readers. Happy citizens, worthy, fine people, but not in the least like the reader Fleet Street seems to be writing for.

These people are not interested in Glyndebourne or vintage claret or opera or the Sitwells or dry as dust economics or tough politics. It is our job to interest them in everything. It requires the highest degree of skill and ingenuity.

Mr. Hearst [American media tycoon William Randolph Hearst] says that his ideal paper is one that causes the following reaction: 'When the reader looks at Page One he says "Gee whizz". When he turns to the second page he says "Holy Moses". And when he turns to the middle pages he says "God Almighty".'

I am not very much in favour of stories of dog shows which describe the scene without telling us who won the championship. A champion dog is a fascinating animal. It must have some peculiarities. It must be fed on some kind of diet. It must have an owner who wears clothes. The descriptive story without facts went out of date even before the twenty-four-page paper died. And I was the leader of the execution party.

News, news, news – that is what we want. You can describe things with the pen of Shakespeare himself, but you cannot beat news in a newspaper.

The gigantic sale of the *Daily Express* should never be used for belittling or mocking or making cheap little people. We must go for the big shots when we want to criticise. We should project our selection of news and features with human understanding, with a generosity of purpose, and with a full sense of the power of a mighty Press, the power to hurt and wound. Always we must guard against the hard-boiled cynical Fleet Street approach.

The master at work. This was the man whose shoes I stepped into with such confidence and high hopes in August 1977. I had taken his philosophy so much to heart that it seemed impossible that I should not succeed. It would have been disrespectful to his memory.

George Scott, then presenting *The Editors* on BBC TV, interviewed me within hours of my being chosen to sit in Christiansen's chair. I told him that my aim quite simply was to restore the paper to the status it had enjoyed under Chris as one of the world's great newspapers. Fred Holtum, a senior BBC TV news executive who had worked with me as a lad at Reuters, wrote that my appearance on *The Editors* must ensure, if all else failed, that 'you have a brilliant future in television'. He must have had a crystal ball in his bonce.

The most gratifying of the letters that came flooding in to congratulate me on my appointment was from Mrs Brenda Christiansen, the great man's widow. After thanking me for my tribute to Chris, she said: 'I wish with all my heart you will be able to bring the *Express* up to its old standards. I think all your predecessors had a hell of a time. May you find it easier. Perhaps Chris will be standing behind your chair as I am sure he is very proud.'

The strangest letter was from another Christiansen. His son Michael, who had been my editor through the sixties at the *Sunday Mirror*. He went on to become editor of the *Daily Mirror*, briefly, but he too succumbed to heart trouble like his father and died in 1984, aged fifty-seven. It was no secret that Mike cherished ambitions to follow his father at the *Express*. We had never hit it off, largely because of my feeling that he regarded me as a cockney upstart too big for his boots. I picked up his letter with some foreboding:

My dear Derek,

So 'tis you who will next step into my father's shoes. I know – because

46

you have told me – that he had high respect for your initiative and enterprise. So in the journalists' pantheon (residence of the gods, *he wrote*) that he probably now occupies I expect there is great satisfaction at the news.

Back here on earth I have more mixed feelings. I always thought you a superb Mirror man, both Sunday and Daily. It was you who doubted my faith, but even now I am a loyal devotee. I suppose the Express is going to challenge the Mirror and Sun under your chieftainship. Well, none better, but I hope the policy proves right for journalism is not just sales, but also commercial and business acumen. The man who can combine all three targets at once is the greatest.

All this sounds pretty carping. I wish you all good fortune and good hunting as Editor.

Sincerely,
Michael Christiansen.

David (now Sir David) English, editor of the *Daily Mail* and one of my main rivals, was far more generous. 'Congratulations and welcome to the club', he wrote. 'In my view, you should have been a member a long time ago.'

4

A Life in the Day

EXECUTIVE stress is an occupational hazard for every editor. Some say it is the toughest job of all, though no doubt racing drivers or SAS men would disagree. There is certainly nothing quite like running a newspaper. This chapter describes a typical day in the editor's chair, though some details have been changed to avoid embarrassment . . .

THE phone's ringing in the outer office. No secretary in yet. Mustn't grumble. It's only five to ten. I've come in a bit early to run through the final editions, checking whether they tally with the headlines I read over breakfast an hour earlier. There's been a shooting in Paddington, two dead. Heard it on the nine o'clock headlines on radio. The rivals may have picked up the story and done a late slip – changed the page – for the London area. We'll look bloody stupid if we've missed it. Doesn't seem to be anything in any of the others, though I see the *Mirror* is still running its Midland 3-star edition in the London area. Poor sods. Obviously can't get on their late page changes. The secretary's phone rings just as I'm about to buzz the news desk on the internal to find out what time the Paddington murder broke. It's the front hall. Commissionaire speaking. 'The Wing Commander's here, sir . . . says he's got an appointment.'

Wing Commander! What bloody wing commander? I don't want to see him at this ghastly hour. I feel terrible. Hardly any sleep. Was well pissed when I got in at half-past midnight. That dinner went on and on and on until gone eleven. Then like a fool I came in and looked at the paper instead of going straight home. Went to sleep all right. Then, bang!, four o'clock in the morning I'm wide awake,

cold sober, staring into the night. It was hours before I drifted off
again. Pauline rang at seven.

Pauline! Wing Commander! The pieces fall into place. Someone
claiming senior rank in the RAF has been phoning my ex-wife at her
home in the middle of the night, demanding to speak to me.

'Yes, that's okay. Send him up. I want a word with him.' Indeed
I do. So much so that I go to the lift to greet my visitor from the
RAF.

'How dare you? How DARE you!' I yell as soon as he walks into
my office.

Wing Commander X looks at me blankly. Very much senior
officer material. Tall, grave, with a larged beaked nose. He isn't
wearing uniform. The grey-blue greatcoat obviously dates from
RAF days, though someone has sewn on civilian buttons. Obviously
retired. 'You ARE a wing commander?' I ask querulously.

He pulls out some kind of ID card. There's a small colour print
of him in the right-hand corner. This time he has a moustache.

'How dare you phone my ex-wife in Islington at two o'clock in the
morning and demand to see me!' I spell it out. Pauline's call at 7 am
was to say there's a Wing Commander Somebody-or-other who has
to speak to me urgently on a matter of national security. He had
been on several times, the last at two o'clock that morning.

'Two o'clock in the morning! Are you mad? I don't even live
there! We're no longer married.'

'A most charming lady,' he tells me evenly. Well, he's right there.
Pauline told me they had a little chat, that he had some kind of
problem he couldn't tell her about. National security. 'He seems a
nice enough chap,' she said. Two o'clock in the morning! Nice?
That's Pauline.

'It was the only way I could get to you, you see,' the Wing
Commander says. 'You were in the London phone directory.
Daren't go through normal channels,' he says. 'They're everywhere.'
He touches his nose with his forefinger. There's no apology. He
doesn't even sound sorry. Perhaps the man's a nut. 'Hang on,' I tell
him and rush to the outer office. Maria Pemberton, my secretary,
has arrived. 'I've got a nut in there,' I hiss at her. 'Get Security to
have someone on the landing. I think he's okay, but just in case.'

Normally I wouldn't bother, but the death threats in the beautiful

Gothic handwriting have been coming again. *Derek Jameson I am going to kill you*, they say. No punctuation. Snow Hill nick sent a DC round to investigate. The only conclusion he reached was 'Nice writing'. The things they learn at Hendon police college. Perhaps the Wing Commander can write 18-point copperplate. Back in my office, I ask how I can help him.

'I'm a bio-chemist,' he tells me. 'A career officer, but a chemist. Industrial. Top-level stuff. You know the sort of thing. I've been in Ulster. Four years. Working with the truth drug.'

That made me jump. 'How does it affect the situation there?' I ask him.

'It's not that I'm concerned about,' he says. 'It's our own lads. These are mind drugs. We've been struck badly. They've been experimenting on the troops. I've just done two years in hospital. There's no compensation, you see. Not a penny. They can't admit the stuff exists. That's why I've come to you.'

Well, he sounded lucid enough. He was a wing commander and he obviously knew all about chemistry. Thousands of our troops in Northern Ireland affected by a leakage of mind gas. I wrote the headline in my mind: TROOPS IN MIND GAS HORROR. But what about the MoD? Chemical warfare was restricted information, wasn't it? Still, we could always get round it by making it a mystery story. Give the facts, but make it all sound vague. *Army chiefs investigating suspected leak of chemicals . . .* Obviously we would have to check it out.

'Can you prove these allegations?' I looked the Wing Commander squarely in the eye. 'You seem perfectly all right to me.'

'In that case,' he said triumphantly like a man with the winning ace, 'how come that the hair on my head is ginger while that around my balls is bright green!'

For a second I thought it was a hoax, that I had been well and truly had. But he was deadly serious. 'Well, we'll look into it,' I tell him. 'Meanwhile, if I were you, I'd go to the Sunday *Observer*. They're very big on national security there.' I ushered him out to the landing, passing him over to the waiting security man. The poor wingco was obviously what we call a front-hall nutter. They normally never get past main reception. This one had got away with it by phoning Pauline and flashing his ID card.

Tea and the mail next. You can never have too much tea in a newspaper office; it is the universal lubricant. As for the mail, the usual invitations to charity receptions and book launches. Two or three job-seekers of the *How do I become a journalist* variety, a particularly sticky solicitor is demanding damages, costs and equal space for an apology in the Hickey column and the gardening correspondent is threatening to resign if his column next Friday is down to nine inches again. Six schoolboys in Anglesey want the paper to sponsor a natural history expedition to Madagascar and the overnight production report says we were twenty minutes late on the first edition and never caught up all night. That will be the backbench sodding about with those ornamental rules on the front page. Of course, they'll blame Sport.

Letters to the editor from the readers – that famous font of democracy – go direct to the editorial post department. The editor doesn't see them. Today I might find time to read a proof with a handful of letters that the paper intends to publish. All of them will have been processed by the sub-editors' mincing machine to make them uniformly crisp and to the point. Sometimes they actually are written by the subs under various names because so many genuine letters are dull and boring. On top of that, many of those who do write are potty. Some say *all* of them. Advanced cases of paranoia are usually spotted. They generally write in ink of four or five different colours. Letters that rubbish celebrities are often concocted inside the paper because the subs need a picture to liven up the page. My first job on a Fleet Street newspaper was writing readers' letters. I must have broken many hearts feeding the art bench's constant hunger for single-column pictures.

Having dealt with the mail, now's the only chance to read overnight proofs of early feature pages. This is the first time I will have seen much of the material going into the paper. Whatever my view, there is little I can do about it. To scrap stories and pictures will slow down the production process and make the paper late – a far greater problem than a dreary feature. So the most I can do is a few *tickles*, altering a headline here and there or asking for a picture to be cropped differently and remade.

My deputy, big Arthur Firth, ambles in at this stage, clutching his own early proofs. We exchange a few words so that he can add my 'marks' to his own and hand them over to Features before the main editorial conference of the day. Like most editors' deputies, Arthur is a personal friend, on the same wavelength. He can read my mind. Between us, we sort out what we want to see on the feature pages and Arthur will convey these thoughts to the executives concerned, doling out kicks or kudos.

'How many bloody times do we have to tell them we don't want fashion spreads from Sloane Street?' I demand. 'Dresses at 450 quid a whack! It's bloody nonsense. Why can't they go to Marks and Sparks same as the readers?' Arthur will let it be known gently to the fashion department that the editor prefers High Street fashion to haute couture.

They file in for conference at 11 am, departmental heads or their deputies crowding the tweed bench seats lining the walls. As my deputy, Arthur has automatic claim to the armchair adjoining my desk. Everyone faces the editor sitting behind his big, intimidating, leather-topped desk. I glance round, spotting notable absentees in a second, and reach for the internal hotline.

'Hello, news desk? Would you kindly ask Mr Arliss Rhind if he would be good enough to grace us with his presence at morning conference? There are sixteen of us sat here like lemons and we can't very well run a newspaper without knowing what the news is, can we?'

Arliss comes bustling through the door. How is he going to play it – sheepish or angry? 'Sorry, boss,' he mutters, 'been an explosion in Ellesmere Port.' He's the news editor, in charge of reporters and news coverage. A tall, tough Scotsman, another good friend. Editors aim to get their own people in top jobs. Life is difficult enough without permitting enemies to flourish in key positions. Sometimes you have to put up with it. Talking them into voluntary *redundo* can be too expensive.

Conference starts with the news schedule. Arliss goes through the main stories of the day. Who's covering them, how they rate in *Daily Express* terms. He will try particularly to sell stories that his reporters have found – or bought – exclusively for the paper. In theory, these are at a premium since we are on our own with them. Others at the conference are not likely to share the news desk's enthusiasm.

'We've got a good one here on a schoolmaster who's quitting because he's in trouble for clipping a boy round the ear,' says Arliss.

'What did the kid do?' I want to know.

'Spat on a girl in his class.'

'Happens all the time,' someone interjects. 'Teachers can't just go around bashing kids. That's all there is to it.'

'He didn't *bash* him,' says Arliss. 'He just gave him a slight cuff round the ear. What's wrong with that?'

'Well, we'll have a look at it,' I say, playing Solomon. 'Perhaps we'll get a debate going in the paper. When can a teacher discipline an unruly pupil? Does anyone care?'

'What about this murder in the King's Road?' the picture desk wants to know. *What murder?* The TV screen winking in the corner has no mention of murder, but then crime is not one of Ceefax's best subjects. This sounds tasty. The best murders are always committed in places like the King's Road. There are murders and murders in tabloid newspapers. Some will make a front-page splash, others are regarded as *fish 'n' chips* – cheap and tatty – and hardly rate a paragraph. Depends on the social status of the victim and where the crime was committed.

'We don't know the details yet,' says Arliss. 'Still waiting for a statement from the Yard.' He sounds uneasy and is obviously having problems with the story.

'Don't know about that,' says the picture editor indignantly. Tall, precise Andrew Harvey, former London *Standard* man, always eager to be first. 'She was a model. A proper one, not Page 3. Her old lady is a Cruft's breeder. We've got three men out on it already.'

'Why was she killed, where was she found, have they pulled anyone?' The questions come thick and fast.

'We dunno much yet,' says Arliss. 'She was found in a posh flat in one of those houses behind the old Chelsea Town Hall.'

'The *Sun*'s buying up everyone who moves over there,' says Andrew. 'They've already got the next-door neighbour, and the *Mirror* is supposed to have her sister. We think the *Mail* is alongside an ex boyfriend.'

'Christ!' I explode. 'Who have we got?'

'Nobody, at the moment,' says Arliss, 'but don't worry.' He taps his nose, indicating he is on to something.

'We're round at the model agency,' adds Andrew helpfully.

'F*** me,' says the editor. 'Sounds like this one is running away from us.

The inevitable question crosses my mind: 'Who's got the mother?'

One by one the departments go through their work schedules. This is where the paper gets its personality. The weight given to the news, pictures, features and sport under discussion determines the shape of future issues of the paper. Executives float their pet projects, ideas buzz around the room, the editor lays down the law. There are differing opinions. Nobody falls out over them. These are professionals. They all know what makes a good story. If the editor pronounces something 'Rubbish', then it's on to the next item on the agenda.

The foreign desk last. I'm in bad odour with this lot for shutting down the expensive Paris bureau. They even had some ancient retainer of Lord Beaverbrook on the editorial budget. 'Sod all happens in France that Reuters couldn't tell us about in six pars', I told them. They don't like that kind of talk. The more bureaux, the bigger the desk.

'There's been a coach crash outside Dortmund, seven dead.' Foreign editor John Ellison kicks off diffidently. He senses the editor's lack of interest. If he can't tempt the editor, then pictures, production and the rest will be equally blasé.

'Any British?'

'Not among the dead. There may have been one or two tourists on the coach.'

We move on to other stories. Nothing much here. Like the public they serve, popular newspapers care little for what goes on out there in the wide world unless it concerns Britain, though we go through the motions if only because the *Express* was once noted for its superb foreign coverage.

Conference over. The queue in the outer office is bigger than ever. Best time to get a hurried word with the editor is between conference and lunch. In come one or both of the leader writers. What great thoughts will have inspired them today? They are there to reflect the views of the paper. In other words, make sure they don't upset the proprietor. You have to watch them. They are supposed to be in tune politically, but being journalists will twist the lion's tail given half a chance.

I hate leader conferences. What madness – a socialist editor curbing and briefing Tory leader writers! I generally let them get on with it, claiming not to understand their opinions and comments. Leader writers are the intellectual wing, invariably Oxbridge and sometimes marking time in Fleet Street waiting for a Tory seat to come along. I reckon they write their editorials in Latin, then translate them into English so the rest of us have only the vaguest idea what they are talking about.

Editorial comment is the only copy to be sent automatically to the proprietor – and often the only thing in the paper he actually reads. The leader writers' ability to pass judgement on high-flown matters with the correct literary flourish and learned allusion has an important bearing on the climate in the chairman's office. Get it wrong and I could be in the doghouse for days. We'll be all right today. Jimmy Macmillan, chief leader writer, is on deck. He learned his craft at the feet of George Malcolm Thomson, official megaphone of the founding father Lord Beaverbrook. Macmillan is a skilled leader writer, quick and to the point.

The leader column sorted out, the next item on the agenda is to okay the cartoon. Problems here because Michael Cummings, the *Express*'s brilliant political cartoonist, seems to me to be slightly to the right of Attila the Hun, even if he is the son of the legendary liberal commentator A. J. Cummings. With their blazing eyes and sharp, pointed features, Michael's caricatures look a poisonous bunch. He reserves most of his venom for Labour leaders. I recognise Michael's skills, but don't like his drawings. Every day he submits five or six rough outlines and I select the one which seems least cruel. Michael probably takes a different view, but he rarely argues the toss.

As editor, I carry the can for the entire contents of the paper, including the cartoons. Readers who respond angrily to something they see over breakfast might be surprised to know that I may well agree with them. I remember Cummings once produced a naked James (now Lord) Callaghan for the front page to illustrate that the beleaguered Labour premier was shorn of policies to meet Britain's economic and industrial problems. Jim spotted me when he was speaking at an official lunch not long afterwards. 'I see Mr Jameson has me going naked into the conference chamber,' he told his audience. 'I can assure him that I'm not feeling any draught whatsoever.' I was most embarrassed. As for Jim, he probably wrote asking for the original of the cartoon.

By now it's around 12.30 and there are still two or three people hanging around waiting for that magic word with the editor. I run an open-door policy, which means I am available to anyone from the tea boy to a visiting starlet so long as the door between my office and the secretaries' room outside is open. It usually is. Right now Ken Lawrence, the sports editor, wants to know if he can send a writer on a forthcoming rugby tour of Australia and New Zealand. 'Christ, it will cost thousands,' I tell him. 'The *Mail* and *Mirror* are going,' he answers. That settles it. 'Well, we'll have to go then,' I tell him. Ken's face lights up. Someone will be getting a smashing trip. It is a time-honoured ritual. His rival at the *Mirror* will be saying at about this time: 'The *Express* and *Mail* are going . . .'

Another head round the door. A Chapel – office branch – representative from the NUJ (National Union of Journalists). They will have to hold a meeting of the news sub-editors at five o'clock to discuss the management's threat to withdraw late-meal allowances from staff who finish work before 10 pm. I know this is a hot potato. Any move by management to save money at the staff's expense always means big trouble.

'Bloody Nora,' I remonstrate. 'Can't you discuss it at a more reasonable time? Only half the copy will be down by five o'clock. Why not have your meeting after the first edition is closed . . . 7.30, say.'

'No, it will hold up their supper breaks.'

'Well, I mean to say, it's you who wants to hold the bloody meeting. What's wrong with making it earlier, say three o'clock.'

'That's no good. People affected won't be here. A lot of shifts don't start until 4 or 4.30.'

This bloke is not going to give me any comfort. I cave in. We agree to a meeting at five o'clock, but not longer than half an hour, and would the Chapel ask the subs to shovel down as much copy as possible before they stop work. Buzz deputy editor Arthur Firth on the hotline: 'Tell the backbench when they come in that the bloody

Chapel has called a mandatory meeting of the subs for five o'clock over those late-meal allowances. I told them upstairs the Chapel would never wear it. Anyway, they've promised to be back by 5.30 so it could be worse.'

There are still people waiting to see me, half a dozen messages on the desk and several letters to be dictated. It's 12.55 pm and I should have left for lunch ten minutes ago. Euston today and the offices of Collett Dickenson Pearce, the *Express* advertising agents. Frank Lowe is in charge. A bundle of energy and ideas that make him the best advertising brain in Britain – so clever it makes you want to spit. As if to prove the point, he seizes on the fact that I am smoking Benson & Hedges in the gold packet.

'They're one of our accounts,' he says. 'I handled the marketing of those.' That's saying something. All those packets of fags planted amid the Pyramids or the Rockies and the only caption an H.M. Government health warning.

'I couldn't find any tipped cigarettes to suit me after smoking plain for thirty years,' I tell him. 'Then I tried Bensons and was converted on the spot.'

'It's the gold packet,' says Frank. 'People love gold.'

'Rubbish,' I scoff. 'I don't like gold. It's vulgar and ostentatious. I wouldn't touch it.'

'Really?' Frank sounds astonished. 'Show me your watch, then.'

Eighteen-carat gold with a band to match. Eagle-eye Lowe spots that my lighter is gold too. 'So you don't like gold, eh?' I surrender and readily go along with the ideas he bounces around the lunch table on the best way to promote the *Daily Express*. Whether Victor Matthews will come up with the money is another question. He does not like spending vast sums on promotion unless there are guaranteed returns: new readers who will stay with the paper. Nostradamus himself couldn't answer that one.

Back in the office before three o'clock – and feeling virtuous about it. What with the jaw and the brandies and the London traffic it is normally a struggle to be at my desk before 3.20 pm. The old man, if he is about, usually buzzes around 3.30 pm. Sure enough the light on the intercom is winking soon after I take my chair. 'Come down,' he says, and I climb the stairs to his third-floor executive suite, dark and foreboding in heavy walnut.

He weighs me up as I walk to his desk, taking in my suit, shirt and tie. Whether he approves remains a mystery since Victor rarely commits himself to personal comment. Instead he waves me into a chair and pushes over a cutting from *Private Eye* someone has kindly drawn to his attention. It says:

> It is high time that my friends on Hertfordshire County Council investigated the goings-on at Stocks, Victor Lownes' bunny mansion near Tring.
>
> It is no use relying on hacks, since it is they for the most part who make up the bulk of his guests.
>
> This may explain why the *Titsbychristmas* carried no account of last weekend's most disturbing sight: Derek 'Pearly King' Jameson plunging naked into Disgusting's jacuzzi-style pool to the accompanying screams of several young ladies in the water.

'Is that you?' asks Victor. 'Fine goings-on.'

I take in the words, my mind racing. 'No, it wasn't like that,' I tell him. 'It was late at night, in the dark. I had my Marks and Sparks Y-fronts on.' I figure it best not to let on that they soon came off in the water.

'Why d'you want to get involved in the first place?' Victor wants to know.

'Well, all the gossip columnists were there – one of them obviously wrote this. None of them had the bottle to jump in the pool. I did it so they would look like what they are, a bunch of wallies.'

I know Victor will approve. Anything competitive appeals to his finer instincts and he detests gossip columns. More than once he wanted to kill the William Hickey column because it had upset some friend or associate of his. I managed to save it by solemnly assuring him that a newspaper without gossip would lose readers. The closest shave we had came when the *Sunday Express* threw a lunch for Mrs Thatcher and there were problems with the seating plan. Sir Jules Thorn, head of Thorn Industries, should have been next to her, but instead finished up two places along. 'That's all right,' he said cheerfully when someone apologised, 'I didn't want to be there. Every time I sit next to her she asks me for money for the Tory party!'

The enterprising Peter Mackay, then playing the title role of

William Hickey, picked up the story inside the building and made an amusing item of it in his column. Victor was glowering with rage when he got hold of me. 'Get rid of that William Hickey,' he barked. 'I've had more than I can stomach. I've told you before, Derek, I will not have my chums treated in this way. Close it down today.'

'You can't do that,' I stormed back at him. 'Sir Jules didn't mind. He thought it was hilarious. It would be a perfectly valid story in any newspaper. Why should we ban it because it happened in this building? We don't seek special privileges for ourselves. It wouldn't be fair.

'Look at this' – I went to the window and pointed to the office opposite – 'if it had happened at lunch in the NatWest over the road, you would be laughing with everyone else. That's why, if Hickey goes, I'll be out there on the cobbles with them.'

Matthews let it drop. He was a fair man and could see the justice of what I was saying. No doubt some kind soul with his knife in the *Daily Express* had been stirring it up.

These encounters all too often leave me a wreck, shaking with rage and frustration. It is not a feeling that can be shared. To offload personal troubles on my own staff will cause greater problems. No wonder editors have been known to take a drink or two. The worst of it is to work twelve or thirteen hours a day, taking responsibility for every word in the paper, fighting to survive and succeed in the jungle – and along comes some creep behind your back and lands you in it with the governor.

Not that every meeting with Victor Matthews resulted in having my knuckles rapped. We had many cosy chats, often extending into the time I should have been worrying about next morning's front page. The constant sense of urgency that makes a daily newspaper tick was totally lost on the master builder.

Back downstairs the pace is hotting up. Still four or five people to see, letters to write, decisions to be made. The make-up clerk from Advertising is sitting there as solid as Buddha, clutching his dummy of the paper with the advertisements pasted in. Features refuse to take a four-column ad on the centre spread, though I agreed to it previously. I snatch the dummy out of his hand, opening it at the offending page. 'Cobblers,' I tell him. 'I agreed to three columns up and down the page, but it has to be below the fold [halfway point] in the case of four cols. You're not having a full four columns on the centre spread. Piss off!' We argue where the ad should go. He claims it has been sold specifically for 'the middle' – the centre pages – but I know the advertiser will accept a page covering television or the horoscope, among the best-read items in the paper. We agree to put it on Saturday's TV pages. Another problem solved. The clerk goes away loving me. He has been on the paper twenty-seven years and I am the only editor who ever spoke to him directly. I love him, too. He let me get away with it. Nowadays they fill the four centre pages of tabloids with advertisements. Management sacrilege.

Five o'clock. Evening conference. This gathering is primarily to find out what late news is in the offing, the most likely splash with or without pictures for the front page and progress of pages already in the production chain. 'Christ, I've not seen that spread on doggy heroes,' I say. 'It'll be offstone in half an hour,' says the features editor. The *stone,* or composing room, is where pages are completed. 'Bloody hell!' I complain. 'We should have seen that hours ago – the pictures and words went down last night.' Feature pages running late are likely to delay the news pages. 'There was a cock-up with the artwork,' says the features editor. Ah well, there's always a cock-up somewhere.

By six o'clock I'm sitting on the backbench, the nerve centre of the paper. This is the realm of the night editor and his deputies. They select stories and pictures for the news pages and design them in concert with the adjoining art bench. These page designs are handed to the chief sub-editor, whose subs tailor the copy, write headlines and captions and make sure everything specified on the layout reaches the compositors.

Though words and pictures are still flooding in, now is the time for me to make my most important decision of the day: what is going on Page 1. This is the showcase of the paper, whether it turns up on a bookstall or in someone's hands on the train to work. Millions are going to see it. The page must reflect what is happening in the world that is going to interest the readers of my paper. It has to be a strong statement symbolising what we are all about. The backbench puts forward what they consider the best story for the front. Features wants half the page devoted to a puff for the latest contest and the picture desk is pushing an exclusive of a pop singer's wife flashing her knickers.

It is at this point that I impose my personality on the paper. Assuming I know my stuff – and many editors don't have a clue – it is my prerogative to decide the shape of the front page. What weight should we give to the main story? How do we balance the other interests? Usually I write the splash headline myself – five or six words that not only cover the subject, but fit typographically – and crop the main picture to give it maximum impact. The editors most respected are those with the technical skills necessary to make these decisions and if necessary carry them out personally. Everyone on the paper is watching.

There are several options. I can go for the biggest story of the day, which quite often means coming up with exactly the same headline as one or other of the rival tabloids. A real disaster that. It looks feeble on the bookstalls, especially as some people will think the *Express* is lamely following the others. If we splash the main story, then it helps if we have an angle of our own that the others may have missed. Better still to have a major story exclusive to the *Express*. The others may 'lift' it once they have seen your edition. Nobody worries too much about that. It is an everyday occurrence for other papers to steal from their rivals. In a way it is flattering, a signal that you have got them worried. Anyway, I will probably be doing the same to them next time. The important thing is that people in the business know who had the story first. Sometimes it gets a bit hairy, with newspapers threatening to sue for breach of copyright. On a major buy-up, perhaps costing a great deal of money, they will annotate the copy: 'Our lawyers are watching'. Sometimes the in-fighting lands both parties in court.

On this day the decision is more or less made for me. Mary Bell, detained at Her Majesty's pleasure for the past ten years for the manslaughter of two toddlers, has gone on the run from an open prison in Staffordshire. Hers is a name that rouses fierce emotions and it is the obvious front-page lead. The only argument is over the headline: CHILD KILLER ON RUN. Is it fair to Mary Bell? She was only a child of eleven herself at the time of the crime, and it happened all those years ago. We decide the headline is simple, to the point and certainly accurate.

'We can't very well say "Girl caught up in tragedy is missing",' I say. That settles the matter. As it happens, Mary was found within hours.

Page 1 completes the paper. By this time most of the day staff have gone home. For the editor and the top executives, as well as reporters, writers and photographers who want to see their work in the paper, the waiting game begins. There is a lull between last copy going to the composing room at around 7.30 pm and the first copies of the paper being hurriedly delivered by the messenger boys at 10 pm.

Once or twice a week I might go out to a formal dinner or perhaps a first night in the West End. Most nights I hang around the office, perhaps clearing up some of the day's paperwork and making those long overdue phone calls. At some stage I may go upstairs for a drink and chat with any senior management personnel still around. One or two earnest souls will still be hovering in the outer office looking for a meaningful chat about the paper and their role in it.

On occasion I open the booze cupboard tucked away in a corner of my office. Visitors from all ranks, whether a feature writer seeking guidance or a Stockholm editor on holiday, will be invited in for a drink. Executives drift in and out as the word goes round the office: 'The editor has opened his booze cupboard'. Chilled white wine, lager and soft drinks are kept separately in a fridge. Having one of your own, however small, is a badge of office. So are fitted carpets and more than two telephones. Sometimes the chat, smoke and booze in the office are too heavy and I make for one of the office pubs. None of them is more than a few yards from the main door. More drink and shop talk there, only this time it is open house. Anyone can join in. People off the street, messenger boys, compositors, reporters from other papers. Some brave soul, full of booze and bombast, will no doubt turn nasty and rubbish the editor. I can usually fend for myself, though if it gets really difficult one or more of my executives in attendance will get rid of him.

Always in my mind, standing there so polite and interested, is the time ticking away until the first edition is rolling off the presses. You can hear them throbbing in the bowels of the building long before a paper appears. It is the most wonderful sound – like the great engines of some majestic ocean liner. Within minutes of the paper coming up almost every person left in the office has a copy open in front of him or her. I quickly skim through – having read much of it in the proof stage – and am more interested now in what the others are up to. Pirated copies of the rivals will have exchanged hands for ten times the cover price in various back alleys off Fleet Street.

I go through the papers with the team on the backbench. Within minutes they will spot whether any of the others has an exclusive so irresistible that it must be matched immediately. Someone will call over to the adjoining news desk: 'See if we can stand up this front page in the *Mirror* about the hospital running out of pens'. One of the late-duty reporters will start phoning the hospital or Whitehall duty officers, seeking confirmation of the story and perhaps some new angle on it. The Press Association news agency might put out a matching story for all its clients. If it proves impossible to confirm independently, the news desk will consider whether to 'lift' the story. In other words, pinch it by changing the wording here and there so it does not look like a direct steal. Any story with legal ramifications, such as a punch-up or a husband walking out on his wife, has to be treated with caution. If you cannot stand up the story yourself and it proves total rubbish, it could be your paper that is facing a massive claim for libel damages totally devoid of any defence since the story was stolen – and probably embroidered – in the first place.

Having scoured the opposition, the editor discusses the stories he would like to see in the later editions, perhaps suggesting the spike for one or two existing reports that do not appeal to him. 'Load of rubbish that Page 7 lead,' he will say. 'Don't believe a word of it.' Or perhaps: 'That story on Page 5 about Jagger in Tokyo was in the *Mail* this morning. Lose it if you can.'

While all this is going on, the sports editor, Ken Lawrence, will be over to tell me that his pages are the best in Fleet Street and could he change an extra page on the late London edition to get in more pictures of a late match involving Spurs. 'You've already got down five changes,' the night editor wails. 'Any more and we'll be in big trouble.' Late page changes have to be tightly controlled. There is only limited manpower available in the composing room to remake pages and any delays will hold up the presses. That could mean missing the transport shared with other papers. 'No, you can't have more than five changes,' you tell Sport. 'Sorry, mate, we were forty minutes late last night. No can do.'

Nearly midnight. Time to go home. Very tired and a little drunk.

– 5 –

The Daily Star – It's Your Baby!

VICTOR MATTHEWS is said to have dreamed up the idea for the *Daily Star* in his bath. He certainly did not share his inspiration with me, perhaps sensing that the editor of the *Daily Express* would not be jumping with joy at the thought of his bosses setting up another daily newspaper under the same roof.

I had to be told eventually, if only because there was no doubt in the upper echelon of Express Newspapers about who should mastermind the launch of the project soon known to one and all as Matthews' baby: that old veteran of a thousand tabloid wars, Derek Jameson. I wished the project well, but didn't share their enthusiasm. I am all for safeguarding the jobs and security of people in *the print*. However, for myself I wanted nothing more than to look after the *Express*. I was going all out for a sale of three million, which would have put it on fighting terms with the *Sun* and *Mirror*. That was quite enough excitement, thank you very much, without entering fresh fields of conquest. The angels that have looked after me from birth were sending urgent signals to have nothing to do with it. They told me – correctly, as it turned out – that this new project would be my Nemesis.

Not that my feelings came into it. Editors do what they are told. The most lowly person in a newspaper office – the lady scrubbing the canteen floor, say – has more rights than an editor. Change her working conditions, with or without consent, and there will be immediate Chapel action with the threat of a walkout. The editor is on his own. His strength rests solely on how well he gets on with the proprietor. Nobody is going to leap to his defence.

So I had to go along with the new baby. I was being conscripted to play the starring role in Victor's drama, which admittedly was a clever concept and evidence yet again, if any were needed, of his managerial skills.

The great fear in Fleet Street in the lunatic years leading up to Wapping was that someone would come along and scuttle the gravy boat. A large number of people were being paid a great deal for doing very little. This did not make the workers happy and secure. Anything but. They knew their days were numbered. Modern methods of production based on computerised typography rather than hot metal were now commonplace in newspapers across the world. Everywhere, in fact, except Fleet Street. There we were locked into a last-ditch battle by the print unions to preserve the status quo. We struggled to bring out newspapers in an atmosphere of tension and mistrust.

Millions of copies were lost night after night on all titles in a series of niggling disputes. Chapels – union branches – would stop work at the drop of a hat if only to reaffirm that they controlled both labour and production. Any suggestion that management should be allowed to manage was met by maximum obstruction. Not bloody likely. The corollary of that was the end of union power.

Victor Matthews fought a series of preliminary skirmishes with the unions within weeks of his arrival in this lunatic asylum. Like Rupert Murdoch at *The Sun* and the *News of the World*, Matthews quickly established that he was no soft touch, ready to surrender in a matter of hours rather than lose copies to rival newspapers.

It got a bit hairy for a time. The unions behaved even more outrageously than normal in an effort to tame this 'berk from the builders' yard', as one of them described him to me. The windscreen of my car was smashed, a fire was started in the publishing hall where papers are bundled and machine parts were stolen to prevent the presses running. Matthews responded by calling in the police – unheard of in newspapers – and refusing to yield to intimidation. There was not the slightest prospect of that. He had discovered that newspaper workers were paid twice the wages of skilled men in his own building trade for less than half the work. 'It's bloody anarchy,' he told me. 'Don't worry. We'll see them off.'

I threw down the gauntlet on his behalf in an editorial challenging the power of the unions. WE SHALL NOT BE MOVED, promised the headline on the front page. My words spelled out Matthews' response to the dreadful excesses he had found:

> Far too many within the industry have cashed in on the vulnerability of newspapers in a shrinking and highly competitive market. Fleet Street has become a jungle where anyone who dares to oppose excessive and often outrageous demands does so at the eternal risk of instant stoppage and imminent bankruptcy . . . We shall not be moved.

Stirring stuff. While the old Fleet Street was only too eager to tell the rest of the world how to go about its business, it was notoriously shy about discussing its own errors and omissions in public. The Chapels might not like it.

We even poked our nose into the shambles at Times Newspapers, where *The Times* and *Sunday Times* had ceased printing for a year in a dispute over the introduction of new technology and corresponding reductions in manning levels. GUILTY MEN AT *THE TIMES*, screamed the headline on my signed piece. The joke was that the full-page article was full of typographical faults – we call them literals – because the typesetters and proofreaders of the National Graphical Association (NGA) did not approve of the *Express* editor speaking his mind about the anarchy at the *Times*. In the end the Thomson organisation was only too happy to sell off the titles to Rupert Murdoch. Today they are flourishing.

It was not long before the message got through that Matthews was not going to be messed about. I think the unions were relieved to be dealing with someone they could respect. One by one the bastions fell. He got rid of Chapel meetings in working hours and people leaving their workplace for a 'blow' – a break – any time they wished. He won injunctions to prevent staff taking industrial action in support of their mates on other papers – an everyday occurrence at that time – and, most important of all, he won union agreement to consider cuts in manning levels and to allow 'management to manage'.

What made the outsider Victor Matthews so different from the rest of us facing each other across the barricades in Fleet Street was that he set about doing something to stop the rot. Not for him the hours and hours of futile discussion between warring parties refusing to budge. Having got the unions on the run, he was quick to see that behind the bombast and bravado were a bunch of frightened men. They were scared that someone like him was going to destroy their livelihoods. Take away that fear, he said to himself, and they are probably ordinary, decent blokes ready to listen to reason.

In that spirit he rocked the industry early in 1978 with the astonishing proposition: 'Newspapers are not overmanned; they are underworked'.

His words cut through the smog like a laser beam. It opened up to the unions the prospect that they could do business with a newspaper proprietor on the basis that their members would not lose jobs. Matthews followed it up with a brave proposal: the first new daily newspaper in Britain for seventy-five years. He announced in September 1978 that the *Daily Star* would be launched in Manchester and produced primarily by staff surplus to requirements on the *Express* in London, Manchester and Glasgow.

So there was a lot more to the birth of the new baby in the *Sun/Mirror* camp than a sudden flash of inspiration in the bathtub. It was a carefully calculated gamble designed to tackle the problems of overmanning and waste in the industry. Whether this bold plan worked would depend on its editorial expertise. In other words, it was up to me. For years I had been hacking a path through the jungle, bringing out newspapers by cockeyed methods with a recalcitrant work force in the production areas. At last a rescue mission that might bring some sense to the situation. I had to take part. Like it or not, I was in it up to my neck.

For the second time in my life I was to find myself in charge of two rival papers simultaneously, which is total madness in newspaper terms. Managing director Jocelyn Stevens did point this out to Matthews. 'I don't know what are you complaining about,' Victor retorted. 'Two editors for the price of one!'

Stevens was all for me concentrating my efforts on the fledgeling *Star* and giving up the *Express* altogether. Proof yet again that editors count for nothing. In a matter of months I had galvanised the staff of the *Express*, turned the circulation round and made it a strong, lively contender in Fleet Street's circulation battles. My early successes stuck in the craw of the old guard on the *Express* management. I had changed very little of the paper's content, though it certainly was now wrapped up more attractively. The toffee-nosed brigade, unable to make sense of my strategy, started a whispering campaign that I was taking the paper downmarket. 'He'll drive away our biggest car advertisers,' they said in hushed tones.

'Get stuffed,' I would tell them. 'An editor's job is to make readers. That's what I'm doing. The advertising will look after itself.'

The knockers won. They usually do. People who do the actual work in life are invariably too busy to defend themselves against those who go around stirring up trouble. So my reward for all that I had achieved in such a short time was to be told to forget about the *Express*, pack my bags and go off to Manchester to launch a new tabloid. I was having none of it. My contract specified that I was editor of the *Daily Express*. Manchester made me and I love the place. My successes there as a *Mirror* editor had taken me to the top in Fleet Street. It made no sense from my point of view to drop everything, go back to Manchester and start all over again. Victor was quick to see my point. We came to an easy compromise. I would remain editor of the *Express*, but leave the paper in my deputy's care while I brought his new baby into the world. Much to the chagrin of my detractors, the announcement went out that Derek Jameson was appointed editor-in-chief of the *Daily Star* in addition to his duties as editor of the *Daily Express*.

The editor of the *Daily Star* was to be Peter Grimsditch, who had worked with me at the *Sunday Mirror* in Manchester and London. He had been brought into the *Express* organisation on my recommendation to produce dummies for a working-class tabloid evening newspaper in the London area – another old dream of mine that has never come to anything. The people who are supposed to know about these matters reckon advertisers are not interested.

Grimsditch – known to one and all as 'Grimbles' – and myself were landed with a monumental task. Without his manic energy in those early months we would never have made it. I was still mentally with my troops at the *Daily Express*, and the main burden of producing the new paper fell on his shoulders. Not that Grimbles complained. He was, after all, the editor.

Most new publications, be they newspapers or magazines, are in the planning stage for a year or more. We were being ask to produce ours in twelve weeks. It was to be a daily – maximum pressure in production terms – and it was to be published only in Manchester. The editorial staff would comprise anyone we could cajole, coerce or con into giving up safe jobs at the *Express*, bearing in mind the executives on that paper would scream blue murder if we tried to take their most highly rated journalists.

Grimbles was consumed by a great passion to succeed. He turned up everywhere, blond curls flying, eyes ablaze with missionary zeal. You would see him in the morning lurking in the features department of the *Daily Express* in London and then a few hours later holding forth in Yates Wine Lodge, opposite the *Express* headquarters in Great Ancoats, Manchester. All the time talking, talking, talking. Explaining just how and why the *Daily Star*, produced by a handful of true believers in Manchester, was going to take on the mighty *Sun* and *Daily Mirror*, based in Fleet Street, and succeed. He made it sound like he was offering a place on man's first mission to the moon. And it worked. Eighty-six of the 165 journalists on the *Express* in Manchester signed on and another dozen at head office moved over to form the *Star*'s London bureau. Talk about rag, tag and bobtail. Some were first-class journalists, stimulated by the challenge of something new. Others were executives impatient with promotion prospects at the *Express*. Many were no-hopers, people who had got nowhere in long careers at the *Express*. Now they were expecting their talents to be better employed at the *Star*.

It was as well that Matthews knew next to nothing about newspapers. I don't think it occurred to him that this scratch crew in Manchester might find it somewhat difficult to outshine the best efforts of the Fleet Street tabloids, produced with far greater resources in the heart of London.

To add to the problems facing Grimbles and myself, the print distribution was to be limited to the North, spreading to the rest of the country later, a factor that had not inhibited market research 'experts' consulted by London. They predicted that the *Star* would have an initial circulation of 1,250,000. I heard the figure for the first time just days before the launch at a dinner for management, marketing and advertising executives involved in the project.

'You must be mad,' I stormed. 'How the hell do you expect a new paper in an overcrowded market to sell 1,250,000 copies! The *Daily Mirror* doesn't sell many more than that after twenty years printing in Manchester.' I reckoned we would sell around a million in the first days, settling down to 650,000. That is exactly what happened. Not that anyone took the slightest notice.

As Grimbles toiled to solve staffing and production problems, I went hell for leather after publicity. Only £700,000 had been set aside for promotion in the initial print area. The campaign slogan, BRITAIN'S BEST BUY, was designed to capitalise on a cover price of 6p, a penny less than the *Sun*. It all seemed exceedingly dull to me. Our best hope, I figured, was to promote the David and Goliath image. *The little paper, produced by a handful of volunteers in Manchester, taking on the big boys in London . . . A paper printed and produced in the North that cares about people and tackles real issues . . .* That kind of thing.

In tune with these thoughts, it seemed a good idea to me that the *Daily Star* should support Labour. It made sense. The North was still the heartland of Labour's support and we were going after working-class readers of the Tory *Sun* and faint-hearted Labour *Mirror*. Most important of all, it would be splendid for Trafalgar's image to show that, in the name of democracy, they were prepared to support a Labour paper. But would Matthews and the Trafalgar board be that munificent?

A few days later Matthews summoned me to his office, looking graver than usual. 'I've had a word with my chums,' he said. By that I took it he had spoken to the Trafalgar board. 'We think you are right. The paper should be Labour.' I almost gasped with astonishment. This was really something. Matthews was Britain's largest individual donor to Conservative party funds. 'There's just one thing, Derek,' he added ominously. 'Let me make this quite clear. You can support Labour – but we don't want you attacking the Tories.'

So the *Star* came out vigorously for Labour from the start. I regarded it as an important factor in our fight to survive. It was really a move designed to aggravate our main rival, the *Sun*. How dare the *Sun* project Mrs Thatcher as some kind of Joan of Arc when most of its readers were working class who normally voted Labour? To me that was the ultimate con. Within days of my leaving Express

Newspapers in 1980 the *Star* changed its allegiance and backed the Tories. Mrs Thatcher later gave Matthews a peerage. Some people say the two events were linked, though I doubt it. He deserved his gong.

Having got the politics sorted out before we launched, what about *image?* – very much a cult word in those days. 'A folksy, homely, down-to-earth Manchester paper with real values and addressed to real people,' I told anyone who would listen. I aroused a great deal of comment pursuing this theme by asking newsreader Anna Ford how much she paid for her knickers. Needless to say, it came out in the gossip columns that I had asked if she wore knickers.

We were doing a presentation together for the advertising industry at the Mayfair Hotel. I complained that the clothes on most fashion spreads were way beyond the reach of the people reading them. Fashion editors, for instance, appeared to pay £19.95 for a pair of knickers.

'How much do you pay for your knickers?' I asked the lovely Anna.

'About 45p in Marks & Spencer,' she said when she had recovered from the shock.

'Exactly,' I said. 'Just like most women . . . and the knickers in the *Star* will be 45p.'

Incidentally, a prophetic note from the *UK Press Gazette* in its report of that presentation. 'The star of the show', it reported on 18 September, 'was undoubtedly Derek Jameson. After his relaxed and amusing performance, the audience of mainly admen were asking when he was going to desert Fleet Street for a lucrative living at the Palladium.'

I put my gift of the gab, the ability to make people laugh, to devastating use in spreading the word about the new paper. On the actual day of the launch I appeared on five consecutive programmes – Radio 4, *Granada Reports* in Manchester, BBC TV regional news, *The Money Programme* and ITN. 'You must have got a million quid's worth of publicity for that paper,' the then TV mogul Jeremy Isaacs told me.

Charles Wintour, the *Express* director who had led me to Victor Matthews, commented sourly in his book *The Rise and Fall of Fleet Street*: 'Soon Jameson was spending less and less time in Manchester and more and more time on radio and television, his real love, where his ready wit and extravagant persona blossomed with growing success.'

I did it for the *Daily Star*, Charlie. My real love has always been newspapers. That's why I spent forty years working for them.

Bingo to the Rescue

MANCHESTER'S new baby, the *Daily Star*, proudly labelled 'Birthday Issue' and dated Thursday, 2 November 1978, could have been worse. That is about the best anyone could say for it, however well disposed they felt towards the first national daily newspaper for seventy-five years. It certainly was a great achievement by the stalwart band in Manchester, eager to take on Fleet Street, and the fact that they got the paper out at all more than compensated for its errors and omissions.

Most of the top brass had gathered to celebrate the birth with a champagne reception at Manchester's Piccadilly Hotel. They slapped me on the back, told me what a wonderful paper it was and what a marvellous job we had done to get it out in twelve weeks. I thanked them politely. Inwardly I blew a raspberry, though it was good to see Victor Matthews so happy.

He was grinning from ear to ear, most unusual for him, as he waved the paper before the cameras. It was very much his moment, the first daily launch for three-quarters of a century, and he was delighted to be the toast of Manchester. He hoped it would create more jobs and lead to the rebirth of the city as a great newspaper centre.

'I do not believe this could have been done anywhere else in this country but in Manchester, and I do not believe it could be done anywhere else in the world but in this country,' Matthews told the dignitaries assembled for the grand occasion.

Old misery guts here, depressed by the appearance of the paper, couldn't wait to get away from the revelry and make his way to the Midland Hotel, a mile away. Half of Fleet Street was there for the birth, including the editors of the two papers we were out to win readers from – Sir Larry Lamb of *The Sun* and Mike Molloy of the *Daily Mirror*. My kind of people.

'What do you think of it so far?' I yelled at them.

'Rubbish!' they all cried in unison.

Ah, what it is to be among honest men, I thought to myself. Then I got drunk and cried.

Victor Matthews sent a brief memo to the editorial staff on publication day: 'Now that I have had a chance to read the paper, may I say "Well Done!" It was much better than I feared!'

This was a back-handed reference to an interview he had given a few days earlier in which he said the *Daily Star* was not the kind of paper he would have around the house. A strange demonstration of proprietorial support, all the more remarkable because he said it before anyone had actually seen the paper. Since we had been given so little time to produce a new daily there had been no time to turn out early dummy editions. Naturally our enemies seized on Matthews' candid comment with great delight.

Not that the first issue proved him wrong. The staff had taken my view that sex sells to extremes and had gone right over the top on the nipple count. Tabloid readers are all for spicy pictures and stories, but they don't want tits leaping out at them from every page. A well-edited newspaper must always have balance.

The truth is that nothing seems to go right on the first edition of a new publication, not least because the people involved are still learning to work with each other. The *Daily Star* was no exception. Just as the first edition was going to press the lawyer reading copy decided that a story about a horse-doping sensation clearly pointed a finger at one particular trainer. He would undoubtedly sue, so the lawyer trusted we could prove our case beyond reasonable doubt. We could not and dare not risk a libel action on day one. The story had to be killed. Minutes to go and there we were without a splash story to lead the paper!

'Christ! What else have we got?' The cry went up from the backbench as it always does at times like this. We quickly promoted another tale which did not add up to much. At least it provided an appropriate tabloid headline. MODEL'S MYSTERY PLUNGE, I wrote. It concerned a fashion model, Kitty Percy, who had landed in hospital after falling from a window in the Mayfair flat of millionaire playboy John Bentley. Our rivals subsequently got a laugh at my use of the word *plunge*. They reckoned it was only four feet to the ground. Ah, well, that's newspapers. Any port in a storm.

We decided that the best answer to Page 3 in *The Sun* was to find bigger and preferably better boobs of our own. The whole of Page 7 was devoted to the first *Starbird*, a comely lass named Karen Richardson. Thanks to problems finding sufficient advertisers, we had space to spare and devoted a whole page to *crumpet*, as it is known in newspapers, for some considerable time. A mistake because the human form fits more comfortably into a four-column frame – and leaves room for stories alongside.

The strongest thing in the paper was a buy-up – the serialisation of a book by football hero Jimmy Greaves, in his day England's greatest goal scorer, admitting that he was an alcoholic and telling how booze had all but destroyed him. If Jimmy gave us our best read, the picture story that produced most adverse comment was BEAUTY AND THE PRIEST, about a happily married vicar in Shepherd's Bush, West London, whose hobby was painting nudes – lots of 'em. For some reason the public could not take to a priest turning Page 3 art into a hobby and we got heavily criticised for reporting it.

Perhaps the most significant thing about that first day was the contest, nowadays an essential ingredient for every tabloid. DOUBLE YOUR WAGES, we offered, quickly adding in a sub-heading UP TO £100 A WEEK. Readers had to complete six phrases about money (*Where there's muck . . .*) and the sender of the first correct entry opened had his or her wages doubled courtesy of the *Star*. The average wage in those closing months of Jim Callaghan's Labour government was £78.10p a week. We thought it a bright, imaginative contest and there was a good response from the readers. Little did I know that before long I would hit on the greatest circulation gimmick in all history – bingo!

It landed on my desk thanks to a sharp-eyed promotions man, Jack Kendall, who had spotted a form of bingo doing quite well tucked away in a puzzle corner in the *Western Morning News*, the Plymouth provincial daily. Perhaps it could be adapted for the *Daily Star*? Too true, I thought. Here was the dream contest for a working-class audience. The reader did not have to write twenty-five words

on some naff subject like *Why I prefer Southend to St Tropez* . . .
All he or she – obviously most players would be women – had to do
was put a cross through some numbers. So simple even my old Mum
could do it, though personally I always found it difficult. I am not
much good with figures.

There were two major hurdles. Firstly, how would we get the
numbers to the punters? It would be virtually impossible to print an
individual bingo card in each copy of the paper, though of course
we could print the winning combination to guarantee they bought
the *Daily Star*. We solved the problem easily enough by commission-
ing a small jobbing printer on the East Lancs Road to turn out
hundreds of thousands of bingo cards for distribution to newsagents
and on to the readers. Cumbersome, but it worked – because the
demand was so great. This system also had the virtue of making an
independent printer responsible for the numbers. That way nobody
could accuse the paper of fiddles, such as making sure the winners
came from an area where we badly needed circulation gains. That
printer, incidentally, was later to turn out bingo cards for most of
the newspapers and became one of Europe's biggest print shops.

The second problem should have proved impossible to beat.
Bingo obviously was a game of chance. Since no skill was involved
it was clearly a violation of the Gaming and Lotteries Act and
therefore taboo. We took legal advice in the hope of finding a
loophole. Alas, there was none.

'A good idea, but totally illegal,' my legal manager informed me
drily. 'It just can't be done.'

'Well, we're going to do it, anyway,' I said indignantly.

'No, no, old chap,' he went on patiently. 'It's illegal. A clear
violation of the Act. Totally out of the question.'

'Oh, yeah,' I shot back at him. 'Well, tell me this. Who the hell
do you think is going to sue us for giving away money? Any
politician who tried that would be the laughing stock of the nation.'

So I went ahead, making sure my bosses in London did not hear
about that little legal problem. We ran bingo first as an experiment
in the the Northeast editions. Fantastic! At the end of the week sales
in Geordieland were up 35 per cent. Could it be a freak result? We
tried it in the Merseyside editions. Up 32 per cent.

Beyond any shadow of doubt the gods had sent us a winner, that something extra we desperately needed if the poor struggling *Daily Star*, woefully short of resources and coming out of Manchester, was to succeed. I persuaded London to put up prize money and we were away.

By May 1980 sales were 1,162,000 copies a day and climbing. We had taken a modest slice out of the circulation of *The Sun*, much to the delight of its main rival, the *Daily Mirror*, and my policy of making the *Star* a working-class Labour paper, as sexy and frothy as the rest, was paying dividends. More importantly, it was not causing any damage to my first love, the *Daily Express*.

At this point in the *Star*'s fortunes, Sir Larry Lamb editor of *The Sun* persuaded his boss, Rupert Murdoch, that it was time for drastic action. My bingo prize money had been fairly modest, £5,000 rising to £10,000. Now *The Sun* weighed in with its own massive bingo promotion, which it was to maintain with a battery of powerful TV commercials for several years. Against our ten grand it offered a top prize of £85,000, and before long was claiming 'the biggest game in the galaxy.' Needless to say, the *Sun* itself won the ultimate prize, an ever-growing circulation. Unlike other proprietors, Rupert has always understood that you have to spend money to make money. Success feeds on itself. In various guises, bingo ultimately was adopted by newspapers in forty-seven countries. Communist sheets in Eastern Europe took it up. Even the straitlaced London *Times* produced its own top people's version, Portfolio. There were times when the whole mad scramble by get-rich-quick readers led to prizes of £1 million. Without doubt it was the biggest and best circulation builder in all history, far outstripping anything a newspaper could do editorially.

The sad thing is that the paper which began the paper chase benefited least of all. That's Fleet Street. It lifts you up to the heavens, then delivers a mighty kick in the balls.

It was obvious from the start that the *Daily Star* was going to be the Cinderella of the outfit, starved of resources and not much loved by the people at the top. Their philosophy was to produce a new paper without any appreciable increase in overall costs apart from the ink and paper. Of course, it didn't work out that way and the management begrudged every penny we spent in our efforts to compete with the giants in London.

Sir Larry Lamb told *Media World* after we had been in business six months: 'Of course they've taken some of the sales we could have, even some we had, but I'm not frightened. It's not a newspaper, it's a cynical management exercise, a product dreamed up by a couple of managers who wanted to carve a slice of our cake. As such, it is not a living, breathing newspaper that could be loved by millions. If anyone could give it life, it would be Jamie [Derek Jameson], who is damn good and who has experience as well as ability. But he's had to cut himself in two with the *Express* and the *Star* – and that doesn't work. I feel great sympathy for him.'

A shrewd assessment by a tabloid veteran and the most successful editor in the business. The *Sun* certainly figured in Matthews' vision in the bath. 'If the *Daily Express* can't steal from a *Sun* that's out on strike,' he told Jocelyn Stevens, 'then let's start a paper that can.'

Well, we caused Larry a few problems, but there was neither love nor money there on the part of management for us to fulfil that early promise. As a *Peanuts* cartoon pinned on the wall of my office put it: 'There's no heavier burden than a great potential.'

As my main rival said, personally I was suffering a severe case of professional schizophrenia, bouncing back and forth between London and Manchester like a ping-pong ball. In the space of a few months I was editor of the *Express* and editor-in-chief of the *Daily Star*, then editor-in-chief of both papers, and finally editor of the *Daily Star*.

I wrote to Chairman Matthews in January 1980:

I would appreciate reassurance from you in writing that it is not your intention to remove me from the *Daily Express*, irrespective of the fortunes of the *Daily Star*. My main role in life is the job for which I am primarily employed – editor of the *Daily Express*. I cannot easily attach myself to another paper if you are unable to settle my fears on that front. Otherwise I could finish up as a permanent fixture in Manchester, which for me would be turning the clock back five years.

Another vital question is the success or failure of the *Star*. I have every hope of making advances, but my private assessment is a growth rate in the region of 300,000 a year over the next five years. I would not like to be left holding the can for failure to reach targets that experts like myself consider impossible. I remember being criticised over that initial 1,250,000 when my own prediction was 625,000.

We also have a problem with Peter Grimsditch. Basically he does not accept that I should take control of the *Star*, though he would not be against the usual advice and guidance.

It would be extremely dangerous for the *Star* at this time if Peter were removed from office. Quite apart from the bad effect on morale, he is the man at the heart of the paper. Nobody knows the staff or the nuts and bolts of the operation better. Our task would be immensely more difficult if he were not on the scene. I think we should allay his fears.

Matthews sent me one of his single-sentence missives in reply: 'I confirm the arrangement that whilst you are editing the *Star* you should be paid an extra £10,000 p.a. effective from 1st January 1980'. The letter was addressed to me as editor of the *Daily Express*. The lunacy of one person editing two rival tabloid newspapers simultaneously was still lost on the Chairman of the Board.

So the Express Group found itself with two hard-working, dedicated editors in a seething rage over the way they were being treated. I had taken the *Express* to an audited sale of more than 2.5 million copies, a 25 per cent increase, in my second year as editor. Staff morale had never been higher; it was the first real circulation gain in twenty years. Instead of honouring my contract and allowing me to go for the three million beckoning, they insisted I live out of a suitcase in Manchester and look after the *Star*. That paper had a first-class editor of its own, my nominee Peter Grimsditch, the man who had done most of the spadework in getting the project off the ground. Relations between Grimbles and most of Jocelyn Stevens' managers could not have been worse. He was short of everything – staff, production capacity, promotional expenditure, good will – and his screams of pain largely ignored. So far as London was concerned, Jameson was running the paper and Grimbles could go to hell. In the end the situation became intolerable. I copped out and gave up the editorship of the *Daily Express*, to my loyal and able deputy, the late Arthur Firth. I had lost probably the best job of them all. On top of that I had to play Judas by firing Grimsditch and taking over full control of the *Star*. As you will have heard, Fleet Street can be an ugly and ruthless place.

The nasty taste in my mouth never went away. By the end of 1980 I had carried out my brief to see the *Star* well and truly launched, staying with the paper for two years instead of the one originally offered. I asked Victor Matthews for my job back at the *Express*. Nothing doing. He was most kind, readily accepting that he had employed me as editor of the *Express*, but it was Manchester and the *Star* or nothing. I preferred to quit. By now it had become a matter of principle. The chairman paid me two years' salary as compensation, since my contract had been broken.

For the first time in my life I was out on the cobbles, an unemployed editor. The thought filled me with fear. There were more than enough of them about already.

— 7 —
Who Needs Massage Parlours?

THE last thing I wanted in life was to be editor of the *News of the World*. All those scoutmasters on grave charges, brothels in council flats and worried grey-haired mothers left me feeling most depressed. The paper reeked of sanctimonious hypocrisy, the worst sin of all in my book. Nevertheless, I was only too glad to get a job when the call came to take over the paper.

It was November 1981 and nearly a year had passed since parting company with the Express Group and I was now living in a two-roomed flat off the Gray's Inn Road, in Central London, with my girlfriend Ellen Petrie. The idea had been to try to break into show business. Big money and be your own boss. It did not work out quite that way. Progress was slow. I had to serve a kind of apprenticeship, building confidence and contacts by going round TV stations across the country doing what they call gigs on just about every chat and game show in the land.

With bits and pieces of writing and one or two regular slots, I earned reasonable money. Most of it went in alimony payments to my ex-wife Pauline and two sons, Ben and Dan. So I was delighted to be recalled to Fleet Street. It would be good to get back to an editor's salary, liberal expenses and a car and driver after living so frugally for months. Most important, I would be doing what I knew best, producing newspapers. In the heart of Rupert Murdoch's empire, too, so there was every chance eventually of moving on to bigger and better things. *The Sun*, say.

Oddly enough, when the phone call came through to Gray's Inn Road from Peter Stephens I didn't connect it with the *News of the*

World. I thought it was an old acquaintance, Peter Stephens, the distinguished Paris correspondent of the *Mirror* papers.

'What can I do for you, Peter?' I asked him, wondering why he was phoning me.

'I thought we might have a spot of lunch,' he said. We agreed to meet the following Tuesday and he promised to call later with details of the restaurant. I still couldn't understand what the Paris correspondent of a paper I had left four years previously wanted with me. Ellen and I discussed it at great length without getting anywhere. Realisation only dawned when Peter's secretary phoned with the restaurant appointment. It turned out to be Peter Stephens, editorial director of Murdoch's News Group and a former editor of the *NoW* and senior executive on *The Sun*.

Peter is a scholarly-looking chap with a deceptively quiet manner. His great passion in life is Derby County football club, though he was rarely able to indulge it on Saturday afternoons since Rupert had told him to look after the *News of the Screws*, as it is known in the business. He didn't beat about the bush.

'How would you like to be editor of the *News of the World*?' he asked before we had got through starters in the Islington bistro.

'I'd love it,' I lied. 'When do you want me to start?'

It wasn't going to be quite that simple. Barry Askew, the present incumbent, had been in office only seven months. He was formerly a prize-winning editor of the Lancashire *Evening Post* in Preston, but was out of his depth running a mass circulation popular paper. He found Fleet Street a strange, unfriendly place and had not been round long enough to know whether it was going to get any better. Being a new boy, he made strenuous efforts to appear tough – no doubt he thought it was the correct Fleet Street image – and soon starred in *Private Eye* as 'the Beast of Bouverie Street'.

'The thing is,' said Peter, 'Barry's only been here five minutes and Christmas is coming up. If we fire him now it will make Rupert look like a heartless monster. There's also that business with the Palace. Rupert wouldn't want anyone to think that had influenced his decision.'

Askew had achieved instant notoriety by upsetting the Queen when she summoned editors to take tea at Buckingham Palace and discuss Fleet Street's coverage of matters royal. Kelvin MacKenzie, editor of *The Sun*, sensibly turned down the invitation, realising that they would be telling him more than he wanted to know. Askew went – and put his foot in it. Princess Diana had been in the news for leaving her official car, popping into a sweetshop and buying her favourite wine gums. It made a big story at the time. The Queen told the assembled editors she thought it rather sad that her young daughter-in-law, still serving her royal apprenticeship, wasn't even able to go to the village shop without being pursued by photographers.

'She was simply drawing attention to herself,' said Barry gravely. 'Why doesn't she send a servant to do her shopping?'

The Queen gave him a withering look. 'I think that's one of the most pompous things I have ever heard,' she told the editor of Britain's biggest selling newspaper.

Naturally everyone assumed that Barry was fired after only seven months in the job because of the Queen's displeasure. *The Times*, also owned by Rupert Murdoch, had even run an editorial commenting: 'The idea that the Princess might send a servant for the wine gums is pompous if not preposterous.' In fact, the dismissal had nothing to do with Barry's gaffe. Inside the office they took the view it wasn't what he said that mattered so much as the way he looked. Barry was sporting a shining black eye. A difference of opinion with one of his executives.

Rupert had also been appalled by a BBC TV *40 Minutes* documentary sending up the *News of the World*. It included some fascinating footage of photographer Ian Cutler staking out the home of a suspected villain beneath the red-and-white stripes of a British Telecom engineer's awning. Every time the suspect, a pathetic old man in braces, came outdoors the candy stripes moved a few feet along the pavement. Hilarious stuff – unless you happened to own the paper.

What with the problem of the Palace and Christmas coming up, I had to wait for my appointment to be confirmed. It was a nail-biting five weeks. Any day, I thought, Barry could land a major exclusive and win a reprieve without ever knowing he was about to be chopped. As always, the angels were looking after me. Driving back to London from a visit to Scotland just before the holiday, I counted no fewer than twelve rainbows on the road south. I took it as a sign from the angels that all would be well. So it proved. Peter Stephens waited for Christmas to pass – and fired Barry on Boxing Day! I was back home again, this time in a narrow, cobbled thoroughfare to the south of Fleet Street. Bouverie Street, Murdoch's headquarters in Britain, home of *The Sun* and *News of the World*.

For most of the century the *NoW* had been the chronicle of the sexual peccadilloes of the nation, with much of the material coming from lurid court cases. The paper specialised in trial reports that the daily papers either ignored or censored. Many times in the past, reading some report full of explicit and often kinky evidence, I would say 'We'll leave all that to the *Screws*, thank you.'

Now here I was, editing the paper that had become a national institution of the music hall joke variety. The first thing I wanted to do was lose that image. There's not much job satisfaction editing a newspaper that a great many readers slip under the armchair cushion to keep it from the kiddies. One old friend, Cliff Wakefield at Reuters, told me he had once given up a job at the *NoW* before he even started because his mother cried for four days. But I would have to tread carefully. The British are among the world's greatest hypocrites. Much as they might turn up their noses at the *NoW* school of journalism, they still bought the paper in their millions. Any drastic change could break the habit factor and drive away those loyal readers.

Rupert summoned me to supper at his London town house to give me his thoughts. More revelation, more investigation, more sensation seemed to be the order of the day. 'The classic role for the *News of the World*', he spelled out as he carved the chicken, 'is the cabinet minister in the whore's bed.'

Well, I could go along with that easily enough, but he nearly dropped the knife when I told him: 'I don't propose to spend a great chunk of my life investigating massage parlours'.

We had a surreal discussion there and then, amid the splendours of Belgravia, on the function of the massage parlour in everyday life. I took the view that they were the quintessential British compromise, the nearest we would ever get to legalised brothels. Old ladies were not bothered by them, and children did not know what they were. A perfect arrangement. Since they did little harm and probably a great deal of good, what was the point in the *NoW* eternally 'exposing' massage parlour operators?

Rupert didn't see it that way. Forget the mythology about 'the dirty Digger'. He is of Scottish Presbyterian stock, a puritan if anything, who believes in strict moral values. His brow furrowed, head tilting to the left, a sure sign that he was about to explode. 'You've got it all wrong,' he barked. 'Housewives going out shopping with the kids don't want to see a massage parlour in every high street, between the chemist and the butcher.' There was no answer to that.

There were to be many other differences over the next two years. The most fundamental was my conviction that the big, sprawling broadsheet pages of the paper were an anachronism. 'Go tabloid and we'll do to the *Sunday Mirror* and *People* what the *Sun* has done to the *Daily Mirror*,' I told him. 'Clobber 'em. We'll put on 700,000 readers.' Rupert and his executives were not so sure. They felt that it could be a costly mistake. Since the *NoW* already had by far the biggest sale, why tamper with success?

'It'll be on your head, Derek,' said Bruce Matthews, Rupert's chief lieutenant in Britain. 'I wouldn't lose a second's sleep over it,' was my answer. 'That's how sure I am.' In the event, long after my departure, the *NoW* did go tabloid – and put on 700,000 new readers.

Despite my initial reservations, the two years I spent editing the *News of the World* turned out to be a marvellous experience. I was conscious of the paper's place in folklore, and the Sunday papers have always fascinated me. There is nothing quite like them. As so often happens in Fleet Street, the reality at the *NoW* was far removed from the myth. The staff were anything but tacky voyeurs in dirty macs. On the contrary, they were a highly dedicated bunch who tended to be quieter and if anything more stimulating intellectually than journalists on many another paper.

Those called upon to pose as customers in massage parlours and the like were usually freelances working casual shifts. They all understood that the *NoW* required them to make a hasty excuse and leave when those being investigated came up with an illegal, immoral or incriminating suggestion. Anyone suspected of wishing to sample the goods would be out on his ear. The paper took itself seriously and was jealous of its reputation for protecting the public against all manner of villainy.

Coming from a tough background in the East End, the role of moral crusader did not sit easily on my shoulders. I quashed many an investigation because of my conviction that you do not take a sledgehammer to crack a nut. Before my time, a lonely, pathetic bachelor had been caught propositioning young girls he lured to his caravan through an advertisement in a seedy contact magazine. He killed himself hours before the *NoW* published the story. I was horrified at the thought of such a thing happening under my auspices.

Presiding over the reporting staff was Bob Warren, the softly spoken, soberly dressed news editor, who could easily have passed for an English master in a public school. His looks belied the fact that he was a mine of information about the follies and foibles of life in Britain. I used to say he knew more about what was going on in the underworld than the Criminal Records Office.

Day after day he would bombard me with memos about the multifarious dirty deeds that he felt the *NoW* was duty-bound to stamp out. Other executives would be coming up with tips and information from their own sources. At any given time we might have twenty investigations under way, most of them potentially explosive from the libel point of view. Here are some examples:

DEPORTED Mafia man George X involved in gaming machines still operating in this country; planning to come into UK for exhibition. Suggest we find out when and where.

HARRY BLOGGINS MP. Suggest we mount an investigation into the girls whose lives he has wrecked.

BROKEN butterflies of the aristocracy – trying to get alongside wealthy families with daughters on heroin.

WOMEN who sell sex aids at Tupperware-style parties.

COUNCIL house brothels – investigating three cases of sex-for-sale in council properties.

BOGUS Hungarian princess – the lady who has conned Society and charities for years.

MARY X – described as the most successful courtesan in Britain – wants £25,000 for her story.

HARRY X – a top supergrass, just out of prison – has information that would put away senior police officer and solicitor involved in laundering bank raid money.

CHELSEA boutique with wealthy clients is front for vice ring.

Just about every item on the list – and all the other lists – would fall down simply because of Britain's highly restrictive libel laws. Before we could publish any of these stories we would have to find the evidence, get it corroborated and then be able to prove it was in the public interest to go into print with it. The truth might be sacred to every journalist worth a damn. It is not a defence; there has to be justification.

Finding a series of articles that came within the *NoW* orbit without breaking the libel laws was a source of perpetual frustration. Tens of thousands of pounds and endless hours of hard graft were often thrown away pursuing a worthy and important investigation that the office lawyers would kill in minutes.

Trying to beat the system sometimes led us into bizarre decisions. I once commissioned Gloria Stewart, a highly experienced freelance writer, to go to South Africa in pursuit of a tip that the missing Lord Lucan had been sighted there alive and well. Finding Lord Lucan has been Fleet Street's magnificent obsession since he disappeared from the face of the earth in 1974 before police could question him about the murder of the family nanny, Sandra Rivett. At various times he has been reported in just about every corner of the globe. On this occasion, early in 1982, Gloria got a tip from somewhere or other – perhaps it was Rocky Ryan (see Chapter 9) – and persuaded us to finance an expedition to South Africa.

In her luggage was a formal contract:

The arrangements are that the *News of the World* will meet your reasonable expenses in connection with your imminent visit to Africa and will receive in return World Rights to all the Lucan story and all related material.

Assuming you are successful in providing full and complete interviews with Lord Lucan and related pictures and all the material is completely exclusive to the *News of the World*, then we shall pay you, upon publication, the agreed sum of £200,000.

Off Gloria went to South Africa, followed a few days later by Stuart Kuttner, one of my assistant editors. He is a past master at this kind of undercover operation – his Fleet Street nickname in those days was 'Whispering Grass'. If anyone was going to find Lucan, it had to be Stuart. I had one or two calls suggesting they were on the right track. It seemed we were in business.

On a Friday morning, with press day fast approaching, he called me on my private line.

'Where are you?' I wanted to know. He mentioned some obscure place off the beaten track, deep in the African veldt. Stuart was calling from a public call box at the end of the trail. He sounded very excited. Our man was supposed to be in a nearby villa. They had done a reconnaissance and there seemed to be a vital clue on the front lawn.

'What is it?' I wanted to know.

'A dice. Our man's got a big ornamental dice right outside his front door.'

'What's that got to do with it?' I asked.

'Well, he's a compulsive gambler. It's just the kind of thing he would have, isn't it?'

Alas, it was not to be. Another case of mistaken identity.

The *NoW* was not the only paper to make a fool of itself over Lucan. The *Daily Mirror* once published a picture of a chair in a South African restaurant with the caption: *Did Lord Lucan sit here?*

These days, of course, the *NoW* is just another tabloid Sunday paper, not vastly different from the rival *Sunday Mirror* and *Sunday People*. The goings-on at the Magic Fingers' Massage Parlour may still be there, but the seamy side of life no longer dominates the pages. The staff have given up scouring the nation's courtrooms for the stories that made it known as the *News of the Screws*.

Gone, too, are those deadpan headlines that made it such a unique institution. The one that summed them up for me was: CRY OF 'FILTHY BEAST!' IN THE CINEMA. Another device was the simple statement of an everyday fact that made the imagination work overtime, such as: SHE LEFT CHURCH DANCE FOR A

GIN AND ORANGE. The most famous headline of all, back in the seventies, read: NUDIST WELFARE MAN'S MODEL WIFE FELL FOR THE CHINESE HYPNOTIST FROM THE CO-OP BACON FACTORY.

The paper's language was as constrained as the headlines, as if to take the sting out of the purple passages and leave the impression that the sole intent was to report the news. For years the *NoW* was far too gentlemenly to refer to sex at all. They called it 'intimacy'. Similarly, women were not raped; they were 'molested'. This genteel double talk could become highly complicated. It was quite common to read something like this: *Miss X suffered a broken arm, fractured ribs and severe bruising. She had not been molested.*

By my reign, these anachronisms were fast disappearing, though the paper still carried lengthy court reports. They even had a venerable old gentleman of East European origin, Edward Sinclair, who spoke about nine languages. His job was to scour European newspapers and magazines looking for stories that would help the *NoW* maintain its proud boast to be the biggest selling newspaper in the world.

They have got rid of the *Make-Britain-Great-Again*, *Tighten-Your-Belts*, *Beware-of-the-Wreckers* leading articles, an important feature of the paper for half a century or more. Each week a cabinet minister, Opposition leader, Church prelate, up-and-coming MP or trade union boss would be invited to write a piece stating his views. A nice little earner for them – up to £1,000 a time in my day – and useful fig leaf for the paper. It gave us an air of respectability and enabled the *NoW* to boast it was politically independent and fair to all.

Margaret Thatcher was one of my contributors in June, 1983:

> Our task is not yet done. We, the British people, walk taller than we did in 1979. We hold our heads higher. But we still have a long way to go together before we have fully restored the pride and the prosperity that we know should be ours.
>
> We no longer have to worry, as we did four years ago, that inflation is running riot . . .

When the sub-editors wanted to know what headline to put on her words, I told them: 'The future lies ahead!'

These articles must have been much in the mind of Stafford

Somerfield, one of my predecessors, when he wrote a leading article in 1968 fighting off a bid for control of the paper by the socialist millionaire Robert Maxwell, now publisher of the *Mirror* papers. It was a blatantly racist attack. Somerfield, twenty-five years on the *NoW*, referred to Bob as 'formerly Jan Ludwig Hoch' and failed to mention the British Army had commissioned him in the field for gallantry. 'Staff' said the *NoW* was as British as roast beef and Yorkshire pudding and he intended to keep it that way. In other words, Czech-born socialists need not apply. It was, of course, the Australian Rupert Murdoch who won the shares battle for control of the paper in January 1969. He fired Somerfield, editor for ten years, a year later.

Rupert does not like jingoism, though it was not Somerfield's intemperate remarks that got him into trouble so much as the new owner's eternal desire for change. He knew instinctively that the *NoW* had to don a new suit of clothes to survive. The once mighty circulation of 8.5 million had been dropping away for years as the readers got older and their sons and daughters turned to the brighter, brasher tabloids. But any change had to be gradual so as not to break that all-important habit factor.

Along with all the other Murdoch editors, I did my bit to make the paper more relevant to the times. With hindsight, my heart wasn't really in it. I found it sad to see harsh reality catching up with an institution founded in 1843 and for so long the favourite reading of the nation, including most of Her Majesty's judges. Winston Churchill said of the paper: 'Long may it continue to educate and amuse the British race'.

Like me, they really did want to know what happened when the girl left the church dance for a gin and orange.

JUST why Rupert Murdoch fired me after two years is still a mystery. Officially it was because he did not consider me 'up to the tabloid challenge', though that made little sense. I had a big reputation as a tabloid expert and had been pressing since day one for the *NoW* to take on the smaller shape. Rupert can be highly impulsive, acting on instinct, and he may well have been influenced by the fact I was being pressed by several producers to forget newspapers in favour of show business. Perhaps he sensed that was where I belonged. Exactly five years later he summoned me to his Wapping headquarters and offered me the job of chief test pilot for SKY Television, presenting *Jameson Tonight*. An inspired choice. For the fourteen months it ran I was reckoned to be the highest paid man in television.

Personally, my view is that I owe my demise as an editor to the sharks seen now and again off the coasts of Australia.

You could call it the story of my life. A bizarre and unlikely event that turns out to be a stroke of good fortune. It happened this way. The major burden in a Sunday editor's life is that very little occurs in this evil world on Saturdays. Government has shut down for the weekend, the courts do not sit, few people are at work, and while heinous crimes are no doubt committed, they have an unfortunate tendency not to come to light until the following week. In other words, frequently there is little news for the thrusting and ambitious editor to put on his front page come three o'clock Saturday afternoon. He and his executives must contrive to liven up things a bit.

This process is all the more imperative on a Murdoch paper because the boss has a nasty habit of calling his editors from the far corners of the globe at the most awkward times to demand 'What's happening?' Should you answer 'Sod all!' Rupert is inclined to see the problem as a matter of internal rather than universal lassitude. He will almost certainly want to know why he is spending so much money when your useless and idle staff cannot even find a worthwhile story for the front page of his newspaper.

It is precisely to field such difficult questions that editors employ executives like the aforementioned Stuart Kuttner, one of Fleet Street's most adept experts at pulling fat rabbits out of thin hats. At the time in question he was my assistant editor, eager to please, his finely tuned nose picking up distress signals like the radar screen in a lifeboat.

'Have you seen this book by Anthony Grey?' he asked me softly this particular Saturday afternoon as I sat on the backbench glumly surveying the blank layout of the front page of the next day's *News of the World*. God forbid, I might be forced to lead the paper with some boring politician's Saturday speech.

'No, what's that?' I asked with interest. I knew Tony Grey well. A journalist of impeccable reputation, famous the world over as the

Reuters correspondent humiliated by China's Red Guards in the Cultural Revolution of the late 60s and forced to spend 380 days under house arrest in Peking. 'What's he been up to?'

'Well,' says Stuart in his best you-won't-believe-this tones, 'he's written a book claiming Harold Holt was a Chinese communist spy who was smuggled out of Australia on a submarine just as he was about to be exposed.'

I jumped about ten feet in the air, my brain going into top gear. Harold Holt, the prime minister of Australia. Disappeared off the coast of Melbourne while swimming. It was 1956 and he had won a landslide victory for the ruling Country Party only three weeks before. It was generally assumed the sharks had got him. There had always been doubts in my mind about that Harold Holt. Despite the mythology, sharks at most kill two or three humans a year off the coasts of Australia. Why should they pick on a distinguished Conservative statesman just days after he had won a landslide victory? It sounded fishy to me.

Stuart quickly produced words telling a different story. According to Grey, quoting a former Australian Navy officer, Holt had been a Communist since university days and had done a bunk to Peking when he realised the game was up. An unlikely story, now I think about it, since Holt was cut in the same cloth as Mrs Thatcher. However, it seemed all right at the time. Anthony Grey and all that. I wrote the headline: LOST PREMIER WAS RED SPY. We were in business.

Peter Stephens, the editorial director, appeared at my elbow as we were locking up the page in the composing room. He looked worried and muttered something about Australia and what would Rupert make of it. 'But it must be true,' I told him. 'It comes from Anthony Grey.' I made it sound like God himself. Time was pressing and I appeased Peter by putting quotation marks around 'WAS RED SPY'.

Nothing more was said and I forgot the whole thing until months after I had been fired. Walking along Fleet Street, I bumped into one of those faceless men who occupy important posts on newspapers though you are never quite sure what they do. He went through the usual niceties and then said: 'Pity about that Harold Holt business. You would have still been with us.' Taken aback, I explained he was telling me something new.

'Well, the Murdochs and the Holts go back years,' he said. 'Chained together going over to the penal colony, or something. Harold Holt's family were most upset and complained to Dame Anna. That's why you got the chop!'

Dame Anna, of course, being Rupert's formidable mother in Australia. They do say she is the only person in the world he is afraid of. Anyway, I reckon she was entitled to complain. The story turned out to be a load of rubbish.

All the same, how ludicrous that a missing Aussie politician, apparently eaten by sharks, should have brought such an inglorious end to my career in journalism stretching back forty years . . .

—8—

A Clutch of Editors

IT'S an incestuous place, Fleet Street. Just one big mixed-up family. Everyone knows everyone else, or someone who does. Usually they have worked together on another paper, possibly as trainees. The links forged struggling for survival in those early days as a cub reporter last forever. In this strange tribe they work, love, laugh and drink together – and yet wouldn't loan their best friend the price of a phone call if they thought it might benefit another paper.

Having been around longest, I suppose my roots go deepest of all. On every paper in the business there are those with a place in my family tree. Perhaps I gave them a job that changed their lives for ever. Some were wooed and won while working for a rival. Others got a nod from me as bright, ambitious youngsters desperate to crash Fleet Street. Then there is the great host of sub-editors, reporters and photographers who worked with me over the years. Hundreds of them. Men and women, all classes, all shapes and sizes. Just a handful will have made it to the editor's chair; there is very little room at the top of the pyramid.

I spotted each and every aspiring editor who brushed against me well in advance. You can tell them in a second. They are usually giving everyone in earshot the benefit of their views about everything taking place on Mother Earth that might just be of some interest to newspaper readers. With any luck, you may disagree and so give them an oppportunity to read you a lecture on What Makes a Good Story, a favourite pastime in every newspaper pub.

The one area I was totally wrong about was women. There was no way I could see a female running a newspaper. It just would not work. The men, hard as nails and cynical with it, would eat them for breakfast. Damn it, women *cry*. You can't have editors crying! Serves me right that the first woman past the post should be one of my own. Wendy Henry, one of twins (sister Sara is a print union activist turned *Telegraph* executive), daughter of a Manchester street trader.

Wendy first worked for me when I was Northern editor of the *Sunday Mirror* back in the sixties. She was a bouncy, overexuberant freelance with ideas above her station. 'I'm going to be the first woman editor of a national newspaper,' she told me more than once. 'Sorry, Wend, no chance,' I would answer sadly. 'It will never happen. Women can't take the pressure, see. When the world starts falling down around them, they just can't cope, can they?'

Wendy would give me a pitying look and get on with the business of proving her point. She is a brilliant journalist, forever sniffing out the most remarkable stories. Having her hair done one day, she discovered the hairdresser was the daughter of Ruth Ellis, the last woman to be hanged in Britain for murder. It happened bang in the middle of yet another national debate on capital punishment. That's Wendy. Lucky as well as clever. A lady of great flair, brimful of ideas.

After a few years on Kelvin MacKenzie's roller coaster at *The Sun* she was promoted to my old job, editor of the *News of the World* Now that the *NoW* was a tabloid fighting the *Sunday Mirror* and *People* on equal terms, Wendy did wonders with the circulation. It didn't help. She still got the chop, like the rest of us. Her mixture of sex-and-sensation proved too strong for Rupert Murdoch. His major rival, Robert Maxwell at the Mirror Group, picked up the fallen pioneer and made Wendy editor of the *Sunday People*. She came to grief there, too. Maxwell did not approve of her choice of pictures, particularly the cancer-stricken Sammy Davis Jnr. Wendy deserved better. Any other place than newspapers would have given her more time before bringing down the axe. By now she will have learned that while bosses love circulation gains, they must be achieved without any pain on their part.

The second woman editor has fared better: Wendy's old friend, Eve Pollard, who gave up a burgeoning television career because her love for newspapers proved stronger. These days she is the highly successful editor of the *Sunday Mirror*, though with Eve you never know where she is going to turn up next. She has succeeded where Wendy failed by staying middle of the road. Nothing in her paper is going to make the proprietor's family choke over their cornflakes at breakfast on a Sunday morning. Eve knows that is the best way to play the survival stakes. We worked together on the *Sunday Mirror* back in the sixties in the days when she was famed for her sexy fashion spreads. Wendy and Eve have certain assets in common: both are as well endowed upstairs as any Page 3 girl. Rupert said to me once, talking about Eve: 'Now there's a woman I find difficult to look in the eye'.

Eve's husband is another contemporary of mine, though we never worked together. Nicholas Lloyd, Oxford graduate (in history), has always dogged my footsteps, proving yet again what a small, incestuous place Fleet Street has always been. He followed me to become a senior executive at the *Sunday Mirror*, went on to edit the *Sunday People* for a couple of years before succeeding me as editor of the *News of the World* in 1984. He rapidly became one of Rupert's bright young men and was pulled out of the *NoW* to take a course at the Harvard Business School. Nick was to have played a key part in the Wapping revolution. Something went wrong somewhere. He finished up in charge of paper clips and quit to take over another of my former jobs, editor of the *Daily Express*. He produces a bright, lively tabloid. What he desperately lacks is money to promote the paper.

At the *Express*, Nick succeeded Sir Larry Lamb, best known as editor of the soaraway *Sun* for more than a decade after its birth in 1969. One of his top executives at the *Sun* had been Nick Lloyd. Larry was my old adversary and, like myself, is a former *Mirror* man. He it was who took the *Sun* to a circulation of more than four million. Larry received a Thatcher knighthood along the way – his admiration for the Iron Maiden is total, despite the fact he is the son of a Yorkshire coalminer who voted Labour. Larry parted company with Rupert Murdoch in 1981. The reason for the split is something of a mystery. There are suggestions that Rupert resented Larry's knighthood; I don't think he is that small-minded. Anyway, the word is that Rupert turned down a title more than once. Most likely they just tired of each other after all those gruelling years together in the pressure cooker. After a spell in Australia, Larry turned up in Fleet Street again to edit the *Express* in the mid-eighties. In earlier years he had told me more than once I was crazy to stay with the *Daily Express*. That did not inhibit him from taking the job himself, though he appears to have had a bumpy ride until he, too, called it a day. His bosses clearly expected him to work the *Sun* magic all over again. Unfortunately there was one half of the equation missing. A genius named Murdoch, a newspaperman from the cradle who knows precisely what is required from management in the tricky business of resuscitating ailing newspapers. Above all, money and faith.

Larry left my oldest friend in the business behind at the *Daily Express*, associate editor Bernard Shrimsley. While still in our teens at night school – the Stoke Newington Literary Institute, it was called – we talked endlessly about becoming newspaper editors. To us, Fleet Street was a world infinitely more exciting than the latest Bogart film, though the idea that we would play a key part in it must have seemed nonsensical to outsiders. Bernard, a gangling clerk in an insurance office, swapping dreams with a lowly Fleet Street messenger boy over tea and buns in a café after a lesson in *The craft of writing*. All the same, we made it. Our routes were separate; our destination the same. Both of us became successful Northern editors of the *Daily Mirror* in Manchester, the perfect launch pad for our wider ambitions. We went on to hold senior posts at the *Mirror* in London. After a spell editing the Liverpool *Post*, Bernard returned as one of Larry's chief lieutenants. He was editor of *The Sun* and the *News of the World* before going on to launch the *Mail on Sunday*. Similarly, I became editor of the *Daily Express*, launched the *Daily Star*, and finished as editor of the *News of the World*. How strange that those early expectations should have been fulfilled so totally. Not that there is much similarity between us. Bernard is well-spoken, highly literate and the most honest, decent person in newspapers. Having been there myself, I felt for him when he carried the can for teething problems on the *Mail on Sunday* without the slightest justification. Another sacrifice to Circulation, the only god followed to any degree in Fleet Street, though Bernard himself is quite phlegmatic about it. His escape hatch is writing excellent novels.

I envy those with less turbulent careers. The impeccably dressed, well-manicured Sir David English, for instance, editor of the *Daily Mail* for nearly two decades and regarded as the most successful and highly professional of them all. He produces a solid, respectable middle-class newspaper so prissy that it cannot bear the word *tabloid*. It refers to itself as a *compact* newspaper and, close your eyes, calls its bingo game *Casino*. David is one of the few among us to have a background perfectly in tune with the paper he edits. His father was a Bournemouth accountant. He rarely puts a foot wrong – some would accuse him of smug complacency – though in 1977 he almost came to grief when his newspaper published a forged letter containing spurious allegations that British Leyland was engaged in corrupt practices. I think his greatest triumph has been to win the unswerving support of his proprietor, Viscount Rothermere. Perhaps one day he will tell the rest of us how it is done. He now looks certain to achieve the rare distinction of reaching retirement age while still holding office.

Mike Molloy, editor of the *Daily Mirror* for more than a decade, didn't quite make it. He always was Fleet Street's greatest survivor, rising above the manic chase after circulation that makes an editor less secure in his job than a football manager. In the end the system beat him, too. He was succeeded as editor by the more bullish Richard Stott – a senior reporter he had once refused promotion – and went *upstairs* as editor-in-chief of the Mirror Group. It was not a role destined to last long. Editors do not take kindly to guidance from old retainers. Mike took early retirement in 1990 to go and work for himself. He had been at the *Mirror* from boyhood less one brief spell on the now defunct *Daily Sketch*. Where he differs from the rest of us is that by definition he is not a words man; Mike is a graduate of the *Mirror* art bench. Quiet and softly spoken, these days he writes gripping novels where once he used to paint and draw. That he lasted so long at the top is a tribute to his unflappability. Mike, son of a supervisor in the Stationery Office, is a superb poker player and no doubt will turn up again holding all the aces.

Richard Stott, a sanguine character with a barking laugh, had splendid credentials for running the *Mirror*. For more than ten years he had been the paper's top investigative reporter, a role in which we went to battle over his allegations of corruption surrounding the former football manager Don Revie. I didn't think the evidence would stand up in court and delayed publication. When the *Mirror* finally published, long after my departure, Stott's reputation was skyhigh. He went on to take over several key jobs until owner Robert Maxwell felt his claims to occupy the editor's chair could no longer be denied. What made the appointment particularly piquant was that Richard and his main adversary, Kelvin MacKenzie on *The Sun*, had been trainees together with the Ferrari family's freelance news agency in Dartford, Kent. The doyen of the business, Dan Ferrari, was for many years a much respected news editor of the *Daily Mirror*. Just how the young Stott and MacKenzie got on together at Ferrari's has never been told, but at least they were still communicating in later years. That in itself was a novelty. The editors of the *Sun* and *Daily Mirror* normally do not speak to each other. After only a couple of years running the *Mirror*, Richard was suddenly posted back to a job he had held previously, editor of the *Sunday People* in place of Wendy Henry. There was much talk of a Maxwell project eventually to hand over financial control of the paper to Stott and his staff. Although Richard has a keen head for business, it is difficult to believe he gave up the *Mirror* because of a management share offer at some time in the future. Methinks the full story has yet to be told.

The new editor of the *Daily Mirror* at the start of the nineties is another protégé of mine. Roy Greenslade, son of a gas fitter from East London. Getting nowhere fast, Roy almost gave up journalism altogether in the seventies and went to the University of Sussex to read politics. The story goes that his radical opinions underwent drastic review when he held a door open for a girl student and she spat at him: 'Don't patronise me, sexist pig'. In those days he was very much a member of the loony Left and, being an NUJ militant, was avoided like the plague by most editors in Fleet Street. 'You must be mad', colleagues said when I gave Roy a job at the Express Group. It was to be his springboard for an executive job with *The Sun*. He spent five years in charge of features, but fell out with editor Kelvin MacKenzie in 1986 and moved over to become managing editor of the *Sunday Times*. That Sussex honours degree wasn't a waste of time, after all.

Once his feet were under the table at the *Mirror*, it was not long before tradition was restored and the editors of our two leading tabloids once again were not speaking to each other. Within weeks Roy was locked in battle with Kelvin MacKenzie, throwing about angry accusations that the *Sun* was stealing *Mirror* exclusives. For once his slow grin was missing. He even ran an editorial mourning the passing of his old friend's sanity.

Kelvin responded in his usual way with a loud raspberry. He is beyond doubt the most extraordinary character in Fleet Street – and the most successful. Kelvin is not simply editor of *The Sun* – he IS *The Sun*. Like the paper itself, he operates at the top of his voice. Bawling, yelling and swearing when occasion demands, he has taken the paper to a sale of over 4,000,000 and, give or take a few hiccups in the crowded marketplace, held it there against all comers. He understands instinctively what his readers expect of their newspaper. Most editors tend to put it the other way round. Kelvin really is a genius. By identifying totally with his people, he is impervious to anything that might divert him from keeping them happy. That is why he turned down the Queen's invitation to tea. His is the true faith. The very thought of a *Sun* buyer turning to another paper is enough to bring Kelvin out in spots. Most of his readers feel the same way. The toffee-nosed brigade can whinge about *The Sun* and its morals until apoplexy sets in. Balls to them. Kelvin gets on with it. Bang, crash, wallop! Here comes the soaraway *Sun*.

Kelvin never seems to have doubts about anything. Jaw thrust forward, eyes blazing, he charges around the *Sun* office like a dervish, a mischievous grin on his face if there is some scam afoot to screw the opposition. They say Rupert Murdoch pays him by the mile. Relations between them are based on mutual respect. He calls Rupert 'the Boss' and rarely answers back. Rupert in turn must surely know he will never find a better man to edit his most important property.

Years ago, realising his potential, I pulled some strings to lure Kelvin away from *The Sun*, where he was having problems as one of Larry Lamb's lieutenants. For a time he worked as night editor of the *Daily Express* – they are still reeling – but it wasn't long before Rupert won him back and made him Larry's successor. The knockers fancy Kelvin to be a working-class oaf and make much of the fact he is supposed to have gained only one O level. He plays up to the image. After all, it is not a million miles removed from the readership profile.

In fact, he went to a private school, Alleyn's in Dulwich, and his background is very much middle class. I was a neighbour of the MacKenzies when Kelvin and his two brothers, Craig and Drew, were kids growing up in a 'higher income' council estate in South London. Right little terrors they were too. Craig later worked for me as assistant editor at the *News of the World*. He now has the same job on the *Daily Express*. Drew is a successful journalist in New York. Their father was the quiet, somewhat reserved editor of a South London weekly paper. Mary, the boys' mother, a stunning blonde, was in public relations.

Kelvin lives with his wife Jackie and three children in a house surrounded by flowers in the Kent countryside, and no doubt like other tabloid editors he dreams of running some gentle weekly paper where the grateful proprietor appears only at Christmas to hand over a bottle of brandy. No man would have deserved it more.

Another of the tabloid editors, David Montgomery of *Today*, worked for me in Manchester after graduating from the *Mirror*'s former training school in Plymouth. The old timers on the *Mirror* there called him my 'cabin boy' because he looked so young and vulnerable. He was anything but. I remember him hovering outside the door of my office late at night to tell me, in his thick Ulster brogue, that I had the wrong story on the front page. 'Will you piss off' I invited him in turn. But I knew he had what it takes to become an editor. Strong opinions.

I have a warm place in my heart for Brian Hitchen, cuddly editor of the *Daily Star*. He looks like everyone's favourite uncle. Behind the easy grin is a tough newspaperman whose greatest feat was organising the hunt that uncovered the missing Great Train Robber, Ronnie Biggs, in Rio. We worked at the *Mirror* together in our young, ambitious days. His problem on the *Star* remains as it was in my time. Since it does not make money, the management is reluctant to spend the millions needed on promotion if the paper is to expand and develop. Brian's boss, Lord Stevens, tried a different tack by experimenting briefly with soft porn as a means of selling newspapers. It proved disastrous. Sales fell drastically and he soon dissolved his partnership with David Sullivan of *Sunday Sport* and his editor, the late Mike Gabbert. Hitchen was brought in to pick up the pieces and restore the pride of the *Star* and its staff. He did the job brilliantly.

These are just a few of the people I grew up with in newspapers. The only thing we have in common is that all were singled out to become editors. Not that any of us ever made much of our exalted status. Perhaps we are only too well aware that someone is likely to come along and snatch it away.

— 9 —

The People You Meet

HAVING looked at some of the editors, what about those on the other side of the fence? People who do not work for newspapers but who somehow manage to get involved with them more than most. Take the case of Michael Rocco Ryan, assuming that really is his name, a man obsessed by the desire to take newspapers for a ride. He has made a huge success of it, it hurts me to say.

Rocky Ryan, as we call him, is an editor's nightmare. He has fantasies about people in the headlines – the royal family, Colonel Gaddafi, Lord Lucan, Dirty Den and the like – and then sets about convincing newspapers to buy his dreams and publish them as real facts. It all sounds a great wheeze, but it's no fun to be at the receiving end of his barmy tricks. Think of Rocky – and there are many like him – next time you read of some huge settlement being paid out in a libel action.

He had a fixation on me in my days as an editor – no doubt because of my readiness to listen to anyone with a story to tell – and I hatched a plot of my own to put one over him and even the score a bit.

Normally a newspaper's own reporters check out the facts behind a tip and soon discover the truth of the matter – whether it stands up as a story or perhaps is too dangerous legally to publish. Frequently it turns out to be a load of rubbish, though the informant may have acted in good faith.

What makes Rocky Ryan so dangerous is his fiendish cunning. The wild stories he invents could *just* be true, but they are always of the kind that people in the know will not talk about. Having set the trap, Rocky then lays down a false trail by adopting a bizarre array of false names, accents and collaborators. The object of the game is to persuade investigating reporters that the story they are having trouble confirming must be true.

There was the case of Dirty Den – actor Leslie Grantham – being written out of *EastEnders* before it actually happened. The BBC's stock answer in this kind of situation is 'It's news to us'. Well, they would say that, wouldn't they? Don't want to give the plot away. But the tip has come from a BBC secretary and she has an internal memo spelling out Dirty Den's end. A Rocky plant, of course. Another newspaper in hot water.

Psst! Here's a good story. Princess Michael of Kent has been summoned to the Palace for a two-hour dressing down by the Queen over her behaviour. Sounds quite likely, though there's no way the royal press office is going to confirm a story like that. Not to worry. The tip comes from a royal chauffeur and what's more he has the phone number of a lady-in-waiting Princess Michael has upset. In fact she's an out-of-work actress living in Chelsea. Within hours several papers are running the story prominently. Rocky strikes again.

There's no end to this bloke's imagination. I once okayed the expensive business of sending a team to South Africa to find Lord Lucan (see Chapter 7). We were acting on a solid tip that he was living there. Could it have been Rocky? Broadwater Farm rioters being trained by Russians, Colonel Gaddafi executing the killers of WPC Yvonne Fletcher, aristos smuggling cocaine into Britain . . . the list of Rocky's scams is endless.

In his council flat off the North Circular Road in Neasden, Northwest London, this dark, swarthy dream merchant is more than happy to show visitors invoices recording generous payments by newspapers and television.

Rocky's idea of heaven is to find a nice little earner, then see the people he has conned taken to court. He regards journalists as the lowest form of human life, a view that all those invoices have not altered. He does have a soft spot for the posher papers and they in turn frequently pat him on the head, though he has taken them to the cleaners many times.

Who is this rascal who fancies himself to be a crusader? I have only a sketchy idea, though I know him better than most. There was a time when he called me morning, noon and night with his fanciful tales, spitting, snarling and swearing if I dared suggest he was not all there.

Michael Joseph Ryan is probably his name, though he uses Rocco, Salvatore, Sabatini and a score of other aliases. They tend to be of Italian origin. His mother is supposedly Sicilian and his father Irish. At times he claims to be his brother – assuming he has one.

He speaks with a cockney accent, though he frequently lapses into Italian, Irish, American and Latin American. Whatever name he adopts, spotting him on the phone is a simple matter. He invariably reverses the charges, even on local calls. Rocky likes to tell people he is a former SAS man and soldier of fortune. He reckons to be a bodyguard by profession, earning big money protecting millionaire Arabs and the stars. On occasion he decides he is an actor – or film extra. Boxer and stunt man, too, if you like. Personally I think he is a mini-cab driver. He is in his fifties.

One thing I did establish is that he is a genuine cockney and has rubbed shoulders more than most with the criminal fraternity. He counts the Richardsons and Krays among his friends. It was his habit of popping down to Parkhurst top-security prison on the Isle of Wight to visit his pals that gave me the chance to land him in it good and proper.

He kept calling me with stories he had picked up about Peter Sutcliffe, the Yorkshire Ripper – another rich field of endeavour for the Ryans of this world. One day he told me breathlessly that Sutcliffe spent hour after hour in his cell painting. If the money was right, his mates in Parkhurst would smuggle out a picture and sell it through Rocky's good offices to the *News of the World*.

'That's not the half of it,' he added. 'You'll never guess what.'

'What?' I dutifully asked.

'It's a painting of Jesus.'

'Jesus!' I said. 'Everyone paints Jesus.'

'Yes,' says Rocky, 'but it's him. The bastard's painted himself as Jesus!'

Even I had to admit to being taken with the notion of the Yorkshire Ripper painting himself with staring eyes in the garb of Our Saviour. However, there was no way I could trust Rocky Ryan.

He might have got one of his Chelsea mates to do the painting.

If it was the work of Sutcliffe, was it going to be half-inched in the nick and illegally smuggled out? What about copyright? Would it not bring down the wrath of the Home Office? Above all, what about the formidable Mrs Sonia Sutcliffe? – a lady not to be trifled with as others discovered later to their considerable cost. She would have something to say about a newspaper publishing a picture by her husband portraying himself as Jesus.

I did not burden Rocky with my doubts, but kept him guessing by stalling over the price. I offered him £4,000, but he reckoned it was worth £20,000, indicating that 'my clients' might be prepared to accept £15,000. With a nod and a wink, he suggested that former gang leader Charlie Richardson, then coming to the end of a long prison sentence, was involved.

We went our separate ways, ostensibly to consult our superiors. He went straight to the rival *Mirror* building and I had inquiries made as to the artistic talents of one Peter Sutcliffe.

The Ripper was indeed spending much of his time alone in his cell painting like fury. Even better news – there were a set of colour transparencies of his work in existence. We lost no time in securing them through a London freelance news agency.

Rocky called several times the following week, getting more angry as each day went by. Obviously he had got a flea in his ear at other newspapers. He sensed I was up to something, but was led astray by his eagerness to get his hands on loadsamoney. Instead of dropping the matter, he warned of the grave peril in store for both of us if his clients were ripped off.

I kept him on the hop, reassuring him that all would be well and £10,000 was as good as his once we had tied up a few loose ends and he had handed over Sutcliffe's painting. He was at exploding point by the time the paper came out on Sunday with a spread of the Ripper's pictures, some of them not dissimilar to the one he had tried to land on me.

Rocky breathed hell and brimstone when he came on the phone after we published. He knew he had been had, but didn't quite know how. The biter bit. Meanwhile, he had some explaining to do to those hard-nosed clients of his waiting for their lolly.

Funny, I never heard from him again after that.

We had Sonia Sutcliffe's support in publishing the pictures.

Getting to her had not been difficult. She was a regular visitor at the *News of the World* offices, spending a few hours there on Saturdays on her way to Parkhurst to see her husband. He has since been transferred to Broadmoor.

A short, dark, intense woman, I thought there was something familiar about Sonia the first time I saw her in the editorial, making tea for the afternoon shift. It still shook me when I was told that the lady busying herself about the place was Mrs Sutcliffe, wife of the Ripper. Apparently she wanted to break her journey to the prison on the Isle of Wight and felt reasonably secure in our office. Mind you, it did nothing to soften her criticism of the *News of the World* and other papers.

I thought of her visits when the satirical magazine *Private Eye* was ordered to pay Mrs Sutcliffe record libel damages of £600,000 for suggesting she was involved in negotiations to sell her story to a newspaper. There was a more sensible settlement later. At one point the *Eye* approached me for information in its search for fresh evidence, but there was nothing I could do to help.

To be honest, Mrs Sutcliffe was welcome in the editorial so long as there was the slightest chance that she would tell the story of her years with the man who butchered thirteen women. It did not happen. She helped us with one or two news reports about Sutcliffe, but would never accept a penny from anyone. Over the years she could have made a fortune. However, she never budged from her principles. I wonder what Rocky Ryan would have made of that?

Editors are always in the front line where intrigue, double-dealing and downright villainy are concerned. There are so many out there with something to sell, some axe to grind, some dream of scoring through the columns of a newspaper. One of the strangest under-the-counter deals to come my way involved the pictures you see constantly in newspapers and magazines and on television of the Moors murderess Myra Hindley.

By strange coincidence, her tireless champion Lord Longford had been complaining to me that one of the factors detracting from Myra's claim to be a reformed character was that the only picture in existence was the police mugshot of her looking like a blonde gangster's moll. Not long afterwards I got a phone call from a contact who wanted to know if I was interested in a set of colour snaps of Hindley taken in prison. That I was. The price: £3,000 in cash and no questions asked. He said his man would be in touch with me at my home number.

The call came through, but there were to be many false starts before I got my hands on the pictures. We arranged to meet at the Blue Posts pub in the West End. He didn't turn up. Another call said he would be waiting by a certain wall in Bloomsbury. He wasn't there. Next time he called I told him to come to my flat immediately or forget it. The bell rang minutes later and there he was, a nondescript little man in a grubby raincoat. He fished into a pocket and brought out a coloured folder like those you get with your holiday prints.

Inside was the most amazing set of colour prints. This was a different Myra altogether. Soft and smiling, brunette rather than blonde, hugging soft toys. I handed over £3,000 in used notes, just like a gangster film, and insisted he signed a receipt, using any name he liked.

There was much gnashing of teeth on other papers when I came out with a big picture spread headlined: MYRA AS YOU HAVE NEVER SEEN HER BEFORE. The pictures subsequently went into syndication and by now should have earned Express Newspapers about £100,000. Not a bad return on an investment of £3,000.

It's strange how important pictures manage to fall into your lap. Some years ago I launched a campaign seeking to prove that an East End tearaway named George Davis was innocent of armed robbery. He was serving a seventeen-year sentence for a raid on the London Electricity Board offices at Ilford, Essex. His family had succeeded in rousing the East End to his cause, claiming he was the innocent victim of mistaken identity. There were public protests and everywhere graffiti appeared on walls saying 'Davis is innocent OK?' Supporters even ripped up the sacred turf at Headingley in the middle of a Test against the Aussies to draw attention to the campaign. Within days of my newspaper demanding an inquiry into the case he was pardoned by Roy Jenkins (now Lord Jenkins), then Labour Home Secretary. Davis had served less than three years and came out of jail toasting Derek Jameson.

I felt a right idiot a year later when he was caught red-handed carrying out a £50,000 armed robbery on a branch of the Bank of

Cyprus in Seven Sisters Road, Holloway, North London. Davis and five other men were arrested in a punch-up as police waiting in ambush pounced on the gang. One of my crime reporters got a phone call that day telling him to be in a certain place. There he was handed a roll of film, shot from a rooftop beside the bank. The whole story of the raid was there in the pictures, with Davis in the starring role. Caught bang to rights. I made much of our great *Express* picture exclusive, despite the fact someone was making a monkey of me.

Davis got fifteen years, reduced on appeal to eleven years. This time there were no protests. The whole gang pleaded guilty. They had been set up by a mysterious *agent provocateur*, who disappeared from the scene. With remission, Davis was freed in 1984. He was back before long, doing eighteen months for attempted theft of mailbags. My innocent hero!

On another occasion I picked up a phone that everyone was studiously ignoring as it rang shrilly in the editorial.

'I'm one of your readers,' said the voice at the other end. 'You know that paragraph you've got in the paper this morning about a princess being executed for adultery in Saudi Arabia? I've got pictures of that. Would you be interested?'

It turned out to be an engineer working in Saudi Arabia who happened upon the public execution. The crowd was so immersed in the drama before their eyes that nobody noticed the Englishman at the back taking pictures with his camera held up in the air.

'Christ,' I said to him. 'We'll definitely have those. Where are they?'

'In Manchester,' he said, 'in Boots the Chemist.'

We managed to get someone to open up Boots after hours and got the pictures. A colour set of splendid quality. We spread them all over the paper and paid our grateful reader £1,000.

Stern magazine in Germany paid £2,000 for them unseen. The rest of the world followed, and my headline DEATH OF A PRINCESS inspired a film of that name which almost caused the breakdown of relations between Britain and Saudi Arabia. *You never know what surprises might be on the other end when you pick up the telephone in a newspaper office.*

There's no place like newspapers for meeting the most extraordinary characters – and the most unforgettable of them all without doubt in my experience is Mrs Margaret Thatcher. She kindly summoned me to her presence for a little political education, having heard that I was not enamoured of politicians in general and the Conservative Party in particular.

In my case this was roughly the equivalent of a bishop disowning God since at the time I was editor of the *Daily Express*, required reading for several million of her followers.

We met in an oak-lined study in the House of Commons and she gave me a twenty-minute burst of economics, foreign affairs, social policy, people pulling up their socks and how we both wanted the best for everyone.

'There you are,' she said triumphantly as I sat too numb to reply. 'You're exactly the same as me. A social democrat in the true sense of the words.'

What struck me about the meeting was not the lesson in politics so much as the hospitality. Although it was not yet noon, Mrs Thatcher thought it fitting we should cement my instant conversion with a drink. To my astonishment she went to a cabinet in the corner and poured two large tumblers of Scotch, which we proceeded to knock back together. I didn't like to tell her drink has a bad effect on me. Three lagers and I'm anybody's.

It was her warmth and enthusiasm that got to me. My God, I thought, this woman really is human – not a bit like the rather stilted image that comes across on television. I think she still tends to freeze in front of a microphone.

My admiration for this remarkable lady was reinforced recently when I sat down alongside her at a posh lunch at the Inn on the Park hotel.

'I hope it's not going to be that *nouvelle cuisine*,' I told her. 'They give you two marbles and call them potatoes. If you're lucky, you get a braised spring onion for veg.'

'Yes, I know what you mean,' she said. 'Those French certainly know how to make a little go a long way.'

What a character – but I'm afraid my opinion of politicians remains unaltered.

My sympathies are with *The Guardian*'s great parliamentary (and cricket) reporter Norman Shrapnel, who was asked on his retirement from the House why he never left the press gallery to go down to the floor below and meet some of the MPs he had written about for years.

'Dear boy,' he said, 'if I were to go down there and do that, it might dilute my hatred of them.'

— 10 —
The Land of Tittle-tattle

RELATIONS between newspapers and the Palace are vitriolic. The Queen and her family exist in a stuffy, cloistered world surrounded by aides determined to perpetuate the half-baked myth that royals are omnipotent, almost divine beings who must not brush against the likes of us. They share the view of many politicians that we should know only what they care to tell us. We might cherish and uphold them, even meet their costs, but God forbid that we should presume to poke our noses into the way they behave.

Newspapers seek to portray them as they really are, good or bad. It makes them more human. Every time we prove they are real people – like Princess Anne telling photographers to 'Naff off!' – the Palace press office has kittens. The less we are allowed to tell, the more eager we become to tell it. Suppression, censorship, restrictions, red tape and bureaucracy – and we have mountains of them all in Britain – simply whet our appetite.

I threw the Palace into a tizz in 1983 while editor of the *News of the World* by proposing to publish the revelations of a maid, Michelle Riles, a Yorkshire girl who had worked there for two years. She was planning a book described by her agent as 'an Upstairs Downstairs story of passion', but nothing came of it to my knowledge. Somewhere along the line the Palace must have reached out its long arm and quashed her story.

Michelle's chronicle concerned her personal experiences while working there as a maid. It was put to me in no uncertain terms that she was governed by an oath of confidentiality and the Palace would secure an injunction – preventing me from publishing – in the late afternoon on Saturday, 28 May 1983. In other words, the *News of the World* presses would be halted just as they started and the losses to the paper in copies and revenue would be enormous. They had me well and truly over a barrel. I took the only way out and instead ran a story about the girl's mother being concerned for her daughter's safety. This brought about a bitter feud between myself and columnist Chris Hutchins, the man who secured Michelle's story. He now writes the Confidential column in the *Today* newspaper and all is well between us, though I broke the rules by battering him with his own story.

One lady who could tell all is actress Koo Stark, former lover of Prince Andrew. Koo is governed not by any laws of confidentiality; only by her own conscience. Yet nothing in the world would persuade her to break her silence. They say everyone has his or her price. Not Koo. I have got to know her well over the years and she is a remarkable woman. Once I offered her £1 million for the story of her romance with Andrew. I knew it was a property the whole world would be eager to buy, including Hollywood. Nights of passion at the Palace. Meeting the Queen. Who thwarted their plans to marry? Her private pictures. It would have been sweet revenge for the girl spurned largely because of her indiscretion in earlier years when, like many another young actress, she had appeared in soft-porn movies.

Koo would have none of it. Her loyalty to Andrew is total. We were taking tea together in the office of her friend and agent, impresario Michael White. She turned to me, those mesmeric green eyes blazing.

'Never,' she said. 'Not for all the money in the world. It's between him and myself.' She never mentions him by name.

I have the greatest respect for Koo and advised her on taking up a career in photography, even suggesting the title for her first book: *Stark Contrasts*. On my wedding day in 1988 she was working on Broadway, but sent a huge basket of flowers. There aren't many from Fleet Street who would get that treatment.

This might be the moment to confess that newshounds employed by me once booked a room in a Westminster hotel next to that occupied by her mother. They spent hours with their ears glued to an empty glass held against the wall in the hope it would pick up what was happening on the other side.

I called them off on hearing about it, but privately admired their ingenuity. Dirty tricks are a fact of life in newspapers. The competition is fierce, the quest for sensation relentless. All too often reporters and photographers go over the top in their eagerness to land a big story. Often the editor is the last to know, but he carries the can, anyway. Sometimes he comes up with a few tricks of his own.

When Cecil Parkinson resigned over his affair with Sara Keays, I sent him a message reading: 'How refreshing it is to see such honesty in public life.' He called me to say he was delighted to have these comforting words on the blackest day of his life. I offered him the columns of the *News of the World*, Britain's biggest selling paper, to put his side of the story. He almost fell for it, but sadly his lawyers vetoed the idea.

Outrageous behaviour? That's the name of the game. As I said, newspapers are there to tell the public what people in high places would rather they did not know. This *right to know* is an important principle and all too often we journalists knock over the goal posts defending it. There are times when we break our own rules and are persuaded to suppress news. It usually proves a mistake.

I remember a most upset Esther Rantzen coming on the phone when I was editor of the *Daily Express* asking me not to publish an exclusive story we had that she was pregnant by BBC executive Desmond Wilcox and that the next series of *That's Life* was to be cancelled.

'Desi hasn't had a chance to tell his children [by his previous marriage],' Esther said. 'Surely you wouldn't want to cause innocent people harm? It's a purely private matter.'

I could not see what was private about the cancellation of a television series watched by millions, but readily agreed to hold the story for a day while Mr Wilcox sorted out his domestic arrangements. My executives were most annoyed.

The next morning someone at the BBC telephoned an official version of the story to the Press Association news agency and that was the end of our Page 1 exclusive. I was always wary of playing Mr Nice Guy after that.

Diary columns probably cause editors more pain than anything else. Since gossip and tittle-tattle are their stock in trade they are always going to be contentious. Every day one reader or another is going to be left seething by revelations in the paper. Some may even reach for a libel writ. The offending words tend to appear in what newspapers politely call the diary page. The public puts it more accurately: gossip column.

John Cleese was in splendid form in January 1978 with this missive to the William Hickey column, commenting on their efforts to discover what was happening in his marriage to actress Connie Booth:

Dear William Hickey,

You may remember I wrote to you a couple of times last year. I've not received a reply yet, but I am sure you will get round to it sooner or later. I do realise how busy you must be running a column like yours.

One of my friends showed me the piece you wrote about Connie and me just before Christmas. It was, of course, wrong. Connie is not coming to Barbados. The Python team is going there to write and she has never been a member of the Python writing team. Nor has it ever been contemplated that she should come, incidentally. Still, getting this sort of thing right would involve you in a lot of exhausting telephoning so I quite understand why you don't bother.

Obviously you are keen to get some information about us both so let me tell you that in the coming year we shall be planning a reconciliation on March 7, August 10 to 11, and Nov. 22. However, we shall be deciding against it on April 6, July 29, and Dec. 2, as well as one unspecified Wednesday. I will send you a telegram when the Wednesday has been decided.

Also, my Ironing Board is 3ft. 8in. long and my cat's favourite food is 'Munchies' – octopus flavour. If I can think of anything else that will help to keep you all in employment, I'll be in touch.

John Cleese.

At least he did not sue. The letter, by the way, was not shown to me. I read it in a magazine. In newspapers there are executives who take the view that what the editor doesn't know is not going to hurt him. That makes good sense – until a libel writ drops into the In tray and the editor hasn't the faintest idea what it is about.

It was William Hickey that led to a celebrated exchange in November 1978 between the critic and author Auberon Waugh and myself in the columns of *The Spectator*. Hickey had wrongly accused

Right: Hamming it up with Mike Molloy, long-serving editor of the *Daily Mirror*. I was Mike's deputy – until the call came to edit the rival *Daily Express*. (*Daily Mirror*)

Below: August 1977 – and I make it to the top. In the editor's chair at the *Daily Express* in the days when long hair was not considered loutish. As a schoolboy, I had a premonition that this job would be mine – though I would have preferred the *Daily Mirror*! (*Daily Express*)

Above: Margaret Thatcher visits some of the troops on the back bench of the true blue *Daily Express*, an occasion which produced some wry smiles among the staff – they knew the editor was a lifelong socialist. (*Daily Express*)

Left: Yachtswoman Naomi James steps ashore at the end of her epic round-the-world solo voyage in 1978 – and first to greet her is the editor who backed her all the way. The experts reckoned Naomi wouldn't get past the Needles! (*Daily Express*)

Right: Moment of triumph for my *Express* boss, Victor Matthews, as he shows off his very own baby, the *Daily Star*, the first national daily for seventy-five years. I slunk away from the *Star*'s launch party in Manchester in November 1978, depressed by the look of the paper. (Press Association)

Below: Promoting the new *Daily Star* with the aristocratic and explosive Jocelyn Stevens, managing director of Express Newspapers. We were to have many battles, but I admired his dedication. (*Financial Times*)

Left: Tea at the Palace – I take Ellen along to a royal garden party. She would have liked something stronger. In those days she was still battling against the booze. (*Daily Express*)

Below: My Fleet Street pals – from left, *Sun* editor Kelvin MacKenzie, then *Times* editor Charles Wilson, editorial directors Peter Stephens and Dick Parack, the Street's first woman editor Wendy Henry, *Sunday Times* editor Andrew Neil, *Daily Express* editor Nick Lloyd, his associate editor Bernard Shrimsley, *Sunday Mirror* editor Eve Pollard (Mrs Lloyd), *Today* editor David Montgomery, and showbiz friend Derek Jameson. (*The Sun*)

Above: September 1988 and the Town Criers Guild ring out a welcome to newly married Derek and Ellen at Arundel Cathedral – a triumphant conclusion to the bride's long battle against alcoholism that almost destroyed her.

Below: Editor turned star – Princess Diana jokes with the line-up at a Royal Gala performance at the London Palladium. Joe Brown and Alvin Stardust are beside me with producer Robert Nesbit looking on. What made her laugh? I told the Princess I was petrified. (*Woman*)

Above: Apprentice to the stars – I went on every possible chat and game show, news and current affairs programme in my early days climbing the ladder in show business. Here Gordon Burns puts me through my paces on Granada TV's *The Krypton Factor*. (Granada TV)

Right: Christmas Day 1988 – and it's duty first for this Radio 2 presenter, broadcasting from a lost dogs' home near Newport Pagnell, Bucks. 'Mornin' Mornin', Jameson here' has become a national catchphrase. (*Daily Mirror*)

Above: Welcomed into the BBC family. From left: John Dunn, Paul Jones, the late Ray Moore, Ken Bruce, Brian Matthew, Richard Baker, Bob Holness, Derek Jameson, Angela Rippon, and Gloria Hunniford. (*Daily Mirror*)

Right: 'The Boss' – Rupert Murdoch – with SKY test pilot Derek Jameson and wife Ellen after the launch of his satellite television service. Rupert raised a few eyebrows by inviting me to present a daily chat show – he had fired me a few years earlier as editor of the *News of the World*. (SKY TV)

Left: Up in lights – *Jameson Tonight,* my SKY chat show, finds a home in the old Windmill Theatre, cradle of so much comedy talent. (*Daily Mirror*)

Below: Ellen and I find plenty to smile about at our beach house on the South Coast, named 'Angels' Rest' as a tribute to those kind souls upstairs who have looked after me from early days begging on the streets of the East End. (*The Sun*)

'Bron' of failing to act to help a woman who had written to him threatening to kill herself.

I give the texts in full because they sum up what journalism is all about – two men, totally different in outlook and background, happy to sink their differences in the pleasure they share over the use of words:

A LETTER TO SID – *Spectator, 4 November 1978*

A week ago I had the occasion to buy a copy of the *Daily Express*, something few people do nowadays, because a friend advised me that I was libelled in it. When asked to produce evidence for my theory that the English, as a race, are growing rapidly stupider, as well as less literate, I usually point to the *Sun*, whose intellectual level is so conspicuously lower than the *Mirror*'s of fifteen years ago, or to the *Sunday Times*, whose dismal books page and general intellectual banality may yet send the English back to church, if not to the one surviving literate weekly. Nobody thinks of the *Daily Express* as illustrating the point, partly because it was always nasty, philistine and half-witted, partly because since Mr Victor Matthews bought the newspaper, nobody who might discuss such matters appears to have seen it.

Perhaps it is time we caught up. Matthews has appointed as editor a fellow cockney called Derek Jameson whom I used to know slightly as the amiable, oafish pictures editor of the *Sunday Mirror* when I worked for that newspaper, writing captions for bathing beauties. In those days we never exposed a lady's breast, and I was interested to learn in a recent radio programme that Jameson has taken this scruple with him to the *Express*. The listening millions hear his solemn pledge: 'Us four oz Oim conncerned, ve *Dighly Express* will never cary noppoos'. (As far as I'm concerned, the *Daily Express* will never carry nipples.)

Where on earth, one might ask in that case, does the *Express* think it is going? It is a crude and tasteless thing to mock a man for his accent unless it is upper class, but to ignore Jameson's cockney would be more insulting, like ignoring the man who arrives at a party in a false nose. In appointing him, Matthews plainly intended to make a statement about something or other, whether about the future role of the *Express* or the new role of the cockney in the modern world. Now it falls on us to unravel what the pair of them are trying to say.

On Monday 23 October 1978, the day of which we treat, the banner headline across the top of the *Daily Express* reads: TODAY: MY KINGDOM FOR LOVE. Edward and Mrs Simpson. ALL THIS WEEK

THE STORY THAT ROCKED BRITAIN STARTING ON PAGE 28.
The East End of London, of course, is famous for its devotion to the
Royal Family, so I suppose a few senile cockneys might be expected to
read on; but if they turned to page 28, they would have found it entirely
taken up with the day's TV programmes.

Eventually, on page 23, the *Express*'s aged readers may have found the
Royal Romance retold yet again, this time in unmistakable pastiche of
Sylvie Krin: 'When Lady Furness arrived at Fort Belvedere that Friday
she found Mrs Simpson already having tea with the Prince . . . Mrs
Simpson, sitting with the teapot beside her in the position of "mother",
was saying . . . "And you, Sir? Another cup of your lovely English Tea?
With milk, but I'll not give you any sugar, it's bad for you".'

Finally, on Lord Moyne's yacht, we reach the long-awaited leg-over
situation: 'One night as they walked hand in hand along the deck and a
song faded behind them under the sounds of the sea and the night breeze
. . . she shivered and let go his hand . . . "I must go to my cabin" . . .

'"Shall you be coming out again, later on?"

'"Not tonight, Sir." She kept her voice cool. She curtsied lightly, but
slowly enough to leave some meaning in the action . . .'

Is this ludicrous publication seriously to be called a newspaper? The
question arose in its most poignant form when I saw the libel, glowing
like stacks of £5 notes on a gaming table, from the William Hickey page:
'*Auberon confesses*. He ignored a suicide warning sent to him by a woman
who later died . . .'

No, we must be resolute. After some happy fantasies of spending the
money – re-gilding my picture frames, restoring my Burges settle,
draining and dredging my lake – I wrote Jameson a personal letter which,
as he has not yet had the courtesy to acknowledge, I offer for wider
scrutiny:

Derek Jameson, Esq.,
Editor,
The Daily Express,
Fleet Street,
London, EC4

24 October 1978

WITHOUT PREJUDICE

Dear Sid,

I would not expect you to have much success in trying to follow a
Spectator article, but it might have been prudent to employ a lawyer with

greater powers of concentration before lifting a story from *Spectator* of 21 October 1978, for your Hickey column of 23 October 1978: 'Auberon Confesses'.

This starts 'Writer and critic Auberon Waugh, son of novelist Evelyn, is making the astonishing confession that he ignored a woman who wrote to him threatening to kill herself. Now the woman is dead.'

As anyone who read the *Spectator* article will know, there was no threat contained in the woman's card. She merely stated her intention of killing herself next day. As I did not open the parcel until nine days later, the moment was long since past and the only logical reason for pursuing an enquiry would have been to satisfy vulgar curiosity. After considerable thought I decided against this course of action and wrote the letter reproduced in full in *Spectator* but not, of course, in Hickey.

Your report omits to mention this vital fact, that I knew of her intention only when it was too late to do anything about it. Instead it creates the deliberate impression that I callously turned my back and ignored her 'threats' while the issue was still in doubt. Perhaps in your world it is perfectly acceptable to accuse someone of murder by neglect but the *Daily Express* lawyers, if you still employ any, may suggest that different standards apply elsewhere.

When your reporter, who said he was called 'John Roberts', telephoned I warned him of the danger of trying to compress a complicated and rather sensitive argument into a lurid gossip paragraph. He chirpily replied that he doubted whether this consideration would influence his superiors. In recklessly ignoring this warning, you also printed an account of my conversation with Roberts which is exactly the opposite of what I said:

'Of course the mystery woman was not a "totally strange woman" to Waugh, as he says in his confession in the small circulation *Spectator* magazine: Yesterday he told me: "Frankly I know she has children. That is why I cannot reveal her name."'

If you ask Roberts to play you his tape of the conversation you will find I explain at great length how I know absolutely nothing about the woman beyond what is in the *Spectator*, but I was not prepared to reveal her name in case she had children.

Yet this false allegation – that I deliberately misled *Spectator* readers on a vital point – is Mr Roberts' only substantive addition to the story which he incompetently lifted from the *Spectator*. He also adds the usual gratuitous pieces of misinformation – that I will be forty next month, that I have written over fifty books – which are what pass for news nowadays,

I suppose, on the *Express*. One day you might teach him how to use the standard reference books.

From my experience of the libel law (possibly not so extensive as your own), I should judge the gravity and recklessness of the main libel to be worth a minimum £5,000 in out of court settlement and any sum you care to name after litigation. The secondary libel – alleging deception of my readers – is of value only in establishing malice.

You may have read that I have a principled objection to suing for libel – even where such a rich and unworthy newspaper as yours is concerned. Alas, this is true although I am sorely tempted on this occasion. The injury is deliberate, damages are tax free. But I give you due warning. I propose to make various utterances on this matter in the course of the next few weeks and months which may well include remarks on the subject of personal habits and fitness for the job of Editor. If these remarks should seem in your judgment to exceed the proper limits of fair comment or good taste, please bear in mind that I am reserving my position over this malicious and unscrupulous attack on my character.

Yours ever,
Bron

Next week (hopefully): the story of Jacqueline – whatever happened to the first Mrs Jameson? The searing account of a marriage that failed; Partners with Pauline – the true-life romance of Sid and his second wife, from languishing looks to leg-over; A Mother Remembers: Mrs Elsie Jameson looks back on struggles with Sid – Part One, nappy rash. All in next week's star-studded *Spectator*. The voice of Britain.

The Spectator published my reply in the next week's issue:

A LETTER FROM SID

Dear Bron,

Sorry, guv, to have caused offence. Dunno wot I must've bin finking abaht to let a hole week go by wivaht replyn' to a toff like Mister Auburn War. You put me in me plice an' no misstake . . .

Really, Bron, you must allow me to teach you cockney idiom, if you could stand the pain. Your version in last week's *Spectator* of how I am supposed to speak ('Us four oz Oim conncerned') was more Street than Street Porter. The local woodworm must have got at you.

Let us turn to the more serious suggestion that I personally had ignored your totally justified complaint that the *Daily Express* William Hickey column implied that you turned your back on a woman who wrote to you saying that she intended to kill herself.

Not guilty. Obviously you were not to know that I have been away from the *Daily Express* for several weeks looking after the launch of a new newspaper. The fact is that I was not responsible for the *Express* at the time that the Hickey piece appeared. The first I knew of your letter was when I read it in *The Spectator* in Manchester last Friday. A two-minute telephone call could have ascertained whether I had received it before you leapt into print blackguarding me. When it comes to checking facts, you aren't any great improvement on William Hickey, are you?

Let that pass. The Hickey piece appalled me when I read it on October 23. You have every reason to be offended by such a distorted account of what happened in the case of this unfortunate woman. It should have been made absolutely clear, if indeed published at all, that you did not see her card until nine days after the day on which she intended killing herself. It was also absurd of Hickey to suggest that the lady was not a total stranger to you.

As editor *in absentia* of the *Daily Express*, I do apologise publicly for the pain that this Hickey report must have caused. Knowing you slightly, I am certain that you would help any person in distress were it in your power to do so. I am very sorry, both personally and professionally. Others are finding out just how this story came to be written.

That does not excuse the crude, offensive tone that you adopt towards me in an entire page of *Spectator*. Your villain has become victim. I was not present when someone had the temerity to write something hurtful about Mr Auberon Waugh. You have neatly turned the situation upside down with a series of spurious assumptions that question my integrity, my professional ability and my fitness to edit newspapers. For good measure you drag in my family and talk of searing romance and Jameson getting his leg over. Next week you hope to tell what happened to my first wife. I will tell you. She died of a brain haemorrhage ten years after our divorce.

Since I share your aversion to the laws of libel, perhaps you and the editor of *Spectator* will extend me the courtesy of space for this letter apologising to you and at the same time rebutting some of your more outrageous statements.

You address me as 'Dear Sid', which is derived from *Private Eye*'s 'Sid Yobbo' (alternating with 'Pearly King'). Presumably these particular insults rest on the fact that I am from the East End, grew up in poverty and left school at fourteen. With all that going for him he's got to be a thick yob, right? You even touchingly suggest in your first sentence that you would not expect me to have much success trying to follow a *Spectator* article.

Would you believe that there are people from the working class who can read and write? I was encouraged at school by teachers who felt there was a distinct possibility that I was cut out for something else than a lorry driver's mate. Their way out, and mine, happened to be literature. They didn't throw the book at me, but the whole bloody library. There was neither the time nor the resources for anything else; a war was going on.

At thirteen I won a national essay competition, which inspired me a year later to seek a job in Fleet Street. Delivering messages. Two years after that I became a trainee reporter and within ten years was a senior executive directing world news services at Reuters. Ask the *Spectator*'s editor about it. His father, Sir Christopher Chancellor, ran the place. Arthur Christiansen recommended me to the *Daily Express* and, to cut a boring story short, ultimately I became deputy editor of the *Daily Mirror* before going back to edit the *Express*. In my first year there, the circulation went up substantially – the first real increase for fourteen years and eight editors. And not a nipple in sight.

You say that you first met me as an 'amiable oaf' at the *Sunday Mirror*, but omitted to mention that I was always courteous and helpful to you. Worth saying because it happened to be a rarity. Most colleagues kept their distance because they felt your presence owed more to Waugh, Downside, Oxford and daddy's old regiment than to any journalistic ability. Since I hate bigotry even more than I detest privilege, I treated you with respect. In any case, my aforementioned library happened to include *Put Out More Flags* and the rest. When you subsequently established a brilliant literary reputation on your own account, I was more than vindicated in my decision to treat you as a decent human being rather than something Hugh Cudlipp had deposited on the mat.

To end at the beginning, sorry that my cockney accent offends your ear. I'm not too crazy either about your piping, emasculated upper-class squeak. Perhaps you should have tried Lancing.

Derek Jameson,
Editor-in-Chief,
Daily Star,
Great Ancoats Street,
Manchester.

Good knockabout stuff guaranteed to get the *literati* going. Some commentators urged that the debate should go on for ever. Bron and I thought one round each was about right. He wrote kindly accepting my apology, said sorry himself and declared he felt I was 'a good egg'.

By way of a postscript, he subsequently described me in *The Spectator* thus: 'Derek Jameson – possibly the last, certainly the greatest, surviving Fleet Street editor of the old school'.

– 11 –

Conduct Unbecoming

NOBODY has ever been able to control the Press, though from time to time those in power make threatening noises and talk loftily of introducing legislation in the forlorn hope that newspapers might conform to what they perceive to be the proper way for it to behave. God help the people if editors ever go about their business to suit politicians, bureaucrats and the self-appointed guardians of public morality: Establishment worthies who fancy they know better than the rest of us what we should be watching on telly or reading over the cornflakes at the breakfast table.

In an ideal world, editors answer to their own conscience and the public they serve. Those readers who regard the editor and the paper he produces as a load of rubbish are free to spend their money elsewhere. It doesn't quite work out that way. The British are a funny lot. In all my life I have rarely heard anyone say a good word for any of the popular papers – and yet they read them by the millions.

As for the integrity and independence of editors – forget it. Like everyone else, we have to pay the rent. That means the papers we turn out first and foremost reflect the views of Viscount Rothermere, Rupert Murdoch, Robert Maxwell and the like. Every office has a grey area known as 'policy', a predetermined set of rules that lays down where the paper stands in any given situation, be it a gruesome murder or a political scandal. The loony Left and others who knock Fleet Street think there is some kind of conspiracy among newspapers, that they get together to decide where to put the boot in. Usually the critics claim that Labour and the trade unions are top of the hit parade. Some even believe editors are summoned to No. 10 on a regular basis to get their instructions.

An interesting scenario, but it is codswallop. Policy is invisible. Nothing is written down and little said. Sherlock Holmes himself would be hard put to find evidence of its existence. It is a distillation of the proprietor's feelings on this, that and the other – they tend to have views on everything – passed on to the editor in their various chats together. The editor in turn conveys what is in the great man's mind to the troops. He might say a word or two at one of the daily conferences or lay down the law to a news or features executive while discussing the paper. Naturally he puts across his own likes and dislikes by the same process.

Sometimes policy is laid down when the proprietor takes exception to something he has read in the paper. He will blow up the editor, who spreads the word to avoid such stories in future. Thus if the man on top has an aversion, say, to Michael Heseltine then that newspaper will not run anything favourable to him until policy is changed. Even his major speeches are likely to be pruned so not to give them too much weight.

Policy is not confined to politics. It covers the whole spectrum of news, features and pictures. The arrangement is so loose that often lines get hopelessly crossed. I remember that the *Mirror* papers for years tried to avoid pictures or stories about snakes. 'Cudlipp hates snakes', senior executives would hiss every time one tried to slither its way into the paper. Apparently Lord Cudlipp, for years the *Mirror*'s editorial director, had been repulsed when he was Hugh Cudlipp, editor of the then *Sunday Pictorial*, by a picture of a python draped round some bright young thing. 'God, how bloody awful,' he said. A remark soon forgotten, but we were still banning snakes thirty years later until someone – it may have been me – asked him why he hated snakes so much. 'Me?' said Hugh, obviously mystified. 'I've got nothing against snakes.'

To be honest, I resented having to kowtow to the wishes of the people upstairs. That presumably is why I am not an editor today. Having been in newspapers from the age of fourteen, clawing my way to the top, I fancied myself to be a better judge of how to serve the public. Naturally my bosses did not see it that way. No doubt they sensed I did not consider them one step removed from God Almighty just because, as was usually the case, they had a head for business or were good at figures.

Rupert Murdoch has a ready answer for anyone who suggests too much power is concentrated in his hands. 'You want to start a newspaper?' he growls. 'Nothing to it. Just go to the bank and ask them to lend you the money.' At least he is a real newspaperman, in the business from the cradle. His newspapers cover the entire spectrum, from sober to sensational, and he does not touch his forelock to the Establishment. But I wouldn't fancy the chances of any editor who argued the toss with him about the contents of his paper. They don't call him 'Boss' for nothing.

He bawled me out in front of my executives when I was editor of the *News of the World*. Having peremptorily summoned the entire team to his presence, he went through the latest issue of the *NoW* page by page and verbally tore them to shreds, spitting our collective efforts all over the floor of his luxurious office. 'If I've told you once, I've told you a thousand times, we don't want pop in the *News of the World*.' He pointed angrily to a piece on the cavortings of some singing idol. 'Leave that to *The Sun*.'

It was too much for me. I turned on Rupert as if someone had shoved a red-hot poker down my trousers. 'What do you mean . . . what do you MEAN!' I screamed out the words. 'Are you telling me, in front of my staff, that we must not do anything in the paper addressed to young people? Let's get this straight, let's have it on the record, since you've brought all these people over here. You are saying that pop stars are of no interest to our twelve million readers, that we should do nothing for the young? Is that it?'

That slowed Rupert down a bit. He thought a moment, then declared brightly: 'Young people are too intelligent to read the *News of the World*!'

See what I mean about proprietors.

They tend to have a blind spot about many ordinary, everyday things that interest the rest of us. Pop stars are high on the list of happenings beyond their comprehension. *How can all that cater-wauling by such an obvious idiot attract so much capital?* Not long after joining the *Daily Express*, Victor Matthews called me to his office, pointed to a picture of Rod Stewart on the front page and enquired solemnly: 'What's this idiot doing on the front page of the *Express*?'

'That "idiot",' I shot back, 'has just brought out a new album. It sold four million copies in a week. That's why he's on the front page. Rod Stewart is big news.'

'Four million!' he said, obviously impressed and quickly dropping the subject. Actually it was nearer a million. Editors have to be cunning. It's bad enough having to put up with the proprietor's whims and fancies without letting him tell you what to put on the front page. Some editors never argue the toss and take everything thrown at them by the people upstairs. They certainly survive longer that way, though their papers tend to be that much more vapid.

Once I asked Victor Matthews why he knew better than anyone else what should go into the paper. The irony was lost on him. He answered without hesitation. 'Well, I've done it all, haven't I? Look at the business me and my chums have built up. You couldn't get as far as I have unless you had it up here,' pointing to his forehead.

He had been proposing that the *Daily Express* should make a somewhat startling contribution to labour relations throughout the nation by demanding that all employees of any firm suffering a wildcat strike should be fired there and then.

'You mean even those not involved in the strike?' I asked innocently.

'That's right,' he said. 'Fire the lot.'

'What's the point of that, then?'

'Well, if you've got a bunch of troublemakers holding a firm to ransom by an unofficial strike, they'll soon come to heel if you dismiss all their workmates. They'd never be able to stand up to the pressure from people in other areas.'

I couldn't believe what I was hearing. 'It doesn't work like that,' I told him. 'Let me give you an example. Take, for instance, a mail-order company in Liverpool. The despatch department, where they send out the parcels, has gone on strike because one of the workers there has been dismissed for bad timekeeping. They're members, say, of the Transport and General Workers, but it's all happened so suddenly that they've yet to get official backing for the strike. The rest of the workforce, mainly housewives doing part-time jobs, are not even in the union. And you're saying they should all be fired on the spot?'

'That's right,' said Victor. 'The people on strike would be back like a shot and they'd think twice before coming out again.'

'Sounds more like an advert for trade unions to me, Chairman,' I told him. 'Far more likely the women would be incensed at being treated so badly over something that had nothing to do with them. Your story would end not with the firm going back to work, but all the women joining the union and the whole lot coming out on official strike.'

We had many chats along these lines. Once I told the Chairman of Express Newspapers that our readers were ordinary men and women in the street. 'They're not all company directors, you know,' I told him.

'No, but they'd like to be,' said Victor.

In theory the proprietor's views should have been passed on to the staff as policy. I made up my own mind about that.

On the whole, proprietors are reasonably tolerant and let their editors get on with it, knowing they are in the front line and take most of the flak. Matthews said publicly on one occasion: 'My editors have freedom, as long as they follow the policy I have laid down.' Those at the top can always blame – or fire – the editor when things go wrong. Cecil King, patrician head of the *Mirror* empire, invariably answered when someone complained to him about the *Daily Mirror*: 'You'll have to talk to the editor about it. I read *The Times* myself.'

The main pressure on editors comes not from the bosses, but from the busybodies who seek to impose controls on the way newspapers behave. They claim to be acting in the public interest, a rather sad proposition because that is precisely what newspapers are supposed to be all about. They are beating not the burglar, but the watchdog. A pretty dismal dog, too, to have aroused the ire of the people he is there to protect.

The Press has been under attack from one source or another since the days of Caxton. Some of us believe that those who scream loudest often have the most to hide. All the same, there is no denying that in recent years criticism had reached such a level that Parliament threatens to introduce legislation to control its wilder excesses. In March 1990 the Press Council rushed out a code of conduct supported by editors in a bid to lower the temperature. National newspapers even appointed their own ombudsmen to investigate complaints and make amends where necessary. Naturally, newspapers did not fall over themselves to report that these measures were in many cases being introduced by the very editors accused of bringing the press into disrepute, or that the newly appointed 'readers' representatives' were primarily newspaper executives, often on the staff of the paper they were supposed to be judging.

As for the code of conduct, like the Ten Commandments it makes good reading. Just how many journalists are going to follow the rules in the frantic climate of tabloid competition is anyone's guess. In my view, any editor who followed the code to the letter would be operating with a hand tied behind his back, much to the delight of his rivals. As day follows night, his good deeds would soon be translated into bad sales. He would be for the chop. When clearing out his desk, presumably he would leave the Press Council's code of conduct in a prominent place for his successor.

Some great thinkers, perhaps better versed in philosophy than communication, claim that the public gets the newspapers it deserves. As is usually the case when those on a higher plane saddle the rest of us with such lofty thoughts, this is patronising and elitist claptrap. People get the newspapers they want. In this country, the choice is as near complete as you will find on earth. Everything from *The Sun* to the *Investor's Chronicle*. Thanks to modern technology, you can even think about publishing a newspaper of your own in the garden shed.

One thing you will learn very swiftly is that your publication, however well intentioned, will have a limited shelf life unless you make it lively and interesting. Since presumably you want to sell copies, which is the object of the exercise, then the more exciting you make the product, the more people will read it. As we know, the things that excite most of the people most of the time are sex and disaster, gossip and scandal, fun and entertainment, sport and television.

It was on this heady diet that the British tabloid press grew rich and fat. The stronger the mixture, the greater the readership. Add a little spice here and there, perhaps some juicy scandal or sensational buy-up, and the circulation will go up and up and up. Late news served piping hot. Unless, of course, your rival comes out with bigger and better scandals. So the crazy waltz goes on for ever.

News and pictures, fashion and features, sporting types and artists, editors and executives, stringers and tipsters, district men and hungry freelances . . . all have but one reason for living. To be best, to have a bigger and better story/picture/feature/contest/stunt than the rest.

It is a harsh and relentless war, these tabloid titans fighting for their share of the cake, and a lot of bystanders get crushed underfoot in the fray. The arrival of modern technology, with its cheap and efficient printing free of union restraints, has given the troops yet more scope for battle. Now it is a free-for-all with greater incentives for the strongest to succeed most. *Bingo, Lotto, Spotto! FIVE MILLION £££s TO BE WON. The Greatest Game in All the Galaxy!*

Into these gladiatorial proceedings, with profits never looking better, comes the prissy, pedantic Press Council, set up as a voluntary body by the newspaper bosses in a feeble attempt to allay public fears. So feeble, in fact, that it was twenty-five years before the Council got around to a joint declaration signed by the editors in support of its code. I can imagine the tortured expression on the face of one or two editors as they were told: *Cut it out, lads, you'll have us all in the dock. You can't go on like this. We'll have to draw up a Code of Conduct.*

Editors in today's climate have to keep their heads down and make the best of it. Faced with a contemptuous public, jittery proprietors, pious politicians and assorted do-gooders, he or she must be seen to be a good and saintly person, most grateful to those clever people at the Press Council. Since I am free to speak, I will tell you why much of the code does not work from an editor's point of view. Let us look at its major provisions:

ACCURACY. It is the duty of newspapers not to publish deliberately or carelessly inaccuracies or statements designed to mislead, and to correct promptly and with due prominence significant inaccuracies which they have published, or misleading statements for which they are responsible, apologising for these where appropriate.

They are talking about the truth, that elusive prize we were always seeking in the old days. So sacred was the true word that I have seen grown men with children weeping because they had been dismissed with ignominy for getting a proper name wrong. I myself, as a young sub-editor on the *Daily Express*, by some mental aberration wrote *Warwick, Worcs.*, instead of *Warwick, Warwicks*. It got into the paper, too, which made it an instant firing offence. I appeared at the feature editor's table next afternoon carrying a bunch of onions. John Macdonald was his name, a hard-nosed Scouse given to pursing his lips and exhaling air loudly at every hiccup in the process of producing features for the world's greatest newspaper, as it called itself. 'What's those for, cock?' he wanted to know.

'I've brought my balls with me,' I told him. 'I know I'm in big trouble.' Angels preserve me; he didn't know what I was talking about. Normally some kind soul passes on big news like A Mistake in a Proper Noun. In this case, nobody had noticed thanks to the close geographical approximation of *Worcs.* to *Warwicks*. I survived. Poor John could hardly fire a sloppy sub-editor for a mistake nobody had seen.

Such tender, loving care for the truth went right through the paper. Any journalist on the staff who got something wrong, allowed *inaccuracies to creep in* as they quaintly put it, was on the carpet with the prospect of instant dismissal. Sin of sins, they had got the paper a bad name. It applied to a spurious report about a politician just as much as a misprint in the racecard. It was all right to be sensational, it was perfectly in order to uncover a scandal, but it had to be true. We lived by the creed laid down by C. P. Scott, the great *Guardian* editor: Comment is free, facts are sacred.

It's not like that today. Every story I read of which I have personal knowledge smacks of careless reporting. Names, dates and facts seem to be wrong as often as they are right. Quotes frequently are of the type that were never quoted anywhere – pure invention. If they have such scant regard for the simple truth of the matter, then what prospect is there that any credibility can be attached to the bigger issues like the story itself and the way it is projected?

These days any tacky old publicity stunt is seized upon as front-page news. It is also generally held that the public get their real news from television so there's no need to worry unduly about matters outside the sex/entertainment/sensation compartment. The important factor is to generate the most excitement. Any gimmick, twist, pun, lie or distortion is acceptable so long as it serves that purpose. Standards have never been lower. They have brought the rails crashing down in their race to be first past the post. People no longer place much trust in anything they read in newspapers. Journalists rank lower in public esteem than estate agents and politicians.

It is most unlikely that the Press will get back to accurate reporting by way of a Press Council edict. Nor do I see editors in today's steamy climate instructing the people they have been driving so hard to change tack completely, to be more concerned with the truth than obtaining another exclusive. To forsake the froth and frippery for solid, hard news values is like asking a fan dancer to perform Chekhov. The responsibility lies with proprietors insisting on higher standards, something that has been happening of late. However, will they at the same time rid themselves of their nasty habit of firing editors who lose circulation?

As for editors apologising when they get it wrong, there are signs that this, too, is becoming common practice. Libel awards of £500,000 and above concentrate the mind wonderfully when a plaintiff is willing to settle for an apology rather than reach for a writ.

OPPORTUNITY TO REPLY: It is the duty of newspapers to allow a fair opportunity for reply when reasonably called for.

This will not cause editors to lose sleep. They are not going to accept the principle that anyone can demand space in their newspaper, though obviously they will be prepared to talk turkey rather than risk legal action. In any case, what is *reasonable*? Furthermore, there are replies and replies. Sometimes a plaintiff can be persuaded to appear among the readers' letters. Fifty quid in the post often helps. At worst, perhaps they will accept a second, more friendly piece in the paper.

PRIVACY. Publishing material or making inquiries about the private lives of individuals without their consent is not acceptable unless these are in the public interest, overriding the right of privacy.

This clause is the heart of the matter, so far as the great debate on control and censorship of the Press is concerned. In June 1990 proprietors and editors were given 'one last chance' to establish a nonstatutory system of self-regulation primarily aimed at improving standards and preventing journalists from intruding into private lives. Otherwise, the Government warned, legislation would be introduced to enforce the recommendations of a committee headed by David Calcutt QC, including replacement of the Press Council by a tougher Press Complaints Commission.

If journalists were left fearful of the consequences of Government controls, the public at large took the view that newspapers had brought it on themselves. Nor was there much sympathy for the holier-than-thou bleat by some journalists that they were being castigated for the sins of their downmarket cousins. The entire Press was on trial. The truth is that newspapers of all shades – from *The Times* to the *Sunday Sport* – are guilty of what others might consider improper conduct.

All of them are composed of stories someone somewhere did not want printed. In a great many cases that presumes they would regard obtaining such a story as intrusive, an invasion of privacy. Newspapers would argue they were simply doing their duty, seeking the facts of a matter they considered the public had a right to know about. Whether the story meets the criterion of being in the public interest is not a factor that brings the news desk to a sudden halt as it goes about its business. They tend to see life in more simple terms. *Will it make a good story?*

What are the boundaries of privacy? Can a person in the public eye have a private life, or is that a contradiction in terms? Does an accountant in Accrington have a greater measure of privacy than a television presenter in Teddington?

One of my favourite newspaper tales concerns the singer Shirley Bassey. Years ago, in her younger days, a rejected suitor named Pepé Davis locked himself into her room at the Cumberland Hotel and produced a pistol, threatening to shoot unless she promised to love him forever. The siege went on for some hours and Davis actually fired a shot. Nobody was hurt, but it cost him a three-year prison sentence. In the middle of all the brouhaha, the head of a *Daily Express* reporter appeared upside down outside the hotel window several floors above Marble Arch. His ankles firmly grasped by two friendly photographers, the newsman tapped politely on the window to attract the attention of Miss Bassey and her uninvited guest. 'Sorry to bother you,' he says politely. 'I wonder if I might have a word . . .'

Highly intrusive, that. There can be few events more intensely private than being locked in a hotel room by a maniac waving a gun. He certainly wasn't looking for publicity and no doubt Shirley Bassey herself was not desperately anxious to see the world sharing her troubles. But was it in the public interest to spread the word? Guns are dangerous and the public has a right to know what the police propose to do when people brandish them in strange places. Or should that be classified information, not available to the public? Perhaps Miss Bassey's fame has a bearing on the matter. Pictures and stories about her appear in the papers all the time. Why not now? Is it perfectly valid to itemise the dresses and shoes in her wardrobe, but not to reveal a threat to her life? Should the reporter have made his intentions known? A note through the door, perhaps, announcing in advance that he planned to risk his neck hanging from a top-floor window and would that be all right?

So who is to decide between private and public, permissible or forbidden? What of the oft-cited cabinet minister who spends the night in his mistress's bed? Certainly a private affair. It enters the public domain only because the man is in the government and therefore presumably not allowed a bit on the side. He is supposed to set a high standard for the rest of us to follow. But what if his wife is an invalid, unable to enjoy sexual relations, and her loving husband has permission to take a mistress? Is that permissible and, if so, does it then become private? In that case, who tells the newspaper? Perhaps all parties should be asked to produce an affidavit before turning down the bedcovers.

It will be argued that the minister's love life has nothing to do with anyone but his immediate family. Years ago John Profumo, Army Minister of the day, angrily denied there was anything improper about his friendship with Christine Keeler, who was what they called in the early sixties 'a good-time girl'. He even lied to the House of Commons about it. It turned out that he was sharing Christine's favours with Evgeny Ivanov, the Soviet naval attaché. Fleet Street discovered this fascinating fact by hotly pursuing the story, despite every attempt by the Establishment to cover it up. Today newspapers would be accused of a gross violation of privacy. They might even be fined half a million for libel.

The Press lives by disclosure. The important question is not how it goes about its business, but the standards of those appointed to do the job. Any queries on that score should be addressed to the proprietor, not the profession. Those who seek reform have missed the simple truth that to take away an editor's right to decide what shall be published is to pass that prerogative elsewhere. Do they seriously believe that the contents of a newspaper should be determined by a politician – or the bureaucrat appointed to represent him?

COMMENT AND FACT. Newspapers are free to be partisan but they should distinguish between comment and fact. Conjecture should not be elevated into statements of fact.

This is a cosy thought, suggesting as it does that newspapers should be fair, balanced and objective. The notion that they should voluntarily keep comment and conjecture out of their news columns betrays a total ignorance of the role and function of newspapers. It is rather like asking the Pope to put in a good word for abortion.

People run newspapers first and foremost to make money. They are not too concerned how this is done, provided the editor keeps the customers happy. However, they are not in the charity business. They exist to make propaganda, as just about every proprietor since Northcliffe has admitted quite freely. Editors are required to support the cause dearest to the proprietor's heart. Normally that they consider best qualified to protect their interests – and their purse.

It usually goes under the name of the Conservative and Unionist party. There are exceptions, of course. Like the others, Robert Maxwell says he runs the *Mirror* papers to make propaganda, but he is a lifelong socialist and supports Labour with qualifications. *The Guardian* and nowadays *The Independent* tend to remain firmly middle-of-the-road. As for the rest, most national newspapers in my lifetime and beyond have rooted loud and clear for the Tories. Indeed, this unswerving support is the clearest possible evidence that the owners' interests come first. It totally ignores the views of the public it so loudly professes to serve. When the electorate undergoes one of its periodic spasms and decides that Labour is the best hope for the country, then the faithful gun dogs bay louder than ever for the Tory Party. To hell with what the public wants. And it is not going to help the cause to limit the proprietor's views to the leader columns under the heading *Comment* or *Opinion*. Less than one reader in six of popular newspapers reads them; that is why they are tucked away on a left-hand page. Even fewer give a toss about the political inclinations of the proprietor.

I have told in the chapter on the birth of the *Daily Star* how I persuaded Trafalgar House that the paper should support Labour, if only to suggest that there is such a thing as democracy and fair play. It was not long before the paper did a quick backflip and changed its colours to true blue. The *Sun*, too, originally supported Labour, not least because it was sired by the old Labour *Daily Herald*. That also underwent a sudden conversion.

When you are batting on such a highly political wicket, the object is to get your opponent out. Short of landing in the High Court on a libel charge, editors do not lose much sleep over how to go about it. Fair play and objective reporting do not come into it. It's a question of any stick to beat a dog. Nothing pleases proprietors more than to see their political enemies dealt a sharp jab in the solar plexus.

Since it is so facile and self-serving, political coverage tends to be a cynical exercise. All too often editors and their staff, particularly political and industrial correspondents, are totally at odds with the cause they are feeding so assiduously. As I have said elsewhere, they have to pay the rent. My guess is that the public can sense the phoney-baloney behind much of politics in popular newspapers and that is why they take such little notice. If the electorate listened to what much of Fleet Street has been telling them *ad nauseam* there would never have been a Labour government in Britain.

I am as guilty as the next man. On 3 May 1979 – election day – I designed a *Daily Express* front page that was nothing more than a Tory election poster – so much so that it was later framed and put up on a wall at Conservative Central Office. It showed a pile of rubbish rotting outside Transport House, Labour's headquarters in London, during a dustmen's strike some months earlier. DON'T FORGET LAST WINTER, screamed the splash headline. Below it were two sub-heads: *Give the girl a chance to make Britain great again* and *Remember – a Liberal vote is a wasted vote*. Other Tory papers came out with similar exhortations to vote Tory. The *Daily*

Mirror stayed true to Premier Jim Callaghan with a huge FOR-
WARD WITH THE PEOPLE – Vote LABOUR today.

 Should these robust views have been confined to the opinion
columns? Of course they should – in an ideal world. Fleet Street, of
course, is a jungle. Will it now become the garden of Eden, courtesy
of HM Government? Some hopes.

> SUBTERFUGE. Newspapers and journalists serving them should use
> straightforward means to obtain information or pictures. Their use of
> subterfuge can be justified only to obtain material which ought to be
> published in the public interest and could not be obtained by other means.

 A fine sentiment, almost impossible to put into practice. How do
you persuade a person, often distraught and being hotly pursued by
the media, that it is in the public interest to cooperate with the very
people he or she is trying so hard to avoid? It would be easy to find
a thousand examples. As we all know, news in newspapers so often
consists of information someone did not want published. It is
impossible to legislate how a newspaper should go about gathering
material. Most resort to underhand methods almost every day. It is
what the business is all about. Ex gratia payments to tipsters, the
cultivation of confidential sources, dirty tricks and double talk. In a
closed society like ours, all too often it is the only way to get the
news. All official information, for instance, is classified unless
somebody in authority clears it for public dissemination. Who is to
be the judge of what is the public interest – the bureaucrat
withholding the news or the reporter chasing the story?

 Let us examine some typical cases:

 In the age of nuclear disarmament, an American unit suddenly
arrives in Suffolk in the dead of night with the latest line in inter-
continental missiles. There is no restriction order – or 'D' (for
Defence) Notice – on the story, though naturally Washington and
Whitehall refuse to say a word. The only answer is to drop fifty quid
to Farmer Fred and take a picture from the roof of his barn.
Subterfuge? Public interest?

 Bishop Gaiters has run off with a chorus girl. No comment and
no pictures. There they are, hand-in-hand on the pier. Should the
photographer jump out from behind the Punch and Judy booth and
snatch a quick picture? Subterfuge, that. Best leave it. Hang on –

there are three photographers from rival papers at the end of the pier. What to do? A prelate of the Established Church. No reason why he shouldn't fall for a pretty dancer. He happens to be a widower. The public will be fascinated, but do they have the right to know? You can imagine the happy snapper working all this out in his brainbox as he tiptoes along the pier!

Inter-Stellar Supermarkets learns that its American cousins have dumped thousands of jars of fish paste because a batch in one store was found to be contaminated. Tests are carried out on the British stocks and they are given the all clear. However, the company does not want to take any chances and decides to get rid of its supply. A checkout girl phones a newspaper. Obviously, the company has acted from the highest motives, but any publicity would be most damaging. Its spokesman refuses to comment. The newspaper, by now suspicious, gets a picture of the dumped fish paste by planting a camera on the checkout girl. Should it publish? There is no public interest. The British supplies are perfectly safe. Unfortunately the newspaper doesn't know that, though its story – obtained by sub-terfuge – saying the fish paste has been dumped is totally accurate.

So much for employing 'straightforward' means to obtain a story to the satisfaction of the wise men and women who would regulate the Press.

PAYMENTS FOR ARTICLES. Payments or offers of payment for stories, pictures or information should not be made to witnesses or potential witnesses in current criminal proceedings or to people engaged in crime or their associates except where the material concerned ought to be published in the public interest and the payment is necessary to enable this to be done.

Another piece of pious nonsense. Why should a newspaper not obtain the story of a crime by the best means possible and publish it for the interest of its readers? There are fictional crimes on television every day of the week. Why not real crimes in news-papers? You may be sure that editors do not throw money around to criminals and/or their associates if it can be avoided.

As an editor, I never understood why some immutable law should decree that it is perfectly in order for thriller writer Sam Smith to put together his highly imaginative version of a string of murders, based on court evidence and newspaper cuttings, and sell it to Hollywood and Random Century for £100,000, while a newspaper is held to have committed a most foul deed if it assigns a writer to the killer's estranged wife and pays her £5,000 for providing expert assistance in piecing together the full and true story.

You see, it's just not the done thing, old boy, to pay money to the family or associate of someone convicted of a crime. Why not? The odds are that the family are innocent and as appalled by the crime as anyone else, and very likely suffering terribly as a result of the villain's activities. Furthermore, they pay criminal lawyers handsomely, don't they? Aren't they, too, benefiting from crime? Come to that, it often happens that lawyers negotiate the sale of material to newspapers on behalf of their clients – for an appropriate fee. The Press Council's rulings in this category are as woolly as most of its declarations. 'Associates' can be held to be a next-door neighbour of a criminal who sells a snapshot taken in his garden to a newspaper. I was censured once for buying the story of Steven Waldorf, the innocent film technician pumped with bullets in Kensington by police who mistakenly took him for a criminal fugitive. The Council reckoned he was an essential witness in the case and should not have been paid to give his version of the ghastly error that almost killed him.

INTRUSION INTO GRIEF. Newspapers and journalists serving them should in general avoid intruding into personal grief. Inquiries should be carried out with sympathy and discretion.

Nobody in his right mind is going to argue with that. The sad truth is that we often do have to intrude at the worst possible moment. I am thinking of the victims of, say, a terrorist bomb that blows up an airliner with the loss of many lives. Newspapermen and women have to carry out the awful task of seeking pictures and background stories. It is always done with total sympathy, though there have been cases of some overzealous idiot snatching a picture from the sideboard while a colleague distracts the family elsewhere. Mercifully such incidents are no longer as common as they were.

We do have reason to be grateful to the Press Council. It has raised standards. Not because editors suddenly became saints, ready to do the bidding of a bunch of busybodies who wish to impose their manners on the rest of us. If anything it has succeeded mostly because its strictures are a constant irritant. One Press Council inquiry can take up hours of a busy editor's time. I used to take the view that I would rather go to Hell and back than get involved in some nitpicking Council investigation.

As an editor, I complained bitterly again and again at its strange decisions. While running the *Daily Express*, I was censured for accusing the National Front of provoking street riots! 'I realise I'm your best customer,' I told the director, 'but this is ridiculous.' He looked puzzled. 'Oh, no,' he said. 'You're not our best customer! *The Guardian* is.' That amused me. Peter Preston, the *Guardian* editor, explained at a later date that his paper attracts more complaints than most because of the high proportion of teachers and social workers among his readers.

As for the ombudsmen employed nowadays to investigate complaints before they get caught up in the cumbersome mechanism of the Press Council, we have yet to determine whether it makes sense for newspaper executives to act as judges in their own cause. The Press Council is still there as a court of last resort.

One thing is certain: the Press Council, fortified by newspapers at last taking direct action internally to improve their behaviour, is infinitely preferable to politicians and their handmaidens setting up a commission designed to control the Press. That is far more likely to be more repressive and unworkable than anything concocted by the Press Council. At best it might frighten some of the maiden aunts of Fleet Street, already hand in glove with the Establishment. At the same time, thou-shalt-not-publish laws could lead to the creation of an underground Press setting out deliberately to defy the bureaucrats by printing every last scrap of material classed as taboo. Compared with that, the editor of *Private Eye* would appear to be highly respectable. They might even give him a knighthood.

– 12 –
Eddy Comes to Town

I COVERED the dramatic events surrounding the closing days of Fleet Street as a reporter. Being out of work, it gave me the opportunity to earn a few bob back where I started in journalism – and at the same time witness the end of an era. These were some of my dispatches.

From *The Guardian*, May 1985:

Like a whirlwind roaring down from Warrington, Mr Eddy Shah arrived in town this week to serve notice on Fleet Street that its days are numbered. Nobody blinked.

A somewhat important item of news, you might think. Needless to say, it was missing in most newspapers the following day. *The Guardian* was one of the few to report Mr Shah's press conference.

All the same, Sir David English of the *Daily Mail* took the brave step of attending personally to discover for himself what Mr Shah is all about.

They even exchanged pleasantries afterwards and agreed to lunch. Could be useful, that, since Sir David's Associated group is locked in litigation with Mr Shah over the contract of Brian MacArthur, who left its *Western Morning News* in a bit of a hurry to edit what is being called the *Daily Shah*.

A few hundred yards from the Press Club where Mr Shah was speaking, news editors were hot-footing into executive suites with the Press Association version of his words so that their more timorous editors might learn the worst.

Mr Shah was preaching revolution, a dirty word if ever there was one. He stepped into the enemy camp with news of an electronic bag of tricks that is going to blow the Street as we know it to smithereens.

A 7-day-a-week newspaper, with more pages, full colour and graphics, later deadlines, cheaper advertising, vastly reduced costs and a work force of 500 where normally we talk in thousands.

As if all that were not bad enough, Mr Shah was also spelling out the message that Fleet Street managements have dug a hole for themselves so deep that it is difficult to see how they are ever going to climb out of it.

Intimidation, industrial blackmail, irresponsible censorship, corruption, greed . . . Mr Shah told those of us who live in the jungle more than we wish to know, thank you very much.

Not that Fleet Street's problems concern him overmuch. Mr Shah has enough on his plate changing all the rules in time to bring out his paper in March next year.

Fleet Street is already light years behind its provincial cousins in computerised technology, but now Eddy Shah has unveiled a new range of electronic tricks that blow the mind of old hot metal hacks like myself.

In essence we will be turning the television screen into a newspaper. And what better man? Journalism has given much of its top talent to television, but Mr Shah is travelling in the opposite direction.

A product of Gordonstoun, he started his career in telly and was once floor manager of Granada's *What the Papers Say*. Perhaps that is where he got the taste. His Warrington-based Messenger Group, having fought and won the battles of 1983, can now produce more pages in two days than the average national tabloid does in a week.

All that is small beer compared with the awesome facts and figures of his new national revealed this week. Forty tabloid pages Monday to Friday, 16 of them in full colour and 16 in partial colour. Forty-eight pages on Saturdays and 64 on Sunday with a 32-page supplement.

The pages are composed totally on computer in London and wired by facsimile transmission to printing plants straddling the motorways, then distributed locally to newsagents who have already agreed to handle the paper.

Selling at 17p, it will cost up to 6p less than its old-fashioned rivals and – perhaps most important of all – will offer advertising in colour at something like a quarter of the Fleet Street rate.

Breakeven point is 300,000 and it could make a profit on 1,500,000 copies without advertising. One comparison: the Mirror Group sells over 25 million copies a week and makes hardly any profit at all.

Mr Shah's workers will be offered shares and profit-sharing, but will not be encouraged to introduce closed shop practices unless the statutory 80 per cent of them vote to do so. There will be just over 100 journalists – as with the launch of Murdoch's *Sun* and the *Daily Star* – and they will be paid Fleet Street rates. Already the poachers are out looking for the right talent. A features editor who saw one of his writers being lunched by a Shah executive roared across the restaurant 'You're not having him!'

That is all par for the course. Fleet Street's real problem is Eddy Shah's mastery of colour and graphics – areas in which they cannot compete.

He is developing a machine that can take pictures off the TV screen, sharpen the image and get into the paper in colour within minutes. Think of that in relation to the Bradford disaster or the Brussels carnage.

There are even plans for photographers to go out not with the usual Nikon, but armed with a video camera which will film scenes that can be relayed back to an office monitor through a telephone. The desk will simply freeze the best shots and print.

With distribution on their own doorstep, the regional printing plants need not start up until 10.30 pm and can run through the night until breakfast television time.

Mr Shah's main problem is going to be getting out enough copies. At present he would be stretched producing 1,500,000 copies a day and has already taken an option on extra presses.

Given strong editorial content, there is little doubt that the *Daily Shah* – the title has yet to be announced [it was to be *Today*, of course] – has so many built-in advantages that it could sell 3,000,000 daily within two years.

Eddy Shah being a middle-of-the-road man, the *Daily Express* and *Daily Mail* will be the most vulnerable, though that colour facility is putting the wind up everyone in the street. Yet still the slumbering giant sleeps.

Thus far only Robert Maxwell has responded vigorously to the threat. He has colour presses on order for the *Mirror* papers, but it will be two years before we see them running.

Much of Fleet Street is on the move, seeking new premises and more modern printing methods in Dockland and elsewhere. These relatively modest plans are meeting massive union resistance, even though Eddy Shah has already made them obsolete.

The *Daily Telegraph*, for instance, is spending more than £100 million to move three miles down the road – 'insane management', Mr Shah calls it – and yet none of its basic methods of production and distribution will change beyond a measure of electronic typesetting.

No wonder Fleet Street has got the wind up. In private, they are saying that the only chance they have to meet the Shah challenge is to shut up shop and start again from scratch.

Of course they were saying that when I arrived to make the tea in 1944. This time, I fancy, it could come true.

What I didn't reveal was that I had come up with the name *Today* while having breakfast with Eddy Shah in the Hyde Park Hotel. I still have the envelope I wrote it on. It was to have had a subheading *IN COLOUR* cut into the masthead since this was the first daily with run-of-the-paper colour printing. For a time Eddy considered appointing me first editor of his revolutionary new tabloid, but turned down the idea in favour of the highly regarded Brian MacArthur. Eddy had decided I was 'a Fleet Street cliché.' In the event, the paper began poorly, he lost control and eventually it passed to Rupert Murdoch. Brian kindly commissioned me to write two columns a week in the new paper. I covered its launch in March 1986 for the *UK Press Gazette*:

BIRTH OF A REVOLUTION

Eddy Shah looks a bit glum. 'We're two hours late,' he tells me. 'Ah, well, not to worry,' I reassure him. 'If this were hot metal, you would be five hours late.'

'Hot metal!' says one of the young sprogs who staff these hi-tech papers. 'What's that?'

That cheers up everyone. It has been a long, cruel and often testy day. At last word comes through that the presses are rolling. *Today* has finally arrived. A difficult birth, to be sure. It could never have been anything else.

A thin cheer goes up from the 100-odd journalists, secretaries and systems men gathered on the first floor of 70 Vauxhall Bridge Road to greet the dawn of a new era – somewhat pre-empted by the dramatic doings at Fort Wapping. The real celebrations will come later, after the first copies come in from the printing plant near Heathrow.

Everyone is worn out. Editor-in-Chief Brian MacArthur has circles like teabags round his eyes. His has been the hardest stint of all. Seven-day weeks in stretches of up to 14 hours daily for months past.

In the end it was a battle between the men and the machine – with technology ahead on points much of the time.

The final aggravating delay was caused by problems in the colour laboratory as they tried to marry cyan, magenta and yellow transparencies to produce a historic on-the-day picture of the Queen in a fetching green outfit wired across the world from Canberra.

The cursed colours wouldn't register properly – and the last thing anyone wanted on Day 1 was a fuzzy picture of Her Majesty up against all those lovely pre-print gravure pictures in the rivals, even if they were taken yonks ago.

Trouble, too, for the layout men and subs putting together final pages as the overloaded system rebelled under the pressure and up came the dreaded word 'Network Failure' on a score of screens – minutes before close copy time.

The resulting pandemonium was the nearest thing on earth to a submarine frantically diving to escape depth charges. Systems men, unaware of the strange hoarding habits of our breed, raced the floor exhorting everyone to abandon all surplus files pronto to save the day.

A great many treasured words disappeared into the nether as the troops abandoned all but essential requirements to meet the computer's voracious appetite. If you ask me, that's what happened to my first column and explains why some outdated dummy copy got into the paper. But this is no time for hard luck stories.

All the same, I said a silent prayer for my hot metal days. You can bully, coerce, charm or even pay subs, comps, lino men, engravers and the rest, but this quietly humming monster, bastard son of Hal in *2001*, refused to listen to any kind of reason. The more you push him, the slower he goes.

'It's like an overloaded lorry climbing a hill – the nearer the top, the harder it becomes until "Poof".' A technician explains it to me patiently as if addressing a child. I think he is German. I don't think he has ever worked in newspapers. It makes me pine to be an editor again.

There is anxiety on every face as the clock ticks on relentlessly. Clusters form round television sets, hoping that the news bulletins will know something they don't about *Today*'s condition. 'Will you turn that down, please, we're trying to get the edition out here,' roars the daily editor, Jonathon Holborow. Ah, well, that's good to know.

'It's like waiting for the Bomb to go off', says someone. 'The back page colour has blown up', says another. In the event, it is the picture of the Queen that has been looking at us from the Picture Desk videogram for the past six hours.

Finally Brian MacArthur brings the good news that all is well and we are running. Magic words. A grateful, admiring staff present him with a John Piper print accompanied by a card showing some poor soul completely submerged in bureaucratic bumph. Just one hand emerges with a placard crying 'Help!'

Paraphrasing Churchill, Brian tells the bright young people now savouring one of the greatest moments of their lives 'We've been through blood, sweat, toil and tears. Tonight we've reached the green fields' –

with a nod at the Queen smiling down in green – 'despite the scoffers, cynics and fair-weather friends. It's a magnificent achievement by all of you.'

But mostly by you and Eddy, I say under my breath. Two men of vision who have produced the world's first all-electronic 7-day newspaper. It has a long way to go, but nobody can take that away from them. History was made in Vauxhall Bridge Road, of all places, on Monday night. I was proud to be there.

The missing link in all this talk of a brave new world was the effect the new technology was going to have on Fleet Street's all-powerful Chapels – union branches – and the FoCs [Fathers of the Chapel] who traditionally controlled production. I wrote these pieces to give their views an airing:

THE MAN IN THE STREET – *UK Press Gazette*, June 1985

Blood on the streets. Someone could finish up getting killed. There's no way the lads will let this bloke Eddy Shah get away with it. Fleet Street is not Warrington.

These chilling words come from someone I have known most of my life. For 50 years less World War II his job has been to wrap up bundles of newspapers into the small hours of the night.

Shorn of the usual jargon, he gives a plain man's view of Eddy Shah's plans and the future of national newspapers from the grass roots level of an ordinary SOGAT member in Fleet Street.

A quiet decent man, this is what he told me as we sat chatting in his lounge on a council estate in East London last Sunday afternoon:

❛Does Shah think we're just going to stand here and see our lives smashed up? Okay, we know they're fat jobs and cushy with it. And there's fiddles everywhere. That's the system. It's always been like that.

Now they reckon they're going to change it all. Our way of life, our jobs, our families. How would you feel if you had children growing up and this bloke comes along with his fancy equipment ready to put you out on the stones?

We don't even think he can do it. How's he going to get his papers out? It's like a big military operation, covering the country from one end to the other in a few hours. It takes a lot of planning and a lot of troops.

What's Shah going to do on his own? Hire an army of unemployed labourers, bung 'em a couple of quid a night and put all our jobs on the line? Where's he going to get this fleet of transport he needs to distribute? Local car hire firms, getting in the way of our vans and our drivers? D'you think blokes who have been in the game for years are going to put up with that?

Union legislation? Don't make me laugh. It's not a question of the union issuing instructions, defying this or that judge. You just put the word round. It's as simple as that. So who are they going to sue?

One day the ink won't arrive. Someone's put a word in the right ear. Or a couple of lads will talk to a print lorry two miles down the road. No newsprint, no paper. It's in our rules. All the courts in the world can't alter that.

Of course I suppose he banks on getting all the Patels [slang for Asian shopkeepers] behind him. There'll be murders if that happens. Blood on the streets. Someone could finish up getting killed.

Not that the retailers are much to worry about. They know what side their bread is buttered on. If they're a few bundles light of *Mirror*s and *Sun*s they'll soon forget about Mr Shah. Injunctions? For a corner shop? A few labels got mixed up, that's all.

Smiths and Menzies. They're our members in there. You can't force a man to handle something. If someone on his committee says it's black, then it's black. It's nothing to do with secondary picketing. It's common sense. We're talking about the man's job.

Of course Shah got away with it in the north. You're talking about the country, aren't you? It's totally different. They're all on low pay or out of jobs. They don't have the strength or the money. They're just producing a handful of little papers. Fleet Street is not Warrington. You can multiply what happened there by 100 if they try it on here.

What about our own guv'nors? They're not going to be all that upset, are they? I mean, it's their living too and they've got the fattest jobs of all. They're not going to help Shah to put us on the street. Wouldn't make sense.

Of course there has to be change. It's got to be done properly. In the right order. When I started in the warehouses there were over 700 men in there. Now it's something over 100. That's the way to do it. They have to give us time.

I know the bosses have got the wind up. They're full of fancy plans to shove us around. What we think never seems to matter. They have this idea of everyone moving out, going into Dockland and all the rest of it.

Who wants to go there? It's like the bleeding desert. We've spent our entire lives here and, with few people coming into the game, most of us are getting on a bit. Nobody's in a hurry to start working somewhere else.

So we'll stick as long as we can. Two or three years and you're that much closer to retirement. **9**

So there you are. The view of the man in the Street. Someone who has never held union office and never made anything extra out of his job other than a few comics for the kids. One last thought. In 50 years the most important people in his life have always been found behind a door marked: *FoC's Office*.

ON THE PICKET LINES – *UK Press Gazette*, Wapping, February 1986

Back from the blazing sun of Tenerife to join pickets shivering in the snow at the perimeter fence of Fort Wapping, a dreadful place to choose for the beginning of the end of Fleet Street. It looks like a concrete mausoleum.

Rupert Murdoch invited me to have a look round inside, but it seemed more fitting to cross the road to the streets where I grew up – what a cruel twist – and talk to the men on the front line.

Comps, platemakers, chippies, messengers, yard marshals, ad clerks, circulation men. Poor sods. They have no chance. Already they look like soldiers who know the battle is lost. They fight on to preserve their dignity and honour.

Over the years these people have driven me potty – the grey hairs are there to prove it – and now my heart goes out to them as we drink foul coffee in plastic beakers beside a makeshift brazier.

Wapping is the crucible, though I find more people and greater activity on the picket lines in Bouverie Street and Gray's Inn Road. The SOGAT and NGA men, standing together for once, feel happier on the pavements they have trod most of their working lives.

What they are looking for is a decent way out. That means fair and reasonable redundancy. They will stand there 24 hours a day in all weathers – some say for as long as a year – until they get it.

Few have any illusions about working again in 'the print'. Only the younger strikers cling to the hope that they will get back on the gravy train.

Each has a story to tell of a lifetime in newspapers. They dwell nostalgically on the good old days. The Lordships they twisted by the tail – Kemsley, Astor, Thomson – are now spoken of as saints. It's all terribly sad.

'I'm a *Times* man,' a platemaker tells me proudly. 'Started at Printing

House Square in 1961. In those days Hugh Astor would come round with a word for everyone.

'"How are you doing, Ian?" he would ask. Now look what they've done to us.'

'What about all these other jobs you've got?' I ask. 'Car hire firms, markets stalls, even a funeral parlour, according to Murdoch.'

They laugh derisively at the suggestion. Again and again I ask them to tell me honestly about their outside work. There are no takers. They claim less than one in ten has a second job, though they admit to doing casual shifts on other papers. As for Rupert's undertaker, they reckon he retired from newspapers five years ago. Similarly they scoff at suggestions that they earn over £500 for a four-day week of less than 20 hours. 'Bullshit,' they say. 'You're talking about a few linotype operators and process men.'

Outside Fort Wapping a passing couple press a £20 note into a striker's hand for their hardship fund just as one of his mates arrives by taxi to join the picket line.

'Hey, Billy,' they yell at him. 'Bloody taxis! You must be doing all right.' He looks sheepish. 'It was the only way I could get here,' he says, waving at the ever-present lines of police and metal barricades.

They are desperate for any scrap of news that might signal an end to their plight. One man stands with headphones tuned into the transistor he hopes will tell him that Eric Hammond has decided to bring out his electricians.

Across the road, safely behind the barriers, a group of journalists emerge, heads down, collars up. They are off in search of a distant pub to find some relief from the electronic command module. 'How d'you feel?' I ask them. 'Shitty,' they say without hesitation.

'Scabs, scabs, scabs,' the strikers chant without much feeling. Oddly enough, there is little resentment against the journalists – who now hold all the cards in the Murdoch empire. Most remember times when they worked when the NUJ was manning picket lines.

Luxury coaches offering winter warmth and reclining seats shuttle back and forth every few minutes – apparently empty. 'They're all lying on the floor', the strikers reckon.

One of those loony Trots who descend like vultures on picket lines ventures: 'It's too peaceful here to make any impression on the public.'

Wrapped up against the bitter weather – most are wearing long johns or pyjamas under their clothes – the strikers ponder whether the arrival of reinforcements from other papers at the weekends will produce a regular rough-house, Warrington style.

'It's going to get a lot worse,' says one. 'Nah. He'll settle,' says another.

There's a fresh rumour every few minutes. The word goes round that Rupert hasn't got enough capacity at Wapping and is about to resume printing in Gray's Inn Road. Someone claims that distribution is below 50 per cent and reckons SOGAT is soon going to sort that out by nobbling the retailers.

'Anyway, we can't lose,' says another. 'EEC regulations lay down that employers must pay four weeks' redundancy for every year worked. He'll have to give us that.'

I risk the question: 'I thought you'd sacked yourselves?' That hurts. 'Bloody nonsense. How can a bloke with a mortgage and a wife and kid "sack himself"?'

Could it be, I asked, that they were badly led by unions fighting to preserve the past, unable to cope with the realities of the electronic age?

They wouldn't wear that. All spoke up loyally for their union leaders. They said there had been a steady rundown in manning levels over the past decade and they were prepared for more drastic cuts in the age of Shah.

'Maxwell did it, but Murdoch didn't want to know. There was never any intention to hold serious negotiations. This was all worked out months ago with the intention of putting us out on the street,' they said.

'You can't erect a fortress in a weekend.'

– 13 –

The Golden Goose

I LIKE to think of myself as the last of the hot metal men. My life in newspapers died as they were putting the last licks of paint to Fortress Wapping, catalyst of the hi-tech revolution about to destroy the jungle that gave me food and shelter. I don't like their new-fangled newsrooms, dust free and softly spoken, where computers set four thousand lines a minute and leave no time for a cup of tea.

Gone are those vats of molten lead bubbling away like so many pools of silver lava, brought to the boil to be shaped and moulded into the typefaces and printing plates that will stamp out as many million sheets of inky paper as the great British public can devour. Same again tomorrow – and the day after that. What an appetite! Keep feeding the brute.

Whenever a dispute threatened, at the drop of a hat, we would slip down to the composing room to see whether they had turned out the heater under the pot hanging like a witch's cauldron from each linotype machine. It kept our seminal lifeline in liquid form. No heater meant bad news. A lengthy dispute. Once the lead hardened in those pots it would be many hours before they could be worked again.

Never mind the management's solemn warning of this, that and the other, which even its authors do not believe. Don't wait for the latest Chapel resolution, mindful of the constant eroding of living standards . . .

Go and see if the bloody pots are out!

God, we loved it there, down among the printers with their constant and cocky claim to be the real heart of the paper, the men who put it together. Compositors, stonehands, case men, linotype operators. The shake, rattle and roll of iron trolleys carrying chases of type to be cast into page moulds, the clickety-clack of linotype

151

machines turning someone's story into print, the crash of a comp's mallet levelling off his forme so that no slug of type shall seek to rise above its neighbour.

They are dirty, smelly, grime-laden places down below where pictures and stories are composed into pages, moulded into papier-mâché, shaped by still more molten lead into circular printing plates, embraced by the rollers of the press, squeezed through a bath of ink and spilled out as newspapers to be counted, bundled and labelled by an army of warehousemen feeding the waiting vans that encircle the building like a mechanical snake.

Standing there amid the clatter, the hum of the presses filling the air like the rumblings of an earthquake, it scarcely dawned on us that we were already an antiquity. These men in boiler-suit blue, some wearing aprons and never a snigger, were merely finishing their time on clapped-out machines in dimly lit ghettoes. Many of the buildings dated from the closing years of the last century when Alfred Harmsworth, son of a poor Irish lawyer settled in London, made the simple discovery that universal education was his passport to fame and fortune. His *Daily Mail* was the first to sell a million copies in 1900. He became Lord Northcliffe soon after, the first baron of the newly emerging popular press.

What made it all possible was Ottmar Mergenthaler's linotype machine, invented in Baltimore in the 1840s, which produced moving type. Instead of a compositor taking up each letter separately by hand, forming words out of the matrices, the linotype could set lines mechanically as on a typewriter at the rate of five lines a minute. It meant the new popular papers could be produced faster and with more pages. The linotype, with a few refinements marginally to improve output, remained the workhorse of the industry until the arrival of new technology. Now type is composed by a photosetter churning out copy at the rate of four thousand lines a minute.

What died at Wapping was not Fleet Street, but Ottmar's magnificent machine and the men who fed off it, the compositors, stereotypers and others who turned the journalists' words into lumps of lead in a printing outfit. Appropriately, the last linotype machine to be seen in national newspapers is a museum piece in the front hall of the *Daily Mail* off Kensington High Street (see jacket).

True – the new, cheaper and more efficient methods of production gave newspapers the necessary spur to move geographically from the dingy premises occupying so much valuable prime land north of the Thames. They are now housed in designer modules, all potted plants and pastel plastic, spread across London from Kensington to the Isle of Dogs. The flickering screen of the VDU rules where once the big, ungainly lino threatened to clout every passer-by with its wonky arm. There is not a greasy overall to be seen in the land of the green-eyed monster. Fleet Street is now merely a part of London EC4, a lush pasture where Japanese and American bankers grow fat.

Most people believe it was the greed of the print unions that killed the Street. They are cast as Luddites, digging their own graves with outrageous demands for ever bigger pay packets for less work while stubbornly refusing to accept the new technology. If anyone doubted this scenario, the fact that his or her favourite newspaper was missing several times a year through labour troubles would prove the bloody-mindedness of the printworkers.

That is only half the story. It overlooks the fact that most of them actually did work most of the time, often in appalling conditions, and managed to deliver their product daily to more than 15 million customers throughout the country, a marketing exercise without parallel. What the print unions did was not kill the old Fleet Street, but delay its demise through industrial evolution with the suicidal zeal of a kamikaze pilot. They fought to the bitter end in a futile effort to preserve their jobs, and then put in some unpaid overtime outside the barricades of Fortress Wapping.

I was one of the pioneers of the revolution that swept away the old order: first chairman of the Mirror Group's development committee charged with the task of converting the *Daily Mirror*, *Sunday Mirror*, *Sunday People*, *Sporting Life* and the now defunct *Reveille* from hot metal to computerised photo-composition. The *Mirror* sent me to the United States for six weeks in 1975 to witness the new methods at first hand. I came back feeling much like Paul on the road to Damascus. Here was an old sweat whose hair had gone grey waiting for type to drop on umpteen thousand editions. Now I had seen the miracle. Imagine tens of thousands of words with barely a mistake. My linotype operators made at least one error every three lines – then got paid again for correcting them. I stood over a TV screen and watched a journalist put together an entire page of the broadsheet *Los Angeles Times* in minutes. It would take the NGA (National Graphical Association) two to three hours to lock up a tabloid page in London, more if they were feeling bolshy.

I wrote of my experience in rapturous terms:

At last a chance for Fleet Street to shake off the doldrums. You have heard all the arguments that inhibit our best efforts to survive . . .

'Hold the run for the big fight. You must be out of your mind.'

'You can't start ****ing about with feature pages at 11 o'clock at night.'

'Christ, we can't ask the comps to reset the whole of Pages 6 and 7.'

'Change that and we'll never get the paper away.'

Now we have the means to sweep all that aside. Not only to produce papers more quickly and efficiently, running with the big news minutes after it happens, but to CHANGE in all directions.

To experiment without fear of rocking the boat, to be bolder in our search for modern ways to communicate, to match the rainbow of colours on the television screen, to arrive on the doorstep in a new suit of clothes.

So what's new that is going to stop the rot? Essentially a piece of equipment called a Visual Display Unit (VDU) – the seeing eye of a computer which feeds on the torrent of words that pours into our newspapers each day. There are parallel advances at all production levels. Graphic scanners to produce pictures, artwork, display ads. Full-page composition on a television screen. Laser letterpress platemaking.

I added that these sophisticated production methods levied a human sacrifice in manpower. There was a halfway house, which involved the computer being limited to producing galleys of type to be cut and pasted on to a page layout. These were jobs that could be handled by retrained printworkers. In other words, the cost in human terms would be less and that, in the end, might well be the most important consideration of all.

Prophetic words. To this day Fleet Street still has a long way to go before achieving full automation. Full-page composition – the entire job done on computer – is hardly known and many papers have not gone beyond the cut-and-paste system. In many offices printworkers operate alongside journalists in producing pages, though their old power has gone. They no longer control the means of production.

It was very much a case of preaching the future when I returned from my American voyage of discovery. The extraordinary thing was that nobody wanted to hear the good word. I remember telling Chapel officials of the NUJ that the journalists would reign supreme under the new system. The printworkers were a dying species. There was nothing they could do that the computer could not do faster and cheaper. The NUJ recoiled in horror. They were not interested in taking jobs held by other unions.

However, the message was not lost on the print unions. At the best of times they were always totally extravagant in their demands, knowing that they rigidly controlled all staff levels and more or less ran the production and distribution departments. Now they would make life even more difficult for proprietors who planned to take their jobs away.

Provincial newspapers had been employing the new technology for a decade or more before the Mirror Group opened the batting in Fleet Street. They gingerly approached the unions for a deal that would allow the switch to some measure of computerised production. That meant buying out the London Scale of Prices, regarded as sacred by union members. For good reason. It encompassed the principles of every agreement on wages, hours and conditions reached over the previous two hundred years. Two hundred years! No wonder Rupert used to go bananas. It was the umbrella under which the NGA maintained the privileges it considered due to the master craftsmen of the industry.

It took years of slow, painstaking negotiations before the *Mirror* production Chapels accepted the inevitable. The cost to the *Mirror* management was colossal. Union members knocking up huge salaries through piecework were bought out with five-figure payouts for loss of 'extra' payments, eight weeks' holiday a year and a 34-hour week. When the dust settled on that lot the *Mirror* discovered it was employing more NGA members than before the negotiations started, thus destroying the whole point of the new technology.

There were other prices to pay. Journalists discovered they had lost their status as the highest paid workers to the compositors. I was Northern editor of the *Daily Mirror* at the time, responsible for the paper in Scotland, Ireland and the North of England, and was apoplectic when I learned that my salary was less than a linotype operator's in London. The NUJ soon banged in a claim for higher wages and a string of perks, including television licence fees and a bonus for going on holiday. At least the *Mirror* papers were able to make some advances in newspaper production, though there were no real changes in manning levels until Robert Maxwell arrived as the new owner in 1984.

The plain truth, though few would face it, was that the workers on the shop floor wanted nothing to do with the new methods. At a national level, the unions generally recognised they would have to go along with the proprietors, though the cost in jobs would be horrendous. However, something could be salvaged through cooperation. The alternative was genocide. They even set up a joint committee with the proprietors in 1976 to find ways of tackling the industry's problems.

Percy Roberts, chief executive of Mirror Group Newspapers, spelled it out: 'Without being emotional or hysterical about it, we really do regard this joint committee as the absolute last chance for the industry. If we do not get it right now – and I am talking about twelve months, not two years – then we might as well wrap up and go home, because there will not be an industry as we know it in five years if we go on behaving in the way we are.'

The joint committee came out with a Programme for Action which offered the printworkers a tempting sweetener. No compulsory redundancies. Workers would leave the industry only on a voluntary basis. In return the unions would allow flexibility in working methods, opening the gates to the new technology. The officers of all print unions recommended the programme, warning that its rejection would lead to compulsory redundancies and newspapers folding. The programme was overwhelmingly rejected by members on the shop floor. Once again they demonstrated that the real strength in Fleet Street rested with the score of Chapels that existed in every newspaper.

Dealing with them was like trying to juggle quicksilver. They knew they were under the cosh and lashed out in all directions. Their demands grew ever more outrageous. By the mid-eighties *Express* lino men were earning £1,100 for a 16-hour week. Even the journalists had never been more difficult, perhaps infected by the sod 'em all atmosphere of the times. In most editorial areas staff put in less than twenty-four actual working hours over four days a week, took seven or eight weeks holiday – plus month-long sabbaticals every four or five years – and enjoyed a string of perks that would not have disgraced Hollywood. But at least the editorial departments still functioned with reasonable efficiency. Cooperation with management in production areas was virtually nonexistent. Week after week millions of copies were lost through trifling disputes that lacked any sanction from national officers. The Chapels were running wild.

The more obstructive the unions became, the more management attitudes hardened. Historically, they had always been a soft touch, ready to surrender to any demand rather than lose a copy to a rival newspaper. With profits plunging to the point where there was little merit in producing newspapers at all, the new breed of proprietors began to get tough. A key factor in the new thinking was the Thatcher government's trade union laws designed to prevent secondary picketing and other excesses. Victor Matthews took on the unions for the first time even before his seat was warm at the *Express*. Faced with a no-nonsense proprietor, they gave more concessions than ever before. Robert Maxwell, veteran of a score of battles with the print unions as the nation's biggest printer, soon began sorting out the tangled mess at the *Mirror*. He got union agreement for two thousand redundancies, an unthinkable proposition under previous managements.

Nowhere was the battle more ferocious than in Bouverie Street. Rupert Murdoch had been fighting the union stranglehold on production since he arrived from Australia in 1968. Victories were few and far between. There was little he could do to shift the status quo on the *News of the World*, his first purchase. He insisted on realistic manning levels for the new *Sun*. The unions accepted reluctantly rather than see the paper disappear altogether. Now both sides were engaged in a constant state of war. Perhaps the unions sensed this shrewd, singular Aussie was going to be the toughest nut of all. They certainly made him pay. For all his hard-nosed approach, at times Rupert was losing more copies than all the other dailies put together.

Working there in the early eighties was a nightmare. As editor of the *News of the World*, I was reminded every day of the power of

...sked for the transcript of a television show in New ...incess Diana was under discussion. I still have a ...e copytaker who took down the words in front of me: *...ext time you want a radio or TV transcript typed do it yourself.* He took the view that it was his job to take down a reporter's words, not handle scripts.

During the Falklands war we were having major problems getting pictures back from the battlefield. The way out was to employ artists to draw graphic war scenes. I employed a talented illustrator named Margaret Keedy. Unfortunately the process workers' Chapel refused to handle her work. 'But she's in their union,' I protested. 'I went out of my way to make sure she had a ticket.' I stormed into the process department. The FoC gravely studied her union card number on the back of the drawing. 'Wrong branch,' he pronounced. 'This is the newspaper branch. She is in the commercial sector.'

'Ah, for Christ's sake,' I objected. 'You're taking earnings away from one of your own members.'

'It's Disraeli, innit?' he suggested.

'You what?'

'Disraeli. Send a gunboat! Put down the natives. Well, this Chapel doesn't support imperialist wars. And we don't handle work by outsiders in support of Thatcherism.'

We went to press with a hole on the page.

With his vast publishing interests in America and Australia, it was not lost on Rupert that most of his problems in Britain could be solved overnight if he could introduce new technology in Britain. The *Sun* and *News of the World* Chapels would not even discuss it. Bruce Matthews, Rupert's managing director in London, told me that at one preliminary meeting the entire union side walked out when he mentioned the dread words. 'We're not here to discuss giving away our jobs,' one of the delegates told him.

This is where the knife was stuck into the side of Fleet Street, amid the lunacy of Bouverie Street and not, as generally supposed, on the picket lines in Warrington where the embattled entrepreneur Eddy Shah was extending his provincial horizons by planning a seven-day newspaper produced and distributed without any help from the print unions. *Today*, as it became, was a brave try and created a timely diversion. But the real battle was to come at Wapping. *Today* itself finished up as part of the Murdoch empire.

Rupert had spent £100 million on newspaper plants at Wapping in Dockland and at Kinning Park in Glasgow, a warning of things to come totally pooh-poohed by the unions. The Scottish print unions had blacked the Glasgow plant for years, claiming it was against Scottish interests to permit the printing of English pages. Most people in the business took the view that it was the interests of the *Mirror*'s sister paper, the *Daily Record*, they were defending, not those of Rob Roy. As for the London plant, ostensibly designed to accommodate a new paper called the *London Post*, nothing would be allowed to move there without the consent of the unions.

The bomb finally fell in January 1986, when Wapping began turning out a section of the *Sunday Times*, a clear declaration of war since it was being done without union agreement. While the rest of us looked on aghast, the print unions responded in their ritualistic manner. *Everyone out, lads.* They knew well enough that a strike would be in breach of their contracts since there was no dispute at either Bouverie Street or the *Times* plant in Gray's Inn Road and they had contemptuously rejected every opportunity of manning agreements to cover Wapping, primarily because they would not accept the principle of a *no strike* deal. Now Murdoch had them by the balls. To stop work over Wapping meant he could dismiss them without any obligation to pay compensation.

Like the final curtain in a medieval tragedy, the printworkers placed a blindfold over their eyes and jumped off the cliff. SOGAT members voted 3,534 to 752 in favour of a strike and the skilled craftsmen of NGA 843 to 117. The majority of the journalists, after some initial gnashing of teeth, defied the instructions of their own NUJ and voted to accept Rupert's offer of an additional £2,000 a year to move to Wapping. Without them the transfer would have been ten times more difficult, if not impossible. s it was, News International lost only one day's editions of *The Sun* and *The Times*. Rupert's meticulous planning had paid off handsomely.

The printworkers, 5,500 of them, went on strike on 24 January 1986. Battles raged on the picket lines outside Fortress Wapping for the next year until the unions threw in the towel, accepting redundancy payments offered by Rupert to bring the bitter dispute to an honourable end.

In their hearts they had known all was lost when Rupert, emulating Eddy Shah, produced his own transport fleet. In every other printing dispute the unions had held the final trump: the vans that carried the papers were driven by SOGAT members. Anyone else behind the wheel would automatically be 'black' in the eyes of both SOGAT men in the wholesale warehouses and the railwaymen. Rupert broke the final link in the union chain with the help of the Aussie TNT haulage company. He happened to be a major shareholder.

Within months of Wapping every other publishing group in Fleet Street announced redundancies and laid plans to move to new plants in Dockland and other parts of London. Direct input by journalists was the order of the day, accompanied by major changes in printing and transport arrangements.

All my working life the unions had scoffed at warnings that their greed would kill the golden goose. In the end I came to believe that the system would never be broken in my lifetime. Now it had happened. The bosses had won back the means of production and, thanks to their refusal to change with the times, the power of the unions was shattered. Ottmar Mergenthaler's huge mechanical typewriter would rattle to their tune no longer. Significantly, the company manufacturing it had long since switched to photosetters.

It was the end of my Fleet Street. Like the printworkers themselves, I was an old hot metal man, too set in my ways to accept the new order. Anyway, for my pains, I loved that hairy, awkward, rude and rumbustious bunch of rascals in 'the print'. Their day was done and mine with it. I would have to go and peddle my talents elsewhere.

First there was a serious problem to be dealt with at home. It had been festering for years, but I had been too involved in newspapers to do much about it. Now it could wait no longer. The lady I loved was hellbent on throwing her life away.

– 14 –

In Love – with a Lame Duck

I'VE suffered a few shocks in my time, but nothing that came within a mile of the macabre sight that greeted me as I stepped into my flat late one Friday night after a tough day at the office.

The place was in darkness, which was odd because my lady should have been home. Although she was likely at any time to lose herself in a bottle of vodka, she normally finished up too paralytic to get through the front door.

I snapped on the switch in the lounge. The lights came on, but the chandelier was hanging from its bare wires a couple of feet from the ceiling. The silk cord of my dressing gown dangled from the broken light fitting. Lying in a crumbled heap on the floor below was Ellen Petrie. The girl I had left home for, deserting my devoted young wife and family, ignoring the advice of my friends. Amid the hurly-burly of producing newspapers at the top I had managed to find time to go overboard for the love of a girl reporter turned crazy drunk.

She had tied the cord tight round her neck, stood on a chair and jumped. Mercifully Ellen's weight had been too much for the light fitting and her pathetic gallows had collapsed.

For a second I thought she might finally have done it, ending the life she had tried to blot out so many times in an alcoholic fog. I quickly dismissed the idea. She couldn't tie knots sober, never mind drunk – and the cord was still hanging from the ceiling.

Sure enough, she was breathing heavily in a drunken coma. I went to the kitchen, filled a saucepan with cold water, came back and flicked it over her face with my fingers. Ellen moaned and groaned,

161

flapped her arms about and finally opened her glazed eyes. She was too far gone for talk. The recriminations would come later. Right now I got hold of her under the armpits and dragged her to the bedroom. She was wearing her red silk negligee with the black lace, though she was anything but alluring. Her face was deathly pale under smudged make-up. She looked like a ravaged Barbie doll.

'*You stupid cow,*' I spat at her through clenched teeth. '*You useless, crazy, drunken idiot.*'

Somehow I got her on to the bed and under the covers. By now my anger was softening into pity. This sad, broken creature had to be in a dreadful state to be so eager to destroy herself. I laid my hand across her forehead, reassuring her of my love, telling her everything would be fine. Eventually she drifted off to sleep. Another crisis over. The next was never far away.

It was the middle of the night. I sat there in the semidarkness, pulling on a cigarette, reflecting that this little drama must have occurred because I stayed late at the office instead of hurrying home to Ellen at our tiny love nest off the Gray's Inn Road. There was I, busy at the *News of the World* chasing dramatic stories to be shared with millions of readers. *All human life is here* was the paper's boast and the editor was locked in a dramatic battle of his own. My story would not be shared with anyone until I found a happy ending.

Our love affair, like so many other great romances, began with a blazing row. It was at a party in December 1976. I had just returned to Fleet Street after a spell editing newspapers in Manchester. We were celebrating a promotion for John Penrose, husband of BBC TV's *Points of View* presenter and *Mirror* columnist Anne Robinson. I arrived in the upstairs room of a local pub feeling highly pleased with myself. My front page in next day's *Daily Mirror* looked certain to sink the offerings of rival newspapers. SEX PISTOLS IN FOUR-LETTER TV SHOCKER, said the splash headline. The New Wave punk group had raised hell on a teatime television show, forcing presenter Bill Grundy to abandon ship when their language and behaviour became uncontrollable.

Standing there among my newspaper pals sipping a half of lager, I was suddenly confronted by this bossy madam brandishing a copy of the first edition, which had just been delivered to the Princess Louisa in Holborn, up the road from Fleet Street.

'Are you responsible for this?' she demanded, pointing to my headline. 'THAT'S not a page 1 story!' she spat at me.

I couldn't believe my ears. Newspaper pubs are full of smart alecs ready to tell the editor how to run his paper. Normally they don't get around to doing it until late at night when they have sunk enough pints to throw discretion to the wind. This particular noisy lady interested me. It was still early and she was a complete stranger. Quite a looker, too. Tall, with long auburn hair and a jumper *under* her blouse. That was different.

'How dare you?' I said, going straight into the attack. 'Don't you tell me what to put on the front page. I was producing papers when you were still in nappies.'

She didn't flinch. 'That story should not have been on page 1,' she repeated.

The sparks were flying and already the sexual chemistry was in overdrive. We were igniting each other. Face to face, eyes locked, we engaged in verbal battle. When the time came for me to go back to the office to 'check the rivals' – see what the other papers were up to – I invited her along. To see how a proper newspaper was run. It turned out she worked on the Mirror Group's now defunct weekly *Reveille*. We collected her coat, a huge fun-fur which made her look like a honey teddy bear, and took the office car back to Holborn Circus. The Fleet Street gossip machine started working as soon as we left the pub together. I was hot news. A whizz kid brought back to London from Manchester only weeks earlier, appointed managing editor and installed in a luxury service flat in St James's, off Piccadilly, while I looked around for a house to buy.

When we got to the editor's office, Ellen sank into an armchair, grasping a Scotch out of the booze cupboard as if she had been doing it all her life. She might only be a writer on a small weekly paper, but it wasn't done to appear to be impressed sitting there amid the black leather splendour. She looked on nonchalantly as this strange man with the wild hair and shark's teeth went through the rival papers, snorting derisively from time to time and barking out orders to the night editor and other late-duty executives on what changes he wanted to see in the final editions.

Finally it was time to go. I took Ellen down to the pavement outside to find her a taxi home to Balham, in South London. As we stood there, I pulled out a coin.

'Heads St James's, tails Balham,' I said, flipping the coin. 'St James's,' I told her, glancing down. It had come up tails, but she wasn't to know. A lover's trick that was to change my life. An hour later we were in bed in the rented penthouse. I remember being very impressed by the fact that she had painted toenails in the middle of winter.

The following morning I had just arrived at the office when I got a phone call from an old mate, Peter Grimsditch, who was deputy editor of *Reveille*. The friend, of course, later to edit the *Daily Star*.

'You wouldn't know the whereabouts of one of my feature writers, Ellen Petrie, would you?' he asked blandly.

'At this moment she's in the ladies' loo changing her clothes,' I told him.

It should have ended there. A one-night stand. My lovely Pauline, as good a wife as any man could have, was still in Manchester with our five-year-old son, Ben, awaiting the call from dad to make the move to London. There was another compelling reason why I should not get involved elsewhere. Pauline was pregnant.

I knew it was wrong and was going to cause terrible heartache, but I was hooked. The more I contemplated breaking with this wild creature I had met in London, the more obsessed I became. The very thought of not seeing her again left me trembling. By the following week when we had our first date, a trip to the cinema to see the remake of *King Kong*, we were already heavily involved. It was one of those relationships where in a very short time you already feel as if you have been together for years.

I had never been smitten with a lady writer before so I enjoyed hearing all about the jobs she was doing and took a great pride in seeing her by-line on some feature or another. Ellen seemed to have a genuine love for newspapers and delighted in showing me her latest efforts. She was anxious to improve her journalistic skills and glad of my experience and advice. For the first time I had someone who understood the newspaper business and loved it as much as I did.

Extramarital affairs are common enough in our profession. Though we were playing a dangerous game, I never hid my love for Ellen. In the long evening hours waiting for the first edition to come up, we would go out to dinner or stand around talking shop in the *Stab*. We were a couple and most people accepted that the relationship was none of their business. It was a painful yet exhilarating time. On the one hand I felt desperately guilty about my wife and family. On the other, I was madly in love and just couldn't keep away from Ellen.

In those early days we broke up many times. Again and again I decided to do the decent thing and be a faithful husband. I even took out a mortgage on a four-storey house in trendy Islington, where Pauline joined me with Ben and our newly born son, Dan. But for all my good intentions, the partings from Ellen never lasted more than a few hours before I would telephone her or search the Fleet Street pubs until I found her.

There were some who tried to warn me with stories of wild behaviour and whispered rumours of the men Ellen had known before me, including the son of a wealthy Arab businessman. These served to excite me even more. Ellen didn't deny the stories but was always reluctant to be pressed on details of her previous life. She had been married to a Scottish journalist called Gavin Petrie. They had lived a nice middle-class existence in a semi-detached in Beckenham, Kent.

Her only explanation for walking away from all that cosy domesticity was that she had been restless. She was already separated when we met and, having spent most of the year moving from flat to flat with an assortment of other unattached girls, was now living with her parents back in South London. When the house in Beckenham was sold she would buy a flat of her own.

In her married life she had never wanted children and I was impressed and relieved that this independent, self-supporting career girl was adamant that she would never marry again. I was never much good as a husband. Domestic life always came second to the pressure-cooker world of newspapers. Even without the other women – and there had been quite a few – I was always too consumed by my job to give proper attention to being a husband and father. Ellen understood that the *Mirror* came first. Many times I told her: 'I should be working my balls off, not involved in an affair with you.'

In the event, I managed to do both and keep the marriage going.

It was a bumpy ride, though my reputation as a tough newspaper-man stayed intact. It came as no surprise a few months later to be summoned to lunch by Victor Matthews. Since Trafalgar House had just acquired Express Newspapers it was quite obvious where destiny was taking me.

Within hours he had made me editor of the floundering *Daily Express*. Significantly, in view of the way my life was to unfold, the new job led to my first major television appearance – an hour-long profile and interview on BBC TV's *The Editors*. Ellen bought me a new shirt and tie. In brown. A colour I never wore. To please her, I put them on for the telly.

The programme did me – and the *Express* – a power of good. For the first time the public heard how this unlikely lad from the East End, a bastard raised in extreme poverty in a home for waifs and strays, had taken himself off to Fleet Street at the age of fourteen, got a job as a messenger boy, and clawed his way up the ladder until he now sat in the editor's chair of one of the world's top newspapers.

While I got down to the problems of the *Express*, Ellen was busy celebrating my appointment. At the end of that first long, hot day in August 1977 I had arranged to meet her in the front hall of the so-called Black Lubyianka, at that time *Express* headquarters in Fleet Street.

It was time to go home. I stepped jauntily out of the lift, happy with my early efforts to revitalise the paper, knowing Ellen was to join me from the Poppinjay, the *Express* pub next door, where she had been pushing out the boat with assorted members of my staff only too eager to please the new editor's bird.

Horrors! Oh God, let the earth open and swallow me up. There she was, flat on her face on the floor, skirt riding up, pissed out of her head. In the front hall of that black marbled palace in full view of security men, messengers and passing reporters, photographers, sub-editors and executives. What if the sage of Auchtermuchty, the ferocious John Junor, editor of my sister paper, the *Sunday Express*, should happen this way? I could be finished before I had even started. Bad news travels fast in newspapers, especially when the new editor's lady is in the starring role. Somehow I got her out of there to the haven of the editor's car, parked in its usual VIP space in the alleyway alongside the office.

'She's been celebrating,' I said lamely to the waiting chauffeur, a tall, white-haired Scotsman named John Cowan. He took it in his stride without raising half an eyebrow. If nothing else, serving seven editors one after the other teaches discretion. No doubt he had seen it all before in varying degrees of drunken lunacy.

Together we poured Ellen into the back of the sky-blue Jaguar and we made our way to the flat she had rented in Victoria while waiting to move into her own place. I was very angry. My first day in a big new job ruined. 'Can't hold her drink', I thought. Drinking is an occupational hazard in Fleet Street, and at that time it didn't stand out that Ellen drank more than others. Long hours hanging around pubs meant loads of booze, of course. It was the right thing to do socially.

Perhaps she would settle down in her own home. A year to the day after we had met, on 2 December 1977, Ellen moved into a one-bedroomed flat in a mansion block off the Gray's Inn Road. A short taxi ride from her office in Fetter Lane and halfway between the *Express* and my family house in Islington. She had decorated and furnished the flat before moving in. Chocolate-brown settees, white carpets and glass and chrome tables. For the bedroom she had bought a pine four-poster bed with lace drapes. Ruby-red velvet curtains framed the windows. The perfect love nest.

On that first Friday night she held a house-warming party. As midnight approached and the other guests drifted away, I prepared to leave. Without warning, Ellen started a scene. Upset and crying, she held on to me and pleaded with me to stay the night. With a wife waiting at home it was out of the question. 'You don't love me,' she accused. 'Just this once, please. I've never asked before. Please don't leave me.'

It disturbed me to see her so upset, but I was powerless. I couldn't just not go home. Of course I loved her, but Pauline was still my wife. I tried to calm Ellen down and promised to stay until she fell asleep. I arrived home much later than intended. Not to worry. In newspapers there are always plentiful excuses for working late.

The next day, when I telephoned, Ellen didn't mention the incident. It didn't occur to me then that she had no memory of it. I took the view that she was feeling emotional, having got her own home again, and felt sad about being left on her own. She had always accepted that I could not walk out on my wife and children and never asked me to do so. Her outburst again brought matters to a head. Already racked by guilt and divided loyalty, once again I tried to end the affair. It wasn't fair to put her through all this, and I urged her to build a new life for herself with someone who was free. We had a long, sad lunch and agreed to not see each other again.

That evening I turned up on her doorstep. She came to the door with a towel on her head. Underneath, her hair was blue. She had tipped a whole bottle of bleach over it.

'What are you playing at?' I yelled.

With a shrug she told me, 'Dying my hair blonde to start my new life.'

'Your life is with me,' I told her, cradling her in my arms. 'I don't know how, when or where, but we have to be together.'

The next day she looked a fright. Her lovely, long auburn hair was the colour of straw and the same texture. A trip to the hairdresser resulted in it being chopped down to a one-inch length all over.

In the next few years, Ellen's dramatic gestures became more and more outrageous. On that occasion only her hair was a casualty. Later she would try more than once to kill herself.

I continued to lead my double life. The situation at home became increasingly unhappy as I made more and more excuses to be away. Pauline was convinced I was having an affair.

Unlike the *Mirror*, where everybody had known and loved Pauline, at the *Express* Ellen was the woman most often at my side. Being away from all those old friends at the *Mirror* and their disapproval made it easier to make my decision. I was going to leave my wife and children and set up home with Ellen. By now Pauline knew I was involved elsewhere and that it was not a passing affair. I couldn't stand the lying and cheating any more, or the sad and confused look on her face.

Knowing that she had done nothing wrong, that she was a perfect wife and mother, made it all the harder. I knew how much I was hurting her but I had to grab the chance of happiness and emotional fulfilment with Ellen. Very few married men choose the mistress. I know why. It was the hardest thing I ever had to do. On 13 April 1978 I packed my bags and left home.

168

Ellen welcomed me with open arms. We settled into a cosy, domestic routine which would have been idyllic but for my terrible guilt. I took the elder boy, Ben, out every Sunday. If sometimes when I got home Ellen had had too much to drink, I put it down to her insecurity about me and the family commitments.

My position as editor meant we had a glittering social life. There were invitations to parties, receptions, premieres and other first nights. Ellen loved dressing up and having a good time. We were out most nights of the week, and when we had an odd free evening were more than glad to curl up together in front of the television.

Before leaving home I had booked to go on a family holiday to Greece. I didn't tell Ellen, but I still intended to go rather than disappoint Ben, who was then six. I was trying to work out a way to tell my lover when she behaved in a way which made me wonder why I had ever left home for her. She disgraced herself at a family party by getting outrageously drunk and dancing close to some neighbour while his wife and I fumed on the sidelines. Despite protests from her family, I dragged her out and when I got her home I laid my cards on the table. I was blazing with anger. 'I didn't go through all the agony of leaving my wife and children to have you treat me like that,' I told her. 'I would never have left home if I had known you were a drunk. And I'm going back to take them on holiday next month.'

With the plausibility that was to disarm and confuse me so many times in years to come, Ellen owned up. 'I knew you were going to leave me,' she said. 'I could tell you had something on your mind. I guessed you were planning to go home. That's why I behaved so badly.'

We kissed and made up. Over the next few weeks I was back on the emotional seesaw. I reassured Ellen that I wasn't leaving, just fulfilling my obligations to a family holiday. Pauline was prepared to forgive and forget, and saw the holiday as a way of our giving our marriage another chance.

At short notice Ellen booked a holiday in Spain so she was away at the same time as me. I drove her to the airport and returned to spend my last night at the flat alone. Late into the night I sat composing the letter I would leave for her return.

'This should be a thank-you-very-much-it-was-lovely note,' I wrote, 'but I can't do it because I love you so desperately and somehow, some way, I have to get back to you. God help me, we really did fall in love properly and beautifully. Whatever happens, remember that you gave me the best l8 months of my not uneventful life.' I ended: 'Take care – and go easy on the booze.'

The next day I packed all my belongings and moved back home again. Pauline, Ben and I went on holiday in a spirit of friendly truce.

The first day back at the office after the holiday I telephoned Ellen and we met for lunch. 'When are you coming back?' she demanded. I hedged.

'If you are not back by the weeked then it really is all over between us,' she threatened. 'While you were still at home I accepted the situation of being the other woman. But now that we have been living together I am not going back to that half life.'

On the Sunday I packed my bags again and left the matrimonial home for good. Pauline started divorce proceedings.

Beat the Devil

ONCE we had settled down to a permanent relationship, it dawned on me gradually that Ellen's drinking was not due to our hectic life, but went much deeper. She just could not function without liberal doses of booze.

To celebrate being together, we planned a dream holiday in the West Indies. Three weeks in paradise. We were to stay in a beach cottage with golden sands and swaying palm trees under a constant blue sky. On our arrival they showed us not a cottage on the beach, as in the brochure, but a room on the second floor of a prefab block with views over the gardens. It wasn't good enough, Ellen decided. She demanded that the travel rep move us to a beach cottage. Having been assured that we would be transferred in the morning, Ellen refused to unpack or spend any time in the room. She made a beeline for the bar, which was dismally empty, and proceeded to drink until they closed. 'I'm on holiday,' she protested when I suggested we were tired and could do with an early night.

In the morning she again demanded that we be moved, even though the rep tried to explain that the beach cottages were not ready for guests. But one was, and Ellen dug her heels in. We had paid for a beach cottage and we wanted one. The hotel reluctantly moved us half a mile away to the one habitable cottage down by the beach. Our dream holiday was setting up nicely for a nightmare.

We were totally isolated. Darkness fell at six o'clock in the evening and we were left sitting on our verandah, the only light that could be seen for miles around, with Ellen sipping ever-stronger Pina Coladas.

The half-mile walk to the restaurant in the pitch black through tropical vegetation with strange exotic animal cries unnerved us. By the time she arrived at the restaurant, Ellen would need a couple of large brandies to calm her down before dinner. Then she drank more than she ate and still insisted on a couple of nightcaps before making the long, dark journey back to our secluded beach cottage. Back there Ellen settled down to drink some more. I was horrified and sickened.

Tired of trying to cajole me into staying up and having a party, Ellen turned nasty. With eyes full of hate, and sneering contemptuously, she screamed at me: 'I don't love you. I don't want you around me. You make me so bloody unhappy. I want to go home.' The tirade went on for hours. She screamed, cried, threw herself on the bed and pounded her fists. 'We are finished,' she told me over and over again.

Alone in that dark, lonely beach hut miles from civilisation and home, I couldn't believe the raving maniac that the woman I loved had turned into. To add to the horror, in the middle of the night someone tried to break into the cottage. A shrieking huge black pig! It was like a horror film.

The more Ellen screamed 'Take me home' the more I wished I could do just that. I felt trapped, powerless, and wanted to run far away from this demented woman. Finally, exhausted and emotionally drained, she fell asleep. I couldn't. I was battered and torn from her verbal assault. Surely it wasn't just the drink, I thought. Had she been taking pills or smoking the local ganga (cannabis) which she had told me was freely available in that part of the world? Was she mental? Had this alien land with its unfriendly natives and isolation made her flip? I was angry and confused.

The next day Ellen slept for hours at a time. She seemed to be totally worn out, emotionally and physically. She didn't want to discuss the night before, but tried to assure me that whatever she had said was untrue. By that time we agreed we would be glad to go home.

The next few days we hardly left the cottage. Ellen complained that she had caught a bug which made her sick and tired. I was being eaten alive by beach flies during the day and mosquitoes at night. My legs, arms and torso were a mass of bites and sores. We lay on our sickbeds with Ellen moaning under her breath and me cursing all insects that live off human flesh. To add to my problems, I didn't know if Ellen would again turn into that raving monster.

After two weeks we had had enough. We wanted out. The unhelpful travel courier said it wasn't possible to go home earlier than our booked day of departure. I walked into a travel agent in town and told them: 'Get me off this island. I don't care where I go, or what it costs, but I want a flight today.' We took the only suggestion that they could come up with: two first-class seats on an Eastern Airlines plane to New York. I made some phone calls and hastily arranged a meeting of *Daily Express* staff based in America.

An editor descending almost amounts to a royal visit. We were wined and dined and generally shown a good time. After an afternoon's drinking in Costello's bar, a famous watering hole for newspapermen in New York, Ellen retired to her bed. Waking up dehydrated, she ordered from room service a large glass of grapefruit juice and a glass of cold milk. She drank them one after the other and was violently sick. 'Remind me never to mix citrus fruit with milk,' she said later. 'It curdles in your stomach.'

I don't know if it occurred to her that the vast quantities of whisky and Coca-Cola she had thrown down her throat had made her sick. I certainly had no doubts.

Shortly after our return from that diabolical holiday, the Mirror Group decided to close down *Reveille*. It had been losing money for years. All staff were to be absorbed into other publications. Ellen turned into a jittering wreck overnight. For so long *Reveille* had been her womb. She was used to earning daily newspaper wages for weekly magazine work. It was a small staff and most of them had been there for years.

While the closure and reappointment of staff went on, Ellen spent weeks sitting in the fast emptying offices with some of the other lost souls, talking on and on about what would become of them. These long, fruitless sessions were fuelled by generous helpings of booze – all pretence at working gone and no executives hanging around long enough to disapprove of their conduct.

Ellen was among the last to be relocated. The problem was that her boyfriend was editor of a rival newspaper. Finally she was taken on at the *Sunday People* after signing a 'loyalty' clause stating that the paper's interests would come before those of the *Daily Express*. She was frightened of going into the big world of real newspapers with the added burden of being the girlfriend of the editor of the *Daily Express*. As always, she found solace in the bottle.

At the time, I was busy planning the launch of the *Daily Star* and spent several days a week in Manchester. When I was at home in London we were very glad of our time together and, with plenty of opportunities to drink while I was away, she managed to be sober and supportive most of the time. But turning thirty on 14 October 1979 provided a great excuse for a total, drunken blowout. I arrived home at 7 pm to take her out to dinner. She had been drinking since lunchtime. Sprawled on the floor, surrounded by drunken friends with music blaring, Ellen was out for the count.

I sent her mates packing. 'How could you let her get herself into that state?' I stormed at them. 'Look at her!'

Ellen came round and demanded to know where we were going for dinner. 'You're not going anywhere,' I told her. She gathered up some of the empty bottles, glasses and overflowing ashtrays and disappeared into the kitchen to refill her glass.

I felt sick and disgusted and went to bed, trying to sleep and blot out the horrible, drunken scene in the living room. After a couple of hours I sensed that she was too quiet and went to investigate. I found Ellen in the bath with her wrists slashed. I got her out, dried her, bandaged her wrists and put her to bed.

'For Christ's sake,' I roared at her the next day. 'You're sick. You need help. You've got to stop drinking.' I would spit out for the umpteenth time: 'Has it never occurred to you that we never once, ever, any time, have a cross word unless you are on the booze?' It never made the slightest difference.

As always, Ellen was contrite and full of remorse, though she clearly did not want to argue or even talk about it. She meekly went off to Bart's Hospital to get her wrists cleaned up and properly dressed. She had left it too late to have the cuts sewn up and still carries faint scars.

This was to become our way of life for many years. A futile round of drunken binges followed by violent rows, dramatic gestures and tearful reconciliations – filled with promises she could not keep. The main casualty was sleep. She would be at her roaring worst at 3 am, singing and dancing the night away. I would sit watching her, grim-faced and angry, knowing I had to be at the office running a newspaper within a few hours. Any attempt I made to go to bed would end in disaster. She would crash into the bedroom within a few minutes.

'You don't love me,' she would sneer. 'If you did, you'd let me enjoy myself instead of being so MEAN to me. That's you! A bastard, a nasty, rotten bastard who won't even have a drink.

'Well, I HATE you and I'm going out with my friends and we're going to have a great time without you. What's wrong with having a drink? Everyone has a drink. It's just you. You're too bloody miserable to know how to enjoy life. All you know is work, work, work. Why don't you have some FUN!

'Look at you, lying there, making out you're asleep. You can sleep any time. Why do you always want to sleep when I'm enjoying myself? I'm going OUT!'

I would leap out of bed, grab her by the throat and hiss ominously, 'You're not going anywhere, you drunken cow. Step outside that door and I'll kill you!'

Then she would lurch off into the living room. One of her favourite gambits in these drunken hours before dawn was to telephone various friends, relatives and occasional drinking partners. Totally smashed, she would invariably dial the wrong number and awaken some innocent soul in the middle of the night.

Any move by me to stop her lunatic antics would lead to a punch-up. To my undying shame, I would slap her across the face and the furniture would go flying, bottles and glasses crashing to the floor. Given half a chance she would rush from the room, grab one of the many jars of pills lying around and start pouring them down her throat.

To avoid these violent scenes, usually I would just sit there hour after hour in a pathetic attempt at some kind of sanity, staring coldly at her, not saying a word, until she finally surrendered and staggered off to bed. Frequently dawn would be creeping under the curtains before that blissful hour arrived. Alcohol creates maniacal energy.

The years passed. We slipped into the never-never world of periods of alcoholic abuse followed by relatively calm sobriety. Nothing I tried to break the mould with proved equal to the poisonous hold of the bottle. Although I had vowed never to get married again, I offered to do so if it would solve her problems.

'Give up drinking for six months and I'll marry you,' I promised. Ellen refused to accept the challenge.

As long as we weren't married she could still defend the bottle against me. Her response was, 'Okay, we are finished. I always knew you would leave me eventually, so you might as well get out now.'

By February 1980 I was in Manchester full time running the *Daily Star*. Ellen stayed in London and continued working for the *Sunday People*. I was beavering away one night when the news editor told me, 'Great story just came in. A girl was nearly shot while trying to propose to Prince Charles. The bad news . . . the girl is Ellen.'

My heart sank. *What has she done now?* I phoned London. Ellen was being held by the police in Bristol. On a Leap Year stunt for the *People* she had jumped on Prince Charles during a private engagement and, going down on one knee, asked: 'Prince Charles, will you marry me?' Armed bodyguards, fearing for the safety of the heir to the throne, had drawn their guns. Ellen was bundled away and after several hours of interrogation while they checked out her story, she was put on a train back to London under police escort.

The gossip columns had fun with that one. Nigel Dempster in his *Mail* diary informed the Queen that she need not worry. Ellen, by now a divorcee, was the long-time girlfriend of cockney character Derek Jameson, editor of the *Daily Star*. I was furious about being involved in this way in such a stupid stunt, and naturally took the view she would not have dared do it unless she was first tanked up with booze. In the event, it proved the right moment to end Ellen's uncomfortable relationship with the *Sunday People*. She resigned and they didn't try to stop her.

Being freelance suited Ellen fine. She didn't have to go to an office every day. She could work when she liked, and as long as she met the deadlines everyone was happy. It meant she often stayed up all night working at the typewriter with a bottle of Scotch at her side. Always a night owl, she spent most of the day in bed. She always denied she was recovering from too much drink. Her work schedule was erratic. That was the life of a freelance, she tried to convince me.

In December 1980 I parted company with Express Newspapers. Much as I loved Manchester, I wanted to be back in Fleet Street.

Lord Matthews would not hear of it. I had taken the *Star* to a sale of 1,250,000 daily, largely as the result of starting bingo in newspapers. But it still had a long way to go. Since I declined to stay in the North, we parted amicably, and for the first time in nearly forty years I was out of work.

Not to worry. I had two years' wages in my pocket, compensation for loss of office. We headed for Scotland to celebrate New Year with her family. A few days later I drove back down the motorway with Ellen, white, shaken and exhausted. The emotional and drunken binges had taken their toll.

'Everyone celebrates New Year. Everyone gets drunk,' she would tell me defensively. 'Everyone except boring old you who doesn't know what having a good time means.'

January 1981 saw my first venture into the world of show business. Granada Television had signed me to do a pilot of a new late-night magazine programme. We worked on it for a month. It was exciting but nerve-racking. I had appeared on radio and TV numerous times. Now I was running the show.

It was a month of working out the format, gathering guests – never easy for a pilot – preparing interviews and all the time trying to get familiar with the technical workings of a television studio. Cameras, lights, autocue, earpieces. I had my teeth bridged, tried to lose weight and spent hours in rehearsal learning the difficult art of appearing natural and spontaneous on television. It's harder than it looks.

The cast of characters on the show included many of the new alternative comedians, whose toughest job was to remember not to swear on screen. Rik Mayall, Alexei Sayle and French and Saunders made hilariously funny showbiz colleagues. We were trying to find our feet in the world of television, and all of us went on to be hugely famous later.

Although the show had many good elements, Granada bosses did not take up the option to make a series. We were all too raw. Oddly enough, by chance its format was later adopted for my highly successful *Jameson Tonight* show on SKY.

At Easter that year we joined Ellen's parents for a long weekend in Blackpool. Worried about my future and needing reassurance, I went to Gypsy Leah Petulengro, one of the fortune tellers on the Golden Mile. She told me many things about my work and prospects and then asked: 'You're worried about your partner, aren't you? She's a sick person but she will get well.'

'It's not a normal sickness,' I told her.

'I know, love,' she said. 'It's the drink. But she will stop one day. You can be sure of it. She will suddenly just stop.'

Those words were to give me hope many times over the years when the sickness grew worse and I could see no way out.

'One day she'll stop', I would tell myself. If the gypsy had told me it would take another six years, I might not have waited that long.

Offers of television and radio work came regularly that year and I was kept busy making appearances on local stations all over Britain. Whenever they wanted an expert on tabloid newspapers they would send for Jameson. I wrote articles for the media pages of *The Guardian*, did news commentaries for London's Capital Radio and phone-ins for LBC.

I never refused a job, even when it paid only £25. The more exposure I got, the more offers came in. At the end of the year, I counted up my earnings. I had made about the same as a doorman in Fleet Street. So that's show business!

Then, a call came asking me to take over the *News of the World*. I accepted like a shot.

Having me at home had been just what Ellen needed. We were together all the time and though she often still drank too much we got along fine most of the time. Her and me against the world. If she did get angry, it was now usually directed at the way Fleet Street had treated me. She swore revenge on all of those she considered had let me down.

When I was offered the job at the *News of the World* she was at first triumphant, then dejected. As I dressed for my first day back in the editor's chair after a gypsy-like year in show business, Ellen lay on the bed, whining, 'What about me? What will I do all day?'

I told her: 'Have a sleep and I'll call later and see how you are.' I picked up a small glass phial of tinsel dust I had bought her for Christmas. 'That's you, the lady in the bottle,' I said. 'I'll put you in my pocket and take you to work with me.'

Ellen began to pick up some freelance work, and by early evening she would join me in the office or at the local pub for a drink. Sometimes when I phoned, I could tell by her slurred voice that she had made an early start. On these occasions I would try to pacify her. 'I'll be home soon. No reason for you to come down. Stay where you are, I'll see you soon.'

Ellen pissed in the office pub I could well do without. Pretty young girls looking to advance their career by chatting up the editor would send her into a black rage. Although I had been a flirt all my life, I tried not to pay too much attention to any woman. It wasn't worth the aggravation and also I knew that, even if the emotions were fired up by drink, Ellen would get hurt badly at the slightest rejection. I could usually spot trouble brewing and tried to get her out of the pub and home before she flipped.

In May 1982, a few months after I joined the *NoW,* Ellen's brother Gerard died tragically. He was thirty-one years old. Ellen sank into a deep despair and drowned her grief in alcohol. Or at least that was her excuse. She didn't need one, but it helped. She would spend days drinking at home, not bothering to dress or put on make-up. Three months later her mother died, aged fifty-one. The tragic life that Ellen had so often fantasised about now became a reality.

While I worked long and hard at the *News of the World,* constantly under the heavy pressure that is the lot of all editors, Ellen worked where and when she could. Normally a good and capable journalist, by now her brain was becoming so fogged with alcohol that she worked in fits and starts. She operated from home and seemed only able to function in an atmosphere of frenzy and madness. There would be papers and notes scattered everywhere. If I didn't want to read, or be read, page after page of her features she would accuse me of caring nothing about her career.

A good by-line or series in a newspaper would call for a celebration. She would go out, buy the paper and visit the off-licence. For hour after hour she would sit re-reading the piece and drinking. When I arrived home and she was in a state I would often slam out of the door, though it frightened me to leave her too long on her own. I never knew what she would try to do to herself.

Taking overdoses of pills was a regular occurrence. Usually she slept them off. Once, when she was deeply unconscious, lying on the floor, I called an ambulance and she was taken to University College Hospital. I went home to bed, leaving her in hospital attached to a drip. Two hours later she slammed in the door wearing only a hospital gown, open all down the back. She had no clothes, handbag or purse but a kindly taxi driver had taken pity on her and waived the fare.

She had come round in the middle of the night and was livid to learn that I had gone home. She expected me to sit by her bedside praying that she would survive yet another suicide bid. She had pulled the drip out of her arm and created such a scene that the nurses readily agreed to let her sign herself out.

In remorseful mood after going on a spree, she would agree again and again to stop drinking. She rarely lasted more than three days without a drink. Any excuse would do to turn on the tap.

She had actually reached a miraculous ten days without booze just as I lost my job as editor of the *News of the World*.

Ellen's response to bad news was always predictable. 'I'll be able to have a drink now, won't I?'

Sometimes she would even admit that alcohol was a problem. But without specialist knowledge of the true nature of her disease, she would always give it just one more try.

'I'm switching to vodka,' she would tell me. 'It's the whisky that makes me aggressive. I'm on Martini now, it's only 17 per cent proof instead of 40 per cent like spirits. I can drink two and a half bottles of Martini to one bottle of whisky. I'll drink sparkling wine or champagne. No one gets drunk on champagne.'

Ellen did. Once she had started drinking she was powerless to stop. 'Please don't drink too much,' I would plead as she went out of the door. I might as well have spoken to the brick wall.

A few hours later the phone calls would start.

'Sorry, darling, I'm running a bit later than intended. I'll be home soon.'

Another couple of hours would pass and, trying to sound normal, Ellen would ring again. 'I'm on to a great story. This will be a real biggy. I have to stay and get it wrapped up. See you soon.'

Another hour, her voice getting more slurred with each call, she would say, 'I'm just leaving now. I've called a cab.'

The next call would be: 'Bloody taxis. They haven't turned up. I'll have to start again. See you soon. You're not annoyed with me, are you?'

Often this call would be followed by one from a stranger saying, 'We've put Ellen in a cab. She's in a bit of a state. Could you watch out for her?'

Ellen had amazing powers of recovery. Often, after a sleep in the taxi, she would breeze in trying to pretend everything was totally normal. A hard-working career girl with a hectic schedule. If she was game for more drinking, she would start to regale me with stories of her adventures. Where she had been, who she had met, the great stories she would do. From what I could piece together she seemed to cross London several times in an afternoon, from pub to club to someone's house back to a pub. Often she did not know where she had been, why she was there or how she got from one place to the other.

It is pointless to try to argue with drunks. They have an evil, cunning way of turning everything to their own twisted way of thinking. So plausible are they that on many occasions Ellen could have convinced me that black was white. I was the one who had got it wrong. My normal, sober way of life was out of step with the rest of the world. She enjoyed a drink, a chat, a laugh. I was a stuffed shirt who tried to spoil her innocent pleasure. Her friends were still out enjoying themselves; wasn't she good to have come home?

Often, while I prayed that she would shut up and go to bed, Ellen would decide to have a party. With a demonic energy fuelled by all the alcohol, she would play loud music and sing and dance till the early hours. If I suggested that I was going to bed, her false good humour would turn to aggression. Then, exhausted, she would finally collapse. I could get no peace, and in those white-hot nights would lie in bed frustrated, angry and hurt. These emotional outbursts made me feel wretched for days.

In the middle of the night I would write her long, heartfelt letters telling her I just could not go on like this. She was killing the deep, powerful love I had had for her. She was smashing our relationship to pieces. Either she stopped drinking, or I would go. Often I had every intention of leaving. But it is not easy to pick up your bag when you have nowhere else to go and hate the futility, the utter waste, of walking out on a passionate love affair. Damn it, I refused to be beaten by a lousy bottle of booze.

I had left my wife and children for her – now a bottle of whisky was driving me out of my home.

'Why do you always blame the drink?' Ellen would taunt me. 'Why don't you ask why I am so unhappy? Why don't you ask what makes me depressed? Why don't I have a job that is worthy of my capabilities?'

She would do anything to defend that bottle against me and gradually the bottle was winning. I had little strength or interest left to fight it. The great love of my life preferred a bottle of whisky to me.

'If you loved me you would stop,' I pleaded.

'It's not as easy as that,' she argued.

The day after a drunken binge, she would be remorseful. Physically and emotionally wrecked by all the alcohol, she crept around not knowing what she had done the night before, then pull herself together. She would clean up the flat, clean up herself, make up, put on something pretty and cook me a favourite meal.

'We have to talk about last night,' I would tell her.

Her face crumpled and she cried. 'I know you can't stand it much longer, but please don't leave me. I don't know why I do it, I don't mean to. I'll give it up. We'll fight the booze together.'

Another try, another failure. Like millions before her, one drink was too many, a thousand not enough.

After a disastrous libel action against the BBC in February 1984, in which I lost my life savings, Ellen was shocked into some semblance of sober living. An obscure satirical programme on Radio 4 called *Week Ending* had described me as 'an East End boy made bad'. I sued for libel, seeking an apology, and got caught up in the legal treadmill. Four years later the case came up in the High Court. The jury decided that the words I complained about were defamatory, but not malicious. That meant I had to meet all the costs – £75,000. Not only was I unemployed. Now I was broke as well.

It was one of the blackest periods of my life and Ellen knew I was near breaking point. She, drunk and out of control, would have been the final straw. During this period she tried to keep her drinking away from me. This time it really was us against the rest of the world and if we were to survive we had to gather all our resources and work like crazy. With the confidence and grandiosity displayed by so many of her kind, Ellen encouraged me to give show business another try.

'I know you can be a big, big star,' she would tell me. 'This can't be the end of the road for you. You are too powerful. You have too much to give. Don't let them beat you. I don't want you to go back to newspapers as a number three or four. You can make it in television.'

Her enthusiasm and faith in my abilities fired me up. Her support kept me going. Although it was difficult for someone like her with no regard for money, she told me grandly: 'You concentrate on becoming a star. I'll pay the rent.'

And in those next months she did try to be self-supporting. If she had money problems, she didn't burden me with them. Ellen was working constantly, mostly for the *Daily Star*. They thought highly of her and the job satisfaction and respect she received did seem to steady her.

I gave show business my best shot. I appeared on every chat show, quiz show, panel game and discussion programme going, as well as writing columns in various magazines and newspapers. The media exposure was paying off and the work rolled in. Within eighteen months I had earned enough to move us out of the one-bedroomed flat we had shared for so long. We bought a beautiful garden flat in Maida Vale, not far from London's West End. We had an office each. Sheer luxury after so long with Ellen's desk in the living room and mine in the bedroom.

'Now I will be happy for ever,' she told me when we moved in. 'I'll never want anything else.'

Ellen had freedom in her own office. She could escape from me – and I from her. She furnished her office like a bedsitter. Sofa bed, wardrobe, display unit complete with cocktail cabinet, fridge, television, telephone – and a desk. From behind closed doors I could hear the bottles and glasses clinking. Sometimes she would 'work' late into the night and I would hear her making long, drunken phone calls. But now, instead of disturbing me, she would crash out on the sofa bed in her office. She tried to avoid confrontations about her drinking and kept much of it secret from me. Still, I would have had to be blind not to notice that she rarely came home without a plastic bag clinking with bottles.

Just before Christmas 1985 I landed the top job in radio. The old Wogan breakfast slot on BBC Radio 2. I was now a powerful force in broadcasting. We treated ourselves to a holiday in Tenerife. As usual on holiday, Ellen took the view that drinking was a normal activity and there was no reason why she shouldn't spend hours in the hotel bar. One night she drank even more than usual. Another drunken row started.

She screamed at me: 'Look at all I've done for you. I've made you a star. You were nothing when I met you.'

If it hadn't been so painful it would have been comic. As the managing editor of the *Daily Mirror*, I thought I wasn't doing too badly for myself. When she sobered up, I warned her: 'I can't take all the pressures of this new life and you drunk all the time. This is deadly serious. It's me or the booze. You can't have both.'

When we returned from holiday she informed me, 'I'm on a Drinkwatchers' course. It's like Weight Watchers. You have so many units per week.'

For women it was twenty units – each unit being a single measure of spirits. With the two suggested alcohol-free days each week that meant she could have four units per day. It didn't seem much compared with the vast quantities of alcohol that she usually drank. Still, anything was worth a try.

It worked fine for two weeks. Then Ellen decided that four units wasn't much use to her, so she would save up her allowance for the week and have all twenty on one day. Madness. It was like a slimmer having her whole week's calorie allowance all in one go.

On 7 April 1986 I started my show on Radio 2. Ellen settled into a new drinking pattern. She wouldn't start until I had gone to bed at 9.30 pm in the evening for my 5.30 am start. She was getting more and more sick. Physically she looked a wreck and mentally she was anxious and sinking deeper and deeper into a depression. We were coming to the end of the road.

One morning on the radio show I had to interview a man who ran a treatment centre, Broadway Lodge, for alcoholics and drug addicts. I asked him: 'Is it true that people can have just as much trouble giving up booze as heroin?'

'Yes,' he said, 'but at least most people on heroin know they have a problem. Alcoholics usually refuse to accept they are addicted.'

I prayed that Ellen was listening. When I got home she was in tears. 'I phoned the treatment centre,' she told me. 'I would have to go there for five weeks and it costs £5,000.'

'I'll give you the money,' I said. 'You can have the money I was saving to have a conservatory built.'

'But it's not fair,' she cried.

'Look, Ellen,' I tried to make her understand, 'if you had cancer and it could be treated for £5,000 we would pay it. You are sick, you must get help.'

'Let me try it again on my own,' she said. It wasn't long before she again got horribly drunk. She had been missing since lunchtime without even the usual drunken, apologetic phone calls. I had long since given up trying to track her down when she was on a bender.

About ten o'clock at night the doorbell went. 'We have your wife here,' said a male voice on the intercom. Supported by two men, Ellen was slumped like a sack of potatoes, out cold. They carried her into the hall and she lay motionless.

'What happened? Where did you find her?' I asked. They gave the name of a local wine bar, but they didn't know how long she had been in there. When she passed out they had found her address in her handbag and brought her home.

They say God watches over drunks, and it must be true because Ellen always found good Samaritans to look after her. These particular samaritans refused to take any money for their trouble and, having deposited her into my safe keeping, were anxious to be off. They were clearly embarrassed for me.

When she came to the next day, Ellen looked pathetic. She went to have a bath and from the other room I could hear her sobs. I went into the bathroom and she was crying as if her heart would break.

Huge teardrops splashed into the bathwater, and she looked like something out of *Alice in Wonderland* about to be washed away on a sea of tears.

'I know you can't take any more,' she cried. 'You might as well leave me. It's never going to get any better. I'll always be like this. Just go.'

I grabbed her by the shoulders and, almost in tears myself, I said, 'You are very sick. They can help people like you. Please let them help you. You don't need to go on destroying yourself.'

'What are people like me?' she asked sadly.

'You are an alcoholic,' I told her. 'It's a disease. You can get better.'

For once, not denying the accusation I had thrown at her so many times, she sighed and some relief crossed her face. 'Okay, let's see if they can help this alcoholic,' she said. 'I'll try anything to get out of this hell.'

She had finally admitted she was beaten. The gypsy's prediction which had given me a glimmer of hope over the years came back to me. *One day she will stop . . .*

Ellen started to live her life one day at a time on 10 June 1986. It was as if the devil himself had been lifted off our shoulders. She has never taken a drink since. Not even in a sherry trifle.

— 16 —
Fairy Tales
Can Come True

NOW the battle against the booze was won. Together we had
driven out the demon that had all but destroyed her. Gradually
Ellen's health was restored, and once again she was able to reveal
her true personality, so often lost in the past in a sea of booze. She
was fun to be with, amusing and easy-going. Over the years she
became my right-hand woman as well as my lover. What a tragedy
it would have been if the booze had succeeded in not only killing
our love, but ultimately in taking her life too. My conviction that we
rowed only when she was drunk proved to be true. In her new sober
life, we were a perfect couple. Our deep love for each other had
endured and strengthened through all the battles we had fought both
professionally and personally.

Ellen's journalistic work had fallen away as she concentrated on
getting well. My show business career was going from strength to
strength, and it soon proved necessary to get a manager. Ellen was
the obvious choice. She was nervous at first about the responsibility
and her lack of experience, but I assured her we would learn the
tricks of the trade together. Over the years our partnership has
become one of the great success stories. So much so that Ellen is
frequently approached by other aspiring telly personalities asking
her to manage them.

Sadly she has to turn them away. 'What you need to succeed,' she
tells them, 'is Derek's personality plus his forty years' experience in
Fleet Street. I don't think you could manage that.'

We always said we would marry on my sixtieth birthday, in 1989
– if Ellen was not drinking. Now all the obstacles to our lasting

happiness had been removed and I was anxious to get on with it. There was no reason to delay any longer. And what better way to give thanks and celebrate our wonderful good fortune, sharing our happiness with friends and colleagues who had stood by us in good times and bad.

On holiday in Tenerife in January 1988, we decided to announce our engagement publicly. Some people use the personal columns of *The Times*. We chose *The Sun*. To the astonishment of a British holiday village sprawled across a hillside on the Spanish island, I descended with Ellen, *Sun* writer Roslyn Grose and photographer Steve Lewis and announced we were about to celebrate our engagement.

Of course, they all knew me – Auberon Waugh once wrote a learned piece saying I was the best-known male in Britain after Prince Charles – and were delighted to join in. People rushed off to their villas and came back clutching bottles of champagne and cans of lager. The young 'uns put pop music on a ghetto blaster and soon we were having a right old knees-up by the poolside – with the bride-to-be joining the toasts with mineral water.

It was all there in next day's *Sun*, including the headline: DEREK DOES THE DECENT THING WITH A £40 RING. I had decided that a Canary Islands gemstone, olivina, would make an appropriate engagement ring – and was delighted when my bright idea turned out to cost only forty quid! The future Mrs Jameson was furious to learn on our return home that my good housekeeping had become public knowledge. She marched me out to the jewellers and I had to fork out £1,000 for a proper three-diamond engagement ring. I tried to keep it quiet. Fat chance. A photographer and reporter from the local paper were there even before we got out of the shop.

I was all for a quiet wedding, especially as it was my third, but have always taken the view it is a lady's privilege to decide how she would like to tie the knot. After all, they do say it is a woman's greatest day. With Ellen's sobriety, she had rediscovered her faith in God. He had answered so many of our fervent prayers and her recovery from that terrible addiction was nothing short of miraculous. Naturally she believed that this union, surely made in heaven, should be given the blessing of a holy ceremony.

That was fine by me if it was going to make my bride happy. I myself follow no religion and, indeed, being born a bastard of dubious parentage, have never been baptised. But I do believe in a divine power, whoever He may be, and was quite happy to go along with Ellen's plans.

Of course it wasn't going to be easy. We had both been married before. They had been civil marriages and as such not recognised by the Catholic Church, of which Ellen was once again a practising member. Her parish priest, Father Frank Leonard, then at Our Lady of Lourdes Church in Harrow Road, West London, agreed to help with the documentation necessary for permission to marry in church. Father Frank thought we would get the necessary consent, but it could take some time. We would have to be patient. There was a mountain of paperwork to be filled in and lots of questions to be answered before the Catholic Marriage Tribunal reached their decision. In the event, it took so long I was convinced the matter had gone before the Pope himself.

However, I knew we would get there in the end. Refusal to let us marry at the altar would have meant the Catholic Church had recognised the authority of a civil marriage – as well as making front-page headlines.

Two months after we had made the initial approach, Father Frank brought the happy news. The Catholic Marriage Tribunal had given their permission for us to be married in church. Father Frank explained that as my first wife, Jackie, had died and my subsequent marriage had been in a register office, as far as canon law was concerned I was a free man. Ellen had never been married or divorced in the eyes of the Church, so she was in the clear.

We had hate mail from some members of the public, who thought the whole thing was a fiddle. 'How much did you pay?' more than one wanted to know. 'Why was I refused permission?' In fact, we neither sought nor received any special favours. I have always made it a principle in life to be treated like anyone else. What the knockers failed to understand was that their first marriage must have taken place in church, which rules out remarriage unless the Vatican takes the rare step of granting an annulment.

Most of my fans were genuinely pleased for us, and their best wishes flooded in. Many listeners seemed to regard the wedding as a family event and they sent greetings cards by the thousand, horseshoes, black cats, silver bells, four-leaf clovers and small household gifts. One fan made a beautiful embroidered ring cushion, an American wedding tradition. The cushion with the wedding rings on is carried down the aisle by the pageboy.

Having been the bearer of our good news, Father Frank said: 'I suppose you will want to get married in a pretty parish church out in the country.'

We both took a deep breath and told him: 'We are planning to try for Arundel Cathedral. Our cottage in Worthing is in that diocese.'

When he recovered from the shock, he smiled and said, 'Okay, I'll do what I can to help.' Sadly for us, he was off that summer to work with Mother Teresa in Ethiopia so would not be able to perform the ceremony himself.

So began another round of questions, form-filling and waiting for permission. Canon Anthony Whale, the priest in charge of the cathedral in the beautiful Sussex town of Arundel, was happy to marry us there. 'It all sounds jolly good fun to me,' he said.

His idea of fun did not seem to be shared by His Grace, the Bishop of Arundel and Brighton, Cormac Murphy O'Connor. To him, the thought of a big public wedding with a divorced celebrity must have been a nightmare.

The message came down the line from the Bishop: 'Couldn't you make the wedding a little more discreet? Why not hold it early in the morning, with just close family present, before people are up and about?'

I explained that it really would turn into a circus if we tried to keep this wedding secret. Fleet Street photographers would be hiding in the confessional box at the crack of dawn and swinging from the chandeliers just to get their pictures.

After more weeks of nail-biting, we were on holiday at our cottage in Worthing when I took a telephone call from Canon Whale. Ellen was upstairs printing out the last chapter of the first volume of my autobiography, *Touched by Angels*, as I called up to her: 'The Bishop says we can get married in Arundel Cathedral.'

She rushed downstairs crying tears of joy, and threw herself into my arms.

But she was soon on the phone to book the cathedral for noon on

3 September 1988. Lots of people pointed out that was the day the war began back in 1939. 'That's okay,' I told them all cheerfully, 'the goodies won.'

Ellen called the Avisford Park Country Hotel in Walberton, five miles from the cathedral, and arranged a grand wedding reception for our 250 guests. She found the place by touring every hotel, restaurant and country pub in Sussex looking for the perfect venue for a summer wedding reception. She had told me excitedly, 'It's got indoor and outdoor swimming pools, tennis courts and a golf course and is set in forty acres of grounds.'

I told her: 'It's a wedding we're organising, not the bloody Olympic Games.' But it was perfect and if, please God, the sun shone down on us most of the celebrations could take place outside.

The hotel was delighted. The owner even had a fountain built in the driveway in our honour. He had seen one in America and had long dreamed of having the same at his hotel. Now we had given him a good reason to have it installed.

Now it was full steam ahead, and with the splendid help of *Woman's Own*, where I was writing a column, Ellen set about organising the showbiz wedding of the year. Invitations and orders of service had to be printed, dresses bought for Ellen and her six bridesmaids, flowers, transport and wedding cake chosen and ordered. No expense was to be spared and I told Ellen, 'It's your wedding day. Do anything you want to make it the best day of your life.'

I marvelled at how that pathetic wreck, drowning in a sea of alcohol, had become an efficient, confident and happy bride-to-be.

In July, while I was in Spain filming for BBC TV, a story broke that parishioners in Arundel were claiming that we had jumped the queue in booking our wedding for September. *The Sun* ran a front-page splash: JAMESON IN CHURCH WEDDING STORM. We kept calm and waited for the storm to blow over. There are some small-minded people about, but they couldn't spoil our joy.

Ellen was worried that the adverse publicity might scare off the Church. Not a bit of it. Lovely, easy-going Canon Whale assured her that Church and cathedral would stand by their decision.

'All the parishioners I have spoken to are very excited about the wedding,' he told us. 'You had better expect a crowd, because many of them are planning to come and cheer you on.'

But when BBC Radio 2 decided to broadcast the wedding live, the Bishop put his foot down. This wasn't a royal wedding, and he wouldn't give permission for the transmission.

Ellen and I got the blame, of course, with one or two sniffy papers claiming it was our idea. In fact, we had nothing to do with it, though we would have been happy to go along with the proposed broadcast if the BBC thought listeners would enjoy it. Judging from all the letters we received asking why it was not being transmitted live on TV, the public *would* have loved it.

During the months of planning, I had had no qualms about getting married for the third time. But at six o'clock on our wedding day, a reporter woke me up with a call asking how I was feeling. 'Bloody awful,' I told him. I had pains in my stomach.

In keeping with tradition, the bride and I had spent the night apart. I had slept in our Worthing cottage and been to the chemist to buy a large bottle of magnesia. Jameson, the man who never suffers nerves in front of television cameras or when speaking in public, was having a bad attack of butterflies in the tummy.

It wasn't getting married that made me feel sick. Rather the thought of this illegitimate son of a kosher butcher standing there at the high altar in Arundel Cathedral, playing the leading role in an ancient Catholic ritual. Ah well, I thought bravely, I'll survive.

Ellen, with her matron of honour, the *Mirror*'s Anne Robinson, was already at the hotel where the reception was to be held. Anne's husband, John Penrose, also a *Mirror* executive, was my best man and he spent the night round the corner from my cottage in the Marine View Hotel, where we had put all our family and friends for the weekend.

As I put on my royal-blue and grey morning suit, complete with topper and gloves to match, there was an urgent ringing at the front door. It was the man from the Brighton *Evening Argus* wanting some copy for his first, pre-wedding, edition. Among the daft questions he put to me was whether I came from Croydon, in Surrey, and could he have some quotes from my father? So much for the nation's favourite cockney bastard! I gave him the benefit of my views on reporters who fail to do their homework.

So I was feeling much better by the time John Penrose arrived to pick me up in a white Rolls for the ten-mile trip to the cathedral. The scene greeting me there almost brought the butterflies back. Thousands of well-wishers were jamming the streets, plus an army of television crews, reporters and photographers. I didn't know how the guests would ever battle their way through and I stood at the huge doors greeting them as they arrived, thus starting a new wedding custom.

Four of my television and radio producers acted as ushers. The satirical magazine *Private Eye* claimed I had ordered them to come dressed as pageboys in satin knickerbockers. In fact, they were dressed like myself in royal-blue morning suits. Pity to spoil a good story, though.

Canon Whale told me that he had had to lock the doors of the church at nine o'clock that morning because fans were flocking into the pews reserved for invited guests. Local police were on hand to control the crowd, and by the time Ellen arrived at the church a few minutes after noon, there were over three thousand people there. She had to abandon her car to walk with her father through the sea of fans. So much for the knockers! Later, watching her arrival on the television news, I was amazed to see that, far from being nervous, she had been giving interviews to the waiting pressmen.

Inside, the cathedral was magnificent. Wooden arches bedecked with summer flowers had been erected over the aisle and a red carpet laid. The marble pillars had been decorated with flowers and ribbons and the altar looked like a florist's shop window. A team of eight, including the flower ladies of the cathedral, had worked for two days to create a dazzling display that made the procession coming down the aisle to the strains of Wagner's Bridal March look like something out of a fairy tale.

First came Canon Whale, followed by Ellen's seven-year-old nephew, Jamie, carrying my fan's decorated cushion with the wedding rings. He wore a navy-blue and white sailor's outfit. Then came the five young bridesmaids – Rochelle, Melanie, Gemma, Kerry, and Sarah – wearing shell-pink shepherdess dresses with layers of lace and hooped skirts. Matron of honour Anne Robinson wore a Scarlett O'Hara off-the-shoulder style in the same shell pink.

When I caught sight of Ellen on her father's arm gliding down the aisle, floating on a twenty-foot train of ruffled silk, I nearly fainted.

She looked like an angel. Her dress was shimmering white, tight-fitting with a huge silver butterfly as the bodice. She had a pearl headband round her forehead and her face was covered in a veil. She carried a trailing bouquet of red and white roses.

Ellen was bathed in an aura of total joy. She appeared incandescent. If there was one moment when I realised without the slightest doubt that our love had won through, this was it. All the pain, the frenzy, the drunken madness, had been driven out. Standing beside me in the majestic cathedral, with its high altar and rich baritone voices enunciating the ancient ritual of marriage, was the woman I loved in her true self. Kind, funny, sharing, beautiful. Brimming over with the richness of life, not slumped on the floor wishing for death. I knew she had been worth fighting for. I had won the toughest battle of all.

The wonderful Monsignor Michael Buckley, a regular contributor on my Radio 2 show, assisted Canon Whale at the altar. After months of worry about being allowed a church wedding, in the event we had two priests marrying us. My four children – Barbara and Peter from the first marriage, and young Ben and Dan from the second – were all guests. The elder two, already in their thirties, read the lessons from the pulpit.

As we signed the register on the altar, in full view of the congregation, a soloist sang 'Amazing Grace'. Few people in the church knew just how important that hymn was to us, but those who did all shed a tear. Ellen squeezed my hand as she heard the words, 'Who saved a wretch like me.' The radiant look on her face filled my heart with love. Now she was Mrs Jameson and we were all set to live happily ever after.

We emerged from the cathedral into brilliant sunshine and a surprise guard of honour from the Guild of Town Criers. I am their only honorary member – a tribute to my foghorn voice. It added another magical element to the proceedings. Ellen had been disappointed when she first learned that the cathedral had no bells. She had wanted to come out of church with all the bells ringing. And she did. The town criers clanged their huge bells for all they were worth.

We made our way to the vintage open-topped Rolls-Royce showered in confetti and congratulations. When the crowd started to sing 'I'm getting married in the morning' Ellen and I stood up in the back of the car, joining in.

The biggest laugh of the day came at the reception when Lord Cudlipp, a legendary figure in Fleet Street, said in a speech there were so many eminent and powerful people in the church, he thought he was at a gangster's funeral – until he realised the priests were smiling.

It was a true multi-media event with guests from newspapers, radio, television, magazines and the world of publishing.

'The editor of *The Times* introduced me to the editor of *The Sun*,' said Lord Cudlipp. 'That would never have happened in my day.'

The ladies were delighted when I invited Ellen to give a wedding speech. Why shouldn't the bride have her say? It's her day. This bride must have been taking lessons from her new husband because she spoke up loud and clear and gave everyone a good laugh.

My old mum, Elsie, was ill during the day, though she insisted we should not worry about her. She had to be brought to the church in a wheelchair and spent most of the reception lying in bed upstairs at the hotel. The doctor had given permission for her to attend the wedding only after she promised to go into hospital the next day for a cancer operation. 'You can't stop me,' she told the doctor. 'This isn't a police state – yet!' That's Mum! But she kept the promise we wrung out of her, had the operation – and made a good recovery. Sadly the cancer remained in her system. She survived for one more year and died peacefully in 1989 at the splendid age of eighty.

On the evening of the wedding the family went to a private party in the Marine View Hotel. With Ellen still wearing her scarlet going-away outfit, we held each other close and danced to Chris de Burgh's hit, 'Lady In Red' – since banned by the Catholic Church in Ireland! Ellen's eyes sparkled and she brushed away a tear. Like all good fairy stories, this one had a happy ending.

Few that day realised it had been such a momentous occasion for us. We had beaten the devil and thanked God by exchanging our vows before the world. Now we were surrounded by the love of our friends.

We did not forget to say a quiet word of thanks to our great friend, the medium Doris Stokes. She had always been confident that Ellen would crack her drink problem and we would one day marry. She had passed over the previous year. Like everyone else, Doris would have loved the grand occasion.

'Thank you, Doris,' Ellen and I whispered to each other – as we always do when things go right. We reckon good old Stokesy is up there, egging on the angels, making it all come true for us.

How to Succeed in Showbiz

FLASHBULBS popped as the tall, elegant blonde approached me with her hand outstretched in greeting, though she lowered her eyes shyly. We were standing in the wings of the London Palladium.

'That was marvellous,' said Princess Diana. 'Were you nervous at all?'

'Nervous?' I repeated in shocked tones. 'I was petrified. That's the first time I've performed on stage. Never even done a church hall before.'

She pealed with laughter, her head thrown back, as I added: 'Ah well, if you're going to make it in show business, might as well start at the top and work downwards.' I thought it best to draw a veil over the fact that my dressing-room mates, Mike Yarwood and Roy Walker, practically had to carry me on to the stage for that Royal Gala charity performance in the summer of 1987.

Rehearsal that afternoon had been a total disaster. Standing there alone in the spotlight, I could see nothing beyond the apron but pitch darkness. As I went through my routine, sending up newspapers and showbiz in my usual way, I was greeted with total silence.

Not so much as a titter from the producer and his team somewhere in the front stalls. I was sure they had applauded the others on the bill – Cilla Black, Barry Humphries, Jeremy Irons, Wayne Sleep, Alvin Stardust, as well as Roy and Mike. The latter tried to reassure me by explaining the rehearsal was simply to fix technical matters like timings, lighting and camera angles, but my tummy had turned upside down when I went out there for real – until the first wave of applause hit me.

That did it. I was as right as rain after that. No wonder people get hooked on the smell of greasepaint, the roar of the crowd and all that theatrical nonsense. And Princess Di's friendly words were the ultimate confirmation. I was now well and truly a star of show business.

Not bad going for an old hack from Fleet Street. Three years earlier I had been unemployed and flat broke after stupidly getting involved in that libel action. Indeed that year, 1984, the one George Orwell warned us about, turned out to be the worst of my life. Oddly enough, being a touch psychic, I had always known it would be.

On 10 January I was fired by Rupert Murdoch as editor of the *News of the World.* Contrary to popular mythology, this was the first and only time I have ever been fired. True, there have been one or two painful partings. I have a tendency to tell proprietors what I think of their tendency to tell editors how to run newspapers. The severance terms were generous and, in truth, the payoff saved me from the bankruptcy court seven weeks later when I lost the libel action.

All the same, I was well and truly on the cobbles. Out of a job, broke and with an ex-wife and two young sons to support as well as keeping myself. As an editor, I had earned around £40,000 a year, plus £6,000 in expenses, and was driven around by a chauffeur in my office limousine. Usually a Jaguar if I could get hold of one.

It seemed extremely unlikely that I would get another job running a newspaper. There aren't too many vacancies for top dog in our business. The prospect before me was to try for a job four or five rungs down the ladder. I did not much fancy going cap in hand to a former rival editor begging for work and probably finishing up as a has-been tucked away in some corner. In my day I have seen too many of these poor sods that passers-by point out with a half-whispered: 'He used to be an editor.'

For starters, Ellen and I did what most people do when their pockets are filled with redundo. We went on holiday to Lanzarote with our friends Lee Everett, former wife of Kenny, and her new husband, actor John Alkin. I was in good heart. Show business was beckoning. Producers everywhere seemed to be after my body.

The first job to turn up was as chief guest on a Yorkshire Televison chat show hosted by Jimmy Young. A long-distance call informed me they were so desperate to get me to Leeds that the producer would hire a private plane to fly me from Lanzarote – and pay a fee of £1,000.

'Forget the private plane,' I told him, 'I can change my ticket. For £1,000, I'm yours.'

When Ellen and I arrived in Leeds, the producer was full of apologies. He hadn't cleared the payment of £1,000 and was in trouble. Would we accept £600? There and then we learned an early lesson is showbiz. Get it in writing.

That wasn't the only problem. When I got in the studio, who should be sitting there in serried ranks waiting to pounce but just about everyone in Britain who had a real or imagined gripe against newspapers. They included football manager Tommy Docherty, Mrs Muriel McKay, widow of the Falklands VC, 'Bishop' Jess Yates, father of Paula Yates, and Mrs Doreen Hill, mother of a student victim of the Yorkshire Ripper.

Their complaints came thick and fast. I got stuck in and did my best to give them a suitable answer. I probably deserved it, but I felt shabbily treated. I don't mind playing the patsy, but I like to know about it beforehand. They had told me it was a programme about newspapers, craftily omitting to mention that I was to be thrown to the wolves.

In fact, I gave such an account of myself that one of the Yorkshire TV producers phoned rapturously afterwards to ask if I were free to make at least twenty-five programmes a year. As usual, I never heard another word. It happens all the time in television.

Two days after the ding-dong in Leeds, unlucky Monday 13 February, I walked into the High Court for a much bigger battle – the libel action. It was to end in disaster for me on the equally ominous 29 February, it being a leap year.

Then a strange thing happened. I suddenly found myself in the public eye as never before. There was sympathy everywhere for the crazy out-of-work editor who had gone to court in a futile attempt to fight for his honour and dignity. Offers came pouring in from all quarters and this time I was able to move away from my usual straitjacket – going on air simply to defend Fleet Street. I did not fancy spending the rest of my life as a press pundit. Now that's what I call really boring.

Even while the trial was still running Thames Television had a car standing by to rush me to the Teddington studios to audition for a spot on the revival of *What's My Line?* Watching the pilot programme, Thames bosses decided I wasn't as lively or spontaneous as they had hoped. I don't know if anyone pointed out that I was fighting for my life in court at the time we recorded it. They gave the job instead to another Fleet Street man, gravel-voiced George Gale.

That's show business. And fate. As things turned out it would have done me no good at all to have been typecast as a game-show panellist. Nice work if you can get it, but the money in that area is peanuts – £200 to £300 a programme compared with the presenter's £2,000 to £3,000. Or in the case of the big boys – £10,000-plus.

Another job that I missed out on at that time was the *Six o'clock Show* on LWT. They gave it to another cockney, Danny Baker. I made some guest appearances on the show, but didn't get the regular commitment and exposure I needed. Producer Greg Dyke – who ironically later became boss of LWT – put up a fight for me to work regularly alongside Michael Aspel, but was overruled upstairs. 'You can still make guest appearances,' he told me lamely in a phone call.

I still find it odd that London's own television station, LWT, has so rarely used the services of the most famous cockney of them all. The fault must lie with me. It has to be the way I talk and my dreadful habit of speaking my mind. My big mouth is always getting me into trouble.

People in high places take a dim view of my accent. It tickles me that some people imagine my rasping cockney tones have been my fortune. I made it in spite of my accent, not because of it. The minute I open my gate there are those who assume I am that illiterate oaf, Sid Yobbo, as *Private Eye* dubbed me all those years ago.

A month after the court case I did my first job at the BBC, a radio interview at Bush House for the World Service. I stuck the security pass they issued on my bathroom mirror, the symbol of an astonishing breakthrough. Where else but in Britain would the public corporation you had taken to the High Court in a messy legal action be paying you a few bob a month later for your views?

Granada TV's *What the Papers Say* also made plentiful use of my newspaper knowledge and I would travel up to Manchester to present the show. I wanted to break away from the ex-editor image, but could not afford to turn down the £400 they paid for a fifteen-minute script.

On the train I once sat with Mike Scott, then Granada programme controller. He could have made me a star overnight if he thought I was worth the risk. We talked about the pilot of a chat show I had made for Granada during my first venture into the world of television three years previously. Like nine out of ten pilots, it had not been taken up.

'The problem with you is that you are too much of a character, larger than life,' he told me. 'There's no way you could be a presenter because you overshadow the guests. You are more interesting than most of them.'

I went home with my tail between my legs, cursing my big mouth, and noted ruefully a few years later that he had no reservations about returning to the role of presenter himself. He now fronts ITV's daytime show *The Time, The Place*.

Recently I was asked to appear on the show with Steve Davis for a debate on really interesting people. Mike Scott challenged me to prove a boast that I could make the telephone directory sound interesting. He handed me one of the thick London directories. I flipped through the pages, seizing on the name Ib.

'What's this! Mr Ib?' I demanded. 'A spy if I ever heard of one. Russian or Chinese? Who is he, what is he? Get a team round there immediately. Find out everything there is to know about the mysterious Mr Ib.'

Lively enough, but what Mr Scott doesn't know – unless he reads this – is that there is no Mr Ib in the telephone directory. I made the name up as he handed me the book.

In those black months following the court case I still was not making enough money to pay the bills, but could at least see a career in show business on the cards. All those minuscule appearances in other people's shows were a kind of apprenticeship.

Fleet Street helped pay the rent. As well as launching a fighting fund, several editors put work my way. I wrote articles for the television pages of *The Sun*, the media pages of *The Guardian*, and even wrote on opera for the *Sunday Times*. It is true when they say that no journalist should ever have to starve. I had my ancient, battered typewriter and was back practising my craft as a freelance hack. 'This old bum for hire', I told the world.

The first consideration in those early months was that I should meet my financial obligations to my ex-wife Pauline and our two sons. Ellen paid the mortgage on our flat off the Gray's Inn Road and our living expenses were modest. Outside of newspapers I took any job offered on the airwaves, however little it paid.

By the end of the year I had established my first permanent niche – a regular spot on TV-am's *Frost on Sunday*, sending up that great British institution, the Sunday papers. I still do it on occasion and some people kindly say it is the best laugh of the week.

But the real break that was to change my life came from the backroom boys of the BBC, the people who make documentary features from a building called Kensington House in Shepherd's Bush, West London. Laurence Rees, one of the army of producers who beaver away there far from the bright lights, had an idea for a series. He proposed gathering footage from all over the world showing how foreigners see the British. Their view of us tended to be bizarre if not totally hostile. The BBC2 series was to be called *Do They Mean Us?* Would I be willing to take it on, taking the rise out of the foreigners sending up the British? In the nicest possible way, of course.

As usually happens in life, I failed to spot that this show was going to make my reputation. It was three weeks before I even responded to Rees' letter asking for a meeting to discuss the project. I agreed to do it readily enough, if only because it would be my own show. But I assumed it would come and go virtually unnoticed.

I could not have been more wrong. As I revealed some of the barmy things foreigners were reporting about Britain, I would ask incredulously: 'Do they mean us? They surely do!' It was a catch phrase that caught on instantly. To this day, five years later, it pursues me everywhere I go. They shout 'Do they mean me!' from the cabs of lorries to the Savoy Grill. I've even had it yelled at me across a street in the Seychelles.

At times the programme pulled an audience touching five million, which is quite phenomenal for a BBC2 documentary. We made three series and packed it in only when the foreign material ran out.

More than anything else it made me a British institution in my own right. The greatest thing of all – it was pure Jameson. Instead of playing my usual role of monkey to other organ grinders, this time I wrote the material and presented the show.

Mary Kenny, writing in the *Daily Mail*, was among the first to spot that perhaps there was something I could offer television. 'Derek Jameson, presenter of *Do They Mean Us?* (BBC2) was the TV discovery of the year for me,' she wrote. 'A brilliant communicator because he's so devastatingly unpretentious and utterly lacking in airs and graces. And his treatment of foreign television is a lot more intelligent than the sneering Clive James.'

The rent money still came from TV-am, where I had become part of the furniture following the collapse of the famous five who inaugurated the station. They put my picture up in the foyer, but never gave me a major role. Once again that cursed accent held me back.

TV-am's Aussie boss Bruce Gyngell clearly preferred the highly professional Anne Diamond and Nick Owen to the rasping tones of Jimmy Greaves and myself, despite the tremendous response us two cockneys had from the audience. Success never comes easily if you're from the working class.

Not to worry. It was beginning to happen. By putting myself about, turning up all over the country in a dozen different guises, I was rapidly becoming known to a vast public. I would travel to Anglia TV in Norwich to play *A Frame with Steve Davis*, pop into the LWT studios on the South Bank to sing *Carmen* with the Welsh National Opera on Mike Parkinson's *All Star Secrets*, drive down to Thames TV in Teddington, Middlesex, as a mystery celebrity on *What's My Line?*, play *Scrabble* on Channel 4 and fly to Border TV in Carlisle to defend Fleet Street. I even worked casual shifts as an ITN reporter, among other things securing a rare interview with *Sun* editor Kelvin MacKenzie.

The programmes might vary, my style remained constant. I was the rough, gruff bloke who said what other people were thinking. Appearing as a guest on ITV's *Around Midnight*, I left presenter Janet Street-Porter twiddling her thumbs while I took on model Vicki Hodge.

'You say you've been with both Prince Andrew and the tough-guy actor John Bindon,' I said to her. 'Which do you prefer, Vicki – the top drawer or a bit of rough?'

'I like the whole wardrobe,' she shot back. The audience erupted, though I don't suppose Miss Street-Porter and her co-presenter, Auberon Waugh, appreciated me taking over their show.

On another occasion I turned up at TV-am and found Anne Diamond most upset. She had been rubbished in the papers that morning by the acid-tongued Nina Myskow, nowadays travelling the same path as myself as a wandering TV and radio performer. 'Don't you worry,' I told Anne on air. 'I've got a message for you, Nina Myskow. Get stuffed!'

Back came a message from the governing IBA – Independent Broadcasting Authority – saying they didn't expect that kind of language at breakfast time.

By the end of that first year I had made more than £20,000 – about half my pay as an editor. I still called myself unemployed, since there was no regular job to go to. I was to discover there is no such thing as overnight success in the world of entertainment. The truth is that you have to serve an apprenticeship, *schlepping* all over the country doing jobs which nobody ever hears about. Though I was not short of work, real success eluded me. I might be a natural on telly, but I had to go out there and prove it to the programme makers. It takes more than half an hour's television to do that. Of course, I always tell people with a grin, it helps if you have run four national newspapers.

It was still a slow, hard slog. In the summer of 1985 my nice little earner at TV-am went up the creek. Frostie disappeared on one of his working trips to America. A fateful call came in from Radio 4. Would I review the Sunday papers in a summer holiday programme they were doing called *Colour Supplement*? This was a real teaser. It was Radio 4, of course, that had turned my life upside down with those harsh words in *Week Ending*.

It did not take long to decide. Pride doesn't pay the rent. Anyway, I'm not one to bear grudges. My script associate on SKY TV's *Jameson Tonight* for a time was Peter Hickey. He is the man who wrote the words 'an East End boy made bad'. Mind you, I let him sweat a bit before giving the go-ahead for him to get the job!

Margo MacDonald, the former SNP MP, presented *Colour Sup-*

plement. I soon stamped the programme with my own particular brand of lunacy. The usual outrageous remarks, followed by that guffaw of laughter. The show was such a success they extended its six-week run to Christmas.

Having made my mark in radio as well as television, I was approached by Radio 2 and asked to stand in for a week in November while Jimmy Young was on holiday. Sue Cook and Angela Rippon were to do a week each, with me in the middle. A thorn between two roses.

That week as the poor man's JY put the seal on my success, I raised a storm, tackling the issues of the day and commenting freely on this and that as I went along. Comment is still a rarity in British broadcasting. The letters flooded in. Eight hundred in a week. Dozens of phone calls on top of that. I finished on Friday, 29 November, my fifty-sixth birthday. 'I'm off now,' I told the listeners. 'See you in the dole queue.'

But I had been noticed in the right places. Even the critics joined in. Jill Neville of *The Listener*, regarded as the top radio critic in the land, said she had been fumbling with the knob on her radio looking for Radio 3 when she came upon this Burglar Bill voice. Me, of course. 'Sign him up', she wrote.

Within days we received a call from Frances Line, the highly perceptive head of music at Radio 2 and the person who decides what goes on the air from day to day. She has since been promoted to Controller, Radio 2, one of the most powerful jobs in the business. Ellen took the call. 'I'll get next year's diary,' she replied when Frances asked if we could meet for lunch. 'I was hoping to do it quicker than that,' said Frances. 'Look, forget lunch. Could we get together real soon? Like now! I can be with you in half an hour.'

Frances jumped in a taxi and told me later that, having secured permission for perhaps the bravest bit of casting in all radio history, she wanted to get everything signed, sealed and delivered before anyone could change their minds.

I had finally made it. The Wogan spot. The biggest and best job in all radio.

Ken Bruce had succeeded Wogan, but it did not work out. I think Ken himself was relieved to be rescheduled to follow me at 9.30 am every morning. More recently he took over the important late-night slot. He certainly has never showed any animosity and sent a telegram on our wedding day: 'Congratulations. Just don't expect me to take over at 9.30.'

My appointment sent a shock wave through the BBC. A former tabloid editor from Fleet Street following in the footsteps of the mighty Wogan? What sacrilege. The old Sid Yobbo image, still haunting me. Even Dave Morris, my own agent at the time, couldn't believe his ears. When I called to say they had given me the job, he exploded incredulously: 'The Wogan spot? What, YOU!'

The news soon reached my former colleagues. *The Sun* broke the story exclusively and it was followed up by the other papers. Of course, they couldn't leave it at that. Some papers tried to suggest aggro between Jimmy Young and myself. In fact, he was the first person to congratulate me on signing up. 'A success for you is a success for Radio 2', he wrote. 'And that is good for all of us.'

All the same, there was a whispering campaign against me inside the Beeb. There were those who just could not believe anyone would be stupid enough to hire an irreverent, outrageous cockney with a voice to match to front the main radio programme of the day. Stories appeared that my ratings were zilch and the show a complete flop. Wishful thinking on their part. In fact, I increased the audience by 25 per cent within weeks and today reach more than 10 million daily – nearly double the figures when I started. It's the most talked about show on radio. My troubles were over the first day I came out with yet another catch phrase: 'Mornin' mornin', Jameson here!'

I had made it – two years after stepping out of the High Court a broken man.

– 18 –
My Friends – the Stars

GOD knows why we are called stars. Take the cameras away and most of us would have a struggle competing with a 60-watt bulb. I've met them all in my time, the handful of men and women like myself fated to descend on millions of homes at the flick of a switch. The one thing we seem to have in common is that none of us bear much resemblance to the image we cultivate so carefully to keep ourselves in front of the bright lights.

Wogan, for instance, is not a barrel of laughs – full of charm and blarney. Michael Aspel might seem silky smooth and unruffled, but he worries all the time. Anneka Rice hates all that running, jumping and leaping about. Rosy-cheeked Sarah Kennedy can be as prickly as a hedgehog. David Frost *is* true to life, no doubt because he never stops long enough to worry about his image.

Jameson has never been called Del Boy outside infants' school. Far from being a cockney rogue, cheeky as a sparrow, he sits quietly listening to opera records behind the thick walls of his castle by the sea.

Offscreen, we tend to be a nervous bunch, querulous and always on edge. It is as if we know the camera does lie and fear someone might come along and reveal the truth that we aren't all that special.

The reigning king, of course, is Mr Terence Wogan. Unlike most of us, he has nothing to worry about – and it shows. Self-satisfaction oozes out of the man who has always been on top, both in radio and television. His adoring public have given him more awards than a marshal in the Red Army. I've been dogging Wogan's footsteps for years, a course I embarked on with relish after first meeting him at an *Express* lunch ten years ago. He was rather subdued, which was understandable. Everyone else around the table worked in newspapers.

'So this is the great man,' I thought to myself. 'If he is the top entertainer in Britain, then I'm in the wrong business.'

We have met several times since I set about changing my circumstances and I have stood in for him three times on his BBC TV chat show, appearing under logos spelling out the name 'Wogan'. I wasn't too delirious about that. Somewhere along the line I seem to have ruffled his feathers a bit. When my book *Touched by Angels* came out it seemed obvious that Wogan would have me on his show. It was a bestseller, written by the man who had taken over his old job at Radio 2. I even got word that his producers were excited at the prospect of a lively exchange.

The interview never happened. It sank without trace on the somewhat feeble suggestion that I had appeared on the show previously and could not be asked back. More likely Wogan was sick of the name Jameson.

It is true that I led Terry a merry dance on my previous appearance. For once, he found it difficult to get a word in edgeways. I even pulled a telephone monitoring device with a rubber suction pad out of my pocket.

'Lick this,' I commanded. Terry looked taken aback, but he went ahead and licked. *'We've got a right one here'*, he must have been thinking to himself.

The invitation to act as Terry's holiday replacement followed that appearance and he will not have missed the fact that my version of the Wogan show leaped dramatically in the top 100, which must have left Britain's top telly personality scratching his head.

Terry got a shock when the famous broadcaster Jack de Manio appeared on his show and told him that Jameson seemed to be hot stuff.

'Yes, he's a great natural broadcaster,' said Terry, gulping visibly.

For all that, there is no real aggro between us. He is a real professional; I'm just an old hack from Fleet Street. He has always been helpful and advised me how to negotiate my contract with the BBC, which proved most useful. I would never have asked that much on my own.

He is a totally different kind of broadcaster from myself. I like to go in hard with tough questions, keeping a smile on my face and always behaving with the utmost courtesy. Because of my years as a journalist, I have the knack of filling my head with fifty facts about a person and can rattle them off like a machine gun as soon as he or she sits down. Most of my chat stems from a few key words scribbled on a piece of paper. All the introductions to guests are written by me.

Terry is from the radio school of broadcasting, an announcer and DJ for twenty years before he became a television personality. His scripts are largely written in advance. There is nothing wrong with that; it is the customary practice. His secret is to make it sound as if he just thinks it all up. But he is still stuck in that formal structure – I call it a verbal straitjacket – and has little chance to be natural and spontaneous, though he manages to appear so.

I am a newspaperman playing at show business and he is an entertainer cast in the role of a journalist. Where he scores over me is with that Irish whimsy, the devil-may-care approach that delights the public. He gazes deeply at his guest, then his face cracks into that broad Irish grin and he has won over another million hearts.

Away from the cameras, he is anything but the man we see on screen. In real life Terry is diffident, almost remote. He is not one for chatting happily with guests and often stays shut in his bleak dressing room at the Shepherd's Bush Theatre in West London until it is time for him to make that grand entrance, the audience whipped into shape by the warm-up man. When I was there it was Felix Bowness of *Hi-de-Hi* fame.

Michael Aspel is another actor, a product of the stage with nicely cultivated vowel sounds just like they teach in drama lessons. He is nothing like a former pipelayer from Battersea, though that is his background. Whenever we meet he is at pains to let me know that his working-class credentials are as good as mine. 'Only yours got lost somewhere along the way!' I tell him with a grin.

I smiled to myself when it was revealed that he was approached by John Howard-Davies, the light-entertainment boss of Thames TV, in the car park at a Twickenham rugby match to take over the late Eamonn Andrews' job on *This Is Your Life*.

It is a job I desperately wanted. I was a boy from the slums, like Eamonn, and am most definitely a man of the people. I knew there were supporters of mine in the *Life* team, that I was on the shortlist and had the advantage of being a Thames star. My series *Headliners* had filled the spot left vacant by Eamonn's death.

No chance, I told everybody. Michael Aspel will get it. I speak with the wrong accent and you are not likely to bump into me in the car park at Twickenham. Apparently they drink champers and eat canapés there while waiting for the match to start. Michael knew what he was doing when he learned to speak proper. What makes him special is that he appears so relaxed, when, by his own admission, he worries about everything to the point of paranoia.

The fact is that those who run television are not comfortable with people like me who sound as if they should be driving a lorry. The programme makers prefer neutral or 'posh' voices, totally ignoring the fact that most of the audience speak the language of the streets.

Look at the rapid rise of Anneka Rice and Sarah Kennedy. Lovely, well-spoken girls, both of them. However, nobody could claim they talk anything like ninety-nine out of a hundred other girls. Theirs is the language of Cheltenham Ladies' College.

You can imagine what some of these awfully nice ladies must think of the likes of me. When I appeared on a pilot for Sarah Kennedy's daytime show at Thames Television they asked the audience, 'What would you like to see more of in the programme?' The cry came back, 'Derek Jameson'. I was not invited back.

Like many another presenter, before and since, she didn't mind Jameson appearing as a sort of cartoon character, but he certainly wasn't going to steal any of her glory. 'Don't patronise me,' she hissed when she was taking the inevitable bash at Fleet Street and I suggested that perhaps I knew more about newspapers than she did.

Sarah, despite being a banker's daughter with a plum in her mouth, has made it to the top by way of *Game for a Laugh* and acting like one of us. She wrote of me: 'We can applaud Derek Jameson . . . Our class system doesn't block the talented and hardworking, however humble. The rub comes when the upper class think they can behave like us and expect us still to curtsey.'

Thank you very much, Ma'am.

Former newsreader Jan Leeming is another who makes me feel uneasy. When we worked together on *I've Got a Secret*, the sparks would really fly and the contest was not limited to the show. One withering look from her would make my toes curl. I got the full blast of her scorn when she discovered I was a former newspaper editor. From that day on I had to answer for all the sins of Fleet Street, especially where the thrice-married Jan Leeming was concerned.

Everyone trod warily in the presence of Madam Leeming and this gave us a useful bonus. Whenever she was on the show, smoked salmon and prawn sandwiches would appear in the artists' green room.

'We couldn't give Miss Leeming cheese sandwiches,' one of the canteen ladies told me in shocked tones when I asked about this conjuring trick.

Jan and I get on much better these days and I think she has forgiven me for being a newspaperman, though she descended like a ton of bricks on me recently for suggesting she was a bit of a tartar.

The lovely Anneka Rice was another panellist on *I've Got a Secret* and her sunny, smiling personality lit up the show. It was easy to see why millions of men fall at her feet, thought anyone who fancied his chances in the studio soon found himself cut dead.

I remember egging on one macho type to chat her up, knowing exactly what would happen. Just as he launched into a graphic account of why she should go hang-gliding with him, Anneka interrupted sweetly: 'Have you met my bloke?' The big, relaxed figure of theatrical producer Nick Allott, the man she was later to marry, was never far away from the girl of a million dreams.

Talking about hang-gliding wasn't much help, either. Anneka groans at the mere mention of her sporty activities on television. I fancy she's a girl who would rather curl up with a good book.

Far from being a dizzy blonde, Anneka is a shrewd business-woman. She owns her own successful production company, markets her own adventure books and designs the Dash range of sports clothes.

Another famous telly star far removed from her image is Anne Diamond. She's supposed to be tough and ruthless – as hard as her name. Not a bit of it. She's quite soft and cuddly.

We have worked together often and I have never come across anyone who got so hurt over what they read about themselves in the newspapers. Rather sad in Anne's case since she must have had the worst press in the history of television. I put it down to the bitchiness in showbiz. Anne has made a lot of enemies in her climb to the top at TV-am. She deserves her success. She is a fully qualified journalist – unlike most of those who knock her – and knows what she is doing.

Anne and Nick Owen, her former TV-am partner who abandoned dawn television is favour of sports programmes, were a joy to work alongside. They succeeded where the famous five failed because they came across as ordinary, down-to-earth performers. The audience could relate to them.

Another big name who helped me through hard times was the late Russell Harty, a lovely man who invited me on to his BBC chat show for no other reason than he had read of my downfall and felt sorry for me. It was an important occasion for me and I was feeling a little apprehensive.

I should have worried. It soon became clear that Russell, relaxed and sharp on air, was a bag of nerves away from the camera. As he welcomed me to London's Greenwood Theatre, I noticed he was dripping with perspiration and wringing his hands with tension. 'What are you getting all het up about?' I asked him. 'You've got nothing to worry about. You're the presenter.'

Sitting in the lounge of Manchester's Midland Hotel with him one day, he was in a dreadful state about the purpose of life, the invasion of privacy and the pressures of show business. He wondered whether he should have remained a teacher.

'Nonsense,' I said. 'We need more tea. Put your hand up.' I raised his hand for him and a waiter was on the spot immediately, ready to stand on his head if Russell had asked.

'There you are,' I said. 'You're a celebrity. You wouldn't have got that treatment if you were a teacher in Yorkshire.' The thought cheered him up immensely.

Incidentally, those people who write to me seeking advice on how to become a TV or radio presenter might be interested in the note Russell sent when I made my first tentative steps in show business: *'Do every quiz/phone-in/chat show/listeners' questions/dog-breeder half-hours/chip shop quorum you can manage. Leave no stone unturned.'*

He was right, too.

Of all those I have worked with, David Frost is the ultimate telly person. Always calm and unruffled, he's not merely a face on camera. He has mastered the system as businessman and programme maker as well as performer. This is the basis of his total confidence in a world where most people suffer with their nerves.

He is another presenter and interviewer who has risen above the class divisions so evident on the telly. 'Good morning, hello and welcome.' It is Frostspeak, neither posh nor poor. The three separate greetings may all be saying the same thing, but they reach out and embrace everyone, whatever their social status.

That's what makes Frostie so clever. He is all things to all people. He can present nonsense like *Through the Keyhole* or interview the President of the United States.

He was the first to give me a regular job, sitting alongside him on the couch at TV-am. 'Lord Jameson is with us,' he booms with a grin that suggests all is well with the world. He says it with such feeling that many really believe I do have a handle. It was Frostie who proclaimed I was 'the great entertainer of today'. Others in show business reaching such a conclusion would have kept very quiet about it. He can do no wrong where I'm concerned.

Jimmy Greaves also held out the hand of friendship to me when I was on the skids. We always have a good laugh together, having both been around a bit in our time. ''Ere, Del, can you understand this geezer?' he asked me once when some wally was wittering on about us getting to the set.

Greavsie has made it as a sports commentator, which is only right and proper since he scored forty-four goals for England; he is not taken seriously in other fields. A great pity because he is a born communicator with a tremendous following. But he has the same problem as myself. Wrong accent.

Mike Parkinson succeeds where Greavsie and Jameson run into difficulties. He is working class, the son of a Yorkshire coalminer, but like Aspel manages to speak in a manner most acceptable to the people who pay the piper. His accent has done him proud. A grammar school boy, he got a pip on his shoulder in the Army while the rest of us were peeling spuds. In the same spirit, Parky went on to conquer the airwaves. In his day he was undisputed king of the chat show.

He has always been kind to me, a fellow journalist, though he doesn't approve of the way I speak. Parky regards me as monster mouth. According to him, the studio technicians have to work behind shields when Jameson is on camera.

My favourite performer is Les Dawson because he has never allowed his success as a writer, comedian and entertainer to go to his head. He is as down-to-earth as the bloke standing next to you in the chip shop.

Appearing as one of his long-suffering panellists on *Blankety Blank*, I loved the way he mingled with the contestants and their families before the show. Shirtsleeves rolled up, laughing like a drain, putting them at their ease. It might not sound much, but I can tell you that many of the big name celebrities in our business are hardly seen when the camera isn't on them. They scuttle in and out of their exclusive dressing rooms like scared rabbits.

Les cheered me up after I had spoken at a men-only night in a club at Barnsley, Yorkshire. I talked about the revolution in communications. They had been expecting a blue comic and gave me the bum's rush, pelting me with bread rolls to help me along my way.

I told Les my troubles and he snorted scornfully. 'You don't want to worry about that, lad,' he said. 'If you get a laugh in Barnsley they give you a free two-week holiday in Malta.'

Su Pollard makes me laugh more than anyone. I could spend the rest of my life watching daft Peggy, the chalet maid, the role Su made famous in *Hi-de-Hi*. She comes bouncing into my Radio 2 bunker from time to time, looking like a daffy owl behind those huge specs, skirt up to here, and wearing one red, one yellow stocking. Ours is a mutual admiration society. I call her Brain of Britain and she refers to me as The Ultimate One.

We presenters on Radio 2 come across as a cosy bunch, which is what you would expect of the station with the biggest audience in Britain. The joke is that we hardly know each other. We meet as a group only at the Beeb's Christmas dinner. So I am at some loss when people ask me the inevitable question: What are the others like? I don't really know, but can tell you how they seem to this amateur playing in the same team.

Like most of us, Jimmy Young is intrigued by what makes politicians tick, the ins and outs of the economy, the barmy bureaucracy of the Common Market or the way trade union leaders behave. Several million housewives identify with him instantly when

214

he asks: 'Minister, a lot of people are worried by what they read in the papers today. Could you explain to us what it means?'

That is his strength. In trying to make sense of it all, the issues of the day become crystal clear to his listeners. He digs away until he is satisfied – and that means the rest of us as well. He is the public listening post.

Gloria Hunniford – Honeybun, the more daring call her – is a real bundle of fun, all kisses and cuddles. Behind the sunny smile is a tough, hard-working showbiz veteran. She was appearing on stage alongside her father, a conjuror, at the age of nine and, like Jimmy Young, was a singer before hosting her own shows. A virtually unknown presenter on Radio Ulster, Gloria got her big break in 1981 when she was asked to stand in for JY when he was on holiday.

She has the heart of a lion. When she smashed her arm playing tennis, she was back at work in a couple of weeks, her arm in a sling. Gloria never told anyone that she was in intense pain. Months later it still hurt to lift her arm, but in her book the show must go on.

I can never quite make out David Jacobs. He is always exceedingly polite, but surely must take a dim view of someone like me. I am everything he is not. Gruff, outspoken, true to my origins.

My mouth drops open with astonishment as I listen to David say things like: 'I don't know whether you ever happen to watch commercial television . . .' I take off my hat to him. He is in his mid-sixties and looks about forty-two, comes from an ordinary background and talks like the Duke of Clarence. I fancy no speck of dust has ever been allowed to settle on his person.

Sorry about the initials, David. My mistake. I'll get them changed one of these days.

The cuddly Scotsman with the dry wit, that is Ken Bruce. A broadcaster's delight. Like his close friend, the late Ray Moore, he is hardly recognised in public until he starts speaking. The voice is unmistakable. We used to have words at 9.30 am every week-day in the days when he took over from me. My aim was to catch him out with some outrageous remark. He was always too quick for me.

He is still in his thirties and will yet become one of the biggest names of all time in broadcasting – not bad going for a lad from Glasgow who once washed cars for a living.

Big John Dunn is the broadcaster we admire most. Calm and unruffled, he makes an art of easy-going chat. Nobody ever gets hurt on the *John Dunn Show*. He really is a gentle giant – 6ft. 7in. tall and smashing with it. The key to his success is that he is so *interested* in everything. When people fail to spot the mystery voice on his programme, he makes them feel it has been a great privilege simply talking to them.

The new girl in class is Judith Chalmers, who already has a huge following as a presenter of *Wish You Were Here* on television. She has always been extremely kind to me, which is what you would expect of a Northern lass, and takes great pains in dealing with the nation's requests. In her own quiet way, I think she is going to become a big star – another housewives' choice.

All of them are skilful broadcasters with something special that makes them so popular with the audience – their love for the people who tune in. It is grand to be a member of the family.

– 19 –
Beating the System

M E, I'm just an ordinary bloke. Nothing special. As I always say, the ugliest man on television and the world's worst DJ. It makes me sound about as appealing as lockjaw at a five-course meal. That does not matter. The important thing is that I am being myself.

The joke is that everyone on the airwaves is supposed to be perfect. We must enunciate to the point of sounding like the speaking clock, be groomed as if living in a hairdresser's and at all times look like a tailor's dummy. God forbid that anyone should swear or behave in any way like real people, unless it is in the name of the drama department and then preferably after nine o'clock at night.

I breezed into show business only too pleased to break some of the rules, as I have been doing for much of my life. I suppose my forty years in newspapers gave me some claim to be different. And so it proved. My famous voice sounds like bath water gurgling down a drain. I am not a trained broadcaster nor an expert on anything. I can't sing, dance or do conjuring tricks.

What I can do is say exactly what I think without looking over my shoulder to see who I am upsetting. If anyone should take exception, the answer is always: 'Well, that's Derek. You can't tell him what to say.'

I can even throw back my head and roar with laughter when something tickles me. That is also a rare commodity. How much real laughter is there on radio and television?

Does anyone ever weep? Sometimes when the news is bad it is difficult for me to hold back the tears. I broke down telling the story of the Zeebrugge ferry disaster and did it again in a programme commemorating the fiftieth anniversary of the Dunkirk evacuation. I see no shame in crying for innocent lives so wantonly thrown away.

Of course it causes some bewilderment when Jameson turns up to make a programme. They seem to think because I speak the language of the street, I must be some kind of cockney Jack-the-lad. When I was standing in for Wogan, the series producer Peter Estall sent me a briefing memo headed: 'Gorblimey!' Words I have never used in my life other than in a joke.

What he was trying to say, I imagine, was that the man-in-the-street had arrived to make a few programmes. I am all for that. That is why I was among the first to welcome the arrival of satellite television in 1989. Rupert Murdoch made no bones about his SKY channels breaking the duopoly of the BBC and ITV. His aim was to liberate the airwaves and present programmes designed for a wider audience than the readers of the *Telegraph* and *Guardian*. There is nothing wrong with them. But there are other people out there, with a different outlook on life. Naturally I was delighted when Rupert called from Wapping to invite me to become a test pilot on SKY. What made his choice all the more poignant was that he had fired me four years earlier as editor of the *News of the World*. Not that such a trifling detail bothered Rupert. 'I've never said a word against this man in my life', Rupert told Andrew Neil, then SKY's chief executive. 'No, you only fired me!' I retorted. We had a good laugh at that.

For more than a year I wrote and presented the main magazine programme *Jameson Tonight* produced for SKY One by a light-entertainment wizard, Michael Hurll. I never felt more at home on the box – it was my Radio 2 programme with pictures! In other words, I was free to do as I pleased without the overplanning that goes into so many chat shows on BBC and ITV.

I played myself instead of being tied down by words written in advance on the Autocue teleprompter, and sat comfortably behind a desk, dispensing with grand entrances and all that posturing and preening nonsense. The important thing to me was to be different. To get away from the same old dreary round of banal questions by changing the subject every few minutes and filling the air with surprises.

Poor old Spike Milligan was thrown into confusion when I said to him: 'Now then, you must have been asked enough stupid questions to last nine lifetimes, so you talk about anything you like, mate.'

Take Pat Boone, the all-American boy grown up. Married his high-school sweetheart, has four beautiful daughters, is spokesman for all the Christian virtues, and singer of sweet songs for decades. Surely you can't be that perfect I put it to him.

Pat confessed he had strayed in his marriage and had had some disastrous business flops.

Sometimes I was the one who finished up surprised. Like when the audience cheered 'spanking' ex-Tory MP Harvey Proctor as he angrily rejected my suggestion that newspapers had every right to expose his kinky activities with underage boys.

Russia's leading rock 'n' roller, Boris Grebenshikov, looked more and more astonished as I went through his sufferings before glasnost arrived in his homeland. At one time, exiled to the icy wastes, Boris' guitarist had icicles in his beard and had to be thawed out to play.

It was all there in notes churned out by the publicity machine.

'I don't know what you're talking about,' said Boris. 'We always have a great time in Russia. It's every bit as good there as in the West.' I made him a Hero of the Soviet Union on the spot.

There were tears, too. The most touching moment was when thirteen-year-old Lee Evans, from Port Talbot, in South Wales, came in to tell us about the smashing poems he wrote in a hospital bed while fighting cancer.

That superb actor Anthony Hopkins, being Welsh himself, came in to read some of them with me and the pair of us sat there fighting off the tears because we didn't want to look soft in front of Lee, the bravest lad I ever met.

Since Wogan has his own Shepherd's Bush Theatre, I wanted my own, too. *Jameson Tonight* came out of the old Windmill Theatre off Piccadilly. Its reputation as the cradle of British comedy talent may well come true yet again in the shape of my sidekick on the show, a young comedian named Shane Richie. He was sensational and I reckon he will go right to the top.

Sadly the show was 'pulled' by SKY executives after fourteen months, despite the fact that Rupert Murdoch had been among its keenest fans. We had done four or five shows a week, interviewing some 2,000 people, but it was costing £4 million a year – far too much for a small audience on a new channel.

Most of the critics ignored it. The non-Murdoch media would have nothing to do with SKY Television and gave us the big freeze. The Murdoch papers kept us at arm's length, wary of being accused of toadying up to the boss, though Gary Bushell in *The Sun* didn't give a damn and made no bones about declaring that we would have been in the top ten on BBC or ITV. Kindest of all was another free spirit, Brian Hitchen, editor of my old paper the *Daily Star*. He wrote a delightful obituary notice in his weekly column:

> If television bosses are not beating a path to Derek Jameson's door, they need their heads looking at – from the inside. Welcoming and friendly as a warm brown teapot on a kitchen table, Derek Jameson is without any doubt the best talk show host in Britain.
>
> His programme on SKY was a nightly parade of the rich and famous and the poor and interesting. It was a show for all the people and fun to watch. Sadly, it has been axed by SKY because it costs £20,000 a week and the infant television station is reportedly feeling the pinch.
>
> Carping SKY insiders have put it about that he wasn't right for the programme. What a load of toffee. Jameson WAS the programme.
>
> Without him the show would have become, like Wogan's, reduced to a procession of stars plugging their latest films, books, and diets . . . the difference between Jameson and almost all the others is that he is a real journalist, not just a talking head.
>
> He does his homework on guests. Which means he doesn't ask damn silly questions like the rest of the talk show gang.
>
> Suddenly hit with the prospect of £250,000 worth of earnings going out of the window, most people would have buried their head in a bucket of whisky.
>
> But not Derek. Saturday morning saw him pecking away at his word processor, labouring over his next book, the follow up to his life story, *Touched by Angels*.
>
> The title is still secret. *Struck by Lightning* sounds about right because he has been hit by lightning before and come bouncing back.
>
> Taking over the Wogan slot should be the next bounce.

Thank you, Brian. Actually the title was *Last of the Hot Metal Men*.

*

So now my time is up. Well, almost. Having passed my sixtieth year, I suppose it is time to think about closing this far too busy mouth for good and giving someone else the chance to get in a word or two. The trouble is that I'm always home when the call comes to sally forth once more . . . It still feels good to be wanted.

I have edited newspapers, written books, made radio and television programmes and yet still don't know how a bastard kid from an East End gutter managed to get up there among the stars. The explanation can only be those angels Ma Wren promised me in that home she ran for waifs and strays.

Writing this in my beautiful white house on the beach – it is called *Angels' Rest* – I wonder what would have happened had I been born into a normal family. The old girl wanted me to be a branch manager in the Co-op. To be honest, I don't think my academic qualifications would have carried me far beyond lorry driver's mate or baker's roundsman.

That was why taking myself off on the No. 6 bus from Hackney Wick to Ludgate Circus proved the single most important act of my entire life.

Fleet Street made me. I could not have had a more wonderful life and, who knows, perhaps my story might do some good. My profession has never been lower in the public esteem. We have gone badly wrong somewhere to come out lower than politicians and estate agents.

I can bear witness that journalism taught me only the best things in life. To be forthright and honest, to care about the people out there without a voice, to love and respect the language, to be fair and decent to all. Most of all, to have a good laugh and want to share it with others.

In that spirit, I leave you with my epitaph – it sums up what this crazy ride on life's merry-go-round has been all about:

In memory of
DEREK JAMESON
the editor who
found the oldest
budgie in Britain

Index

Index

FOR THE BEST IN PAPERBACKS, LOOK FOR THE

In every corner of the world, on every subject under the sun, Penguin represents quality and variety – the very best in publishing today.

For complete information about books available from Penguin – including Puffins, Penguin Classics and Arkana – and how to order them, write to us at the appropriate address below. Please note that for copyright reasons the selection of books varies from country to country.

In the United Kingdom: Please write to *Dept E.P., Penguin Books Ltd, Harmondsworth, Middlesex, UB7 0DA.*

If you have any difficulty in obtaining a title, please send your order with the correct money, plus ten per cent for postage and packaging, to *PO Box No 11, West Drayton, Middlesex*

In the United States: Please write to *Dept BA, Penguin, 299 Murray Hill Parkway, East Rutherford, New Jersey 07073*

In Canada: Please write to *Penguin Books Canada Ltd, 2801 John Street, Markham, Ontario L3R 1B4*

In Australia: Please write to the *Marketing Department, Penguin Books Australia Ltd, P.O. Box 257, Ringwood, Victoria 3134*

In New Zealand: Please write to the *Marketing Department, Penguin Books (NZ) Ltd, Private Bag, Takapuna, Auckland 9*

In India: Please write to *Penguin Overseas Ltd, 706 Eros Apartments, 56 Nehru Place, New Delhi, 110019*

In the Netherlands: Please write to *Penguin Books Netherlands B.V., Postbus 195, NL–1380AD Weesp*

In West Germany: Please write to *Penguin Books Ltd, Friedrichstrasse 10–12, D–6000 Frankfurt/Main 1*

In Spain: Please write to *Alhambra Longman S.A., Fernandez de la Hoz 9, E–28010 Madrid*

In Italy: Please write to *Penguin Italia s.r.l., Via Como 4, I-20096 Pioltello (Milano)*

In France: Please write to *Penguin Books Ltd, 39 Rue de Montmorency, F-75003 Paris*

In Japan: Please write to *Longman Penguin Japan Co Ltd, Yamaguchi Building, 2-12-9 Kanda Jimbocho, Chiyoda-Ku, Tokyo 101*

FOR THE BEST IN PAPERBACKS, LOOK FOR THE

A CHOICE OF PENGUINS

Miss Manners' Guide to Rearing Perfect Children   Judith Martin

'Whether she is discussing playground etiquette or teenage parties, how to cope with toddlers' birthdays or a fiancé abruptly introduced to unsuspecting parents, the author brings to child-rearing the same high-minded hilarity, the same firm insistence on proper behaviour, that made her *Guide to Excruciatingly Good Behaviour* such a huge bestseller'.

The End of the Affair   Graham Greene

The frank, intense account of a love affair and its mystical aftermath. 'For me one of the most true and moving works of my time, in anybody's language' – William Faulkner

The Life of Samuel Johnson   James Boswell

Hailed by Macaulay as the best biography ever written and by Carlyle as a book 'beyond any other product of the eighteenth century', this work today continues to enjoy its status as a classic of the language.

Modernism   Edited by Malcolm Bradbury and James McFarlane

This thoughtful and extensive book examines the literature of the period 1890–1930 and identifies the ideas, the groupings and the social tensions out of which Modernism emerged.

My Life as a Man   Philip Roth

'Roth's best novel . . . no writer alive can sustain a full-length novel at as high a decibel level as Philip Roth' – *Newsweek*. 'Philip Roth is one of the country's finest, most forceful, intelligent and serious contemporary writers' – *The New York Times*

Penguin French Reader   Edited by Simon Lee and David Ricks

Funny, informative and thought-provoking – a selection of workaday samples of modern French, from books and newspapers, circular letters, theatre programmes, brochures – to help you speak French like a native.

A CHOICE OF PENGUINS

Riders in the Chariot Patrick White

'Stands out among contemporary novels like a cathedral surrounded by booths. Its forms, its impulse and its dedication to what is eternal all excite a comparison with religious architecture. Mr White's characters ... have the symbolism of statues and spires' – Maurice Edelman in the *Sunday Times*

London: The Biography of a City Christopher Hibbert

'As teeming with life as the city itself' – *New Yorker*. 'Instructive, exuberant and witty' – *Washington Post*. 'Consistently entertaining' – *Punch*

The Literature of the United States Marcus Cunliffe

A general introduction to the main themes and figures of the American literary scene, from colonial times to the present day. 'A very good book indeed' – D. W. Brogan in the *Guardian*

Selected Stories Nadine Gordimer

'A magnificent collection worthy of all homage' – Graham Greene. 'Nadine Gordimer's work is endowed with an emotional genius so palpable one experiences it like a finger pressing steadily upon the pulse – *Village Voice*

The Decameron Giovanni Boccaccio

A skilful plotter, an instinctive spinner of stories and a craftsman whose prose is by turns poetical, elegant and down to earth, Boccaccio, with his hundred stories of the *Decameron*, has passed into Western literature and folklore, enriching it immeasurably.

Clinging to the Wreckage John Mortimer

The unforgettable, bestselling autobiography of the creator of Rumpole. 'Exceptionally touching and funny' – *The Times*

FOR THE BEST IN PAPERBACKS, LOOK FOR THE

BIOGRAPHY AND AUTOBIOGRAPHY IN PENGUIN

My Father's Island Johanna Angermeyer

In 1935 Johanna's father Hans and his four brothers had fled from Nazi Germany to the Galapagos Islands. Then he died, and his daughter travelled 2,000 miles to the enchanted isles he had loved – there to piece together the story of her parents' incredible lives, their enforced separation and her father's tragic death.

The Secret Lives of Trebitsch Lincoln Bernard Wasserstein

Trebitsch Lincoln was Member of Parliament, international spy, right-wing revolutionary, Buddhist monk – and this century's most extraordinary conman. 'An utterly improbable story ... a biographical scoop' – *Guardian*

Tolstoy A. N. Wilson

'One of the best biographies of our century' – Leon Edel. 'All his skills as a writer, his fire as a critic, his insight as a novelist and his experience of life have come together in this subject' – Peter Levi in the *Independent*

Brian Epstein: The Man Who Made the Beatles Ray Coleman

'An excellent biography of Brian Epstein, the lonely, gifted man whose artistic faith and bond with the Beatles never wavered – and whose recognition of genius created a cultural era, even though it destroyed him' – *Mail on Sunday*

Backcloth Dirk Bogarde

The final volume of Dirk Bogarde's autobiography is not about his acting years but about Dirk Bogarde the man and the people and events that have shaped his life and character. All are remembered with affection, nostalgia and characteristic perception and eloquence.

Searching for Bobby Fischer Fred Waitzkin

Since Bobby Fischer retired from chess in 1975 Americans have been searching for a successor. Fred Waitzkin describes how he helped his gifted son Josh become a leading contender. 'A terrific book for fathers, sons, chess players and the general reader' – Tom Stoppard

Touched by Angels

'My story is simple enough. I grew up poor and hungry on the streets of London's East End and decided at an early age it was better to be rich and successful.'

'With my background and accent, there was only one way I was going to succeed. That was by working my balls off. As always. Time and again in my career I lost out to the old boy network.'

'I loved the Army, every last barmy minute of it. It was obvious that National Service was going to be pure farce.'

'Editor of the *Daily Express*. In many ways the most coveted job of all in the world of newspapers . . . *Now I guess it's really going to get tough.*'

'There I was with this wonderful French mistress . . . every man's fantasy – and she wanted nothing more than to read and watch telly.'

'Years later, I still have nightmares about that childhood. Those early years have dominated my life. That is why I laugh so much. It takes away the pain.'